P9-DBT-280

HARPER FORUM BOOKS

Martin E. Marty, General Editor

NATIONALISM AND RELIGION IN AMERICA

Concepts of American Identity and Mission

HARPER FORUM BOOKS

Martin E. Marty, *General Editor*

Published:

IAN G. BARBOUR
SCIENCE AND RELIGION: New Perspectives on the Dialogue

A. ROY ECKARDT
THE THEOLOGIAN AT WORK: A Common Search for Understanding

JOHN MACQUARRIE
CONTEMPORARY RELIGIOUS THINKERS: From Idealist Metaphysicians to Existential Theologians

GIBSON WINTER
SOCIAL ETHICS: Issues in Ethics and Society

JAMES M. GUSTAFSON & JAMES T. LANEY
ON BEING RESPONSIBLE: Issues in Personal Ethics

EDWIN SCOTT GAUSTAD
RELIGIOUS ISSUES IN AMERICAN HISTORY

SAMUEL SANDMEL
OLD TESTAMENT ISSUES

JOSEPH DABNEY BETTIS
PHENOMENOLOGY OF RELIGION

OWEN C. THOMAS
ATTITUDES TOWARD OTHER RELIGIONS: Some Christian Interpretations

WINTHROP S. HUDSON
NATIONALISM AND RELIGION IN AMERICA: Concepts of American Identity and Mission

Forthcoming:

RICHARD BATEY
NEW TESTAMENT ISSUES

WILLIAM A. SADLER, JR.
PERSONALITY AND RELIGION

IAN T. RAMSEY
PHILOSOPHY OF RELIGION

GILES GUNN
LITERATURE AND RELIGION

NATIONALISM AND RELIGION IN AMERICA

Concepts of American Identity and Mission

edited by

Winthrop S. Hudson

GLOUCESTER, MASS.
PETER SMITH
1978

LIBRARY OF CONGRESS CATALOG CARD NUMBER: 76–109063

ISBN 0-8446-0711-8

Reprinted, 1978, by Permission of
Harper and Row Publishers, Inc.

To three young Americans

DAVID, DOUGLAS, AND RICKY

HARPER FORUM BOOKS

OFTEN dismissed with a shrug or accepted with thoughtless piety in the past, religion today belongs in the forum of study and discussion. In our society, this is particularly evident in both public and private colleges and universities. Scholars are exploring the claims of theology, the religious roots of culture, and the relation between beliefs and the various areas or disciplines of life. Students have not until now had a series of books which could serve as reliable resources for class or private study in a time when inquiry into religion is undertaken with new freedom and a sense of urgency. *Harper Forum Books* are intended for these purposes. Eminent scholars have selected and introduced the readings. Respectful of the spirit of religion as they are, they do not shun controversy. With these books a new generation can confront religion through exposure to significant minds in theology and related humanistic fields.

MARTIN E. MARTY, GENERAL EDITOR
The Divinity School
The University of Chicago

PREFACE

NO ONE can understand American national self-consciousness without taking into account the religious heritage of the American people. At least until World War I, theological language, religious metaphors, and biblical allusions were as characteristic of political discourse and historical writing as they were of sermonic literature. The ringing challenge of Theodore Roosevelt, "We stand at Armageddon and battle for the Lord," was typical of language used by McKinley, Bryan, Wilson, and their predecessors in the political arena. And the massive volumes of George Bancroft, the great exemplar of the historian's craft in America, read like theological treatises, reflecting both the idiom and the assumptions of New England election sermons. Wherever one turns one becomes aware of the pervasiveness of religious language and imagery.

The present volume is designed to aid the reader to grasp the basic themes that have given content to the American sense of identity, mission, and destiny. Selections are provided to illustrate a fundamental rootage in English traditions and their subsequent development when transplanted in American soil. The selections also exhibit a robust faith in a living God (judging, correcting, disciplining, guiding, and directing the American people) being slowly eroded and reduced to the pale affirmations of twentieth-century "civil religion." The selections are repetitive because the themes are repetitive, and the repetition serves the useful purpose of illustrating the uniformity of political discourse in America. Clerical writings are used extensively because the clergy were more apt to give a full exposition of specific concepts, whereas in other writings the concepts were often introduced incidentally as axiomatic assumptions. Most of the themes could be illustrated by snippets drawn from the writings of Tom Paine but their meaning would not be as clear. Major space is given to selections emanating from New England because New England influence was decisive and because New England provides a much broader selection of material. Elsewhere, as Hezekiah Niles discovered, sermons and orations were generally designed "to be heard, not published."[1]

The selections in the Appendix illustrating the English heritage were originally compiled as an opening chapter to provide perspective and background for American developments. It soon became apparent that this extensive block of material at the outset of the volume would be more confusing than illuminating. There will be many readers, however, who will wish to turn to the Appendix for fuller explication of the notion of a chosen and covenanted people and of the purpose and utility of the fast days proclaimed by the Continental Congress during the American Revolution. The Appendix also gives the American sense of historical rootage and links it to the notion of ancient Saxon liberties.

It is well to keep in mind that there are, as Hans Kohn pointed out, two kinds of nationalism. British and American nationalism has tended to be universalistic, inclusive rather than exclusive, in contrast to particularistic forms of nationalism which emphasize "tribal solidarity" and "the diversity and self-sufficiency of nations." Kohn also noted that British nationalism was characterized by a deep moral undercurrent which often tempered the more brutal forms of imperial rule. The demand for and the promise of political, intellectual, and religious liberty was never wholly absent from British imperial politics, nor was the insistence upon equal justice under law. Also present as a moderating force were lingering traces of "the Puritan Revolution's enthusiastic hope and anticipation of the establishment of a universal Kingdom of God on this earth." It was Oliver Cromwell, in the midst of war against Spaniards, who told an English admiral at Jamaica in 1655: "The Lord himself hath a controversy with your enemies. . . . In that respect you fight the Lord's battles. . . . Only the covenant-fear of the Lord be upon you."[2] Fear of the Lord was always a strong antidote to national self-adulation. In America the same moral undercurrent tended to inhibit and restrain (not always successfully) imperial ambitions.

Spelling and punctuation have been modernized throughout, but some ambiguities remain. When "Heaven" and "Providence" are used as synonyms for God, they are capitalized; when they are used to denote either a place or an action, they are not. The context, however, does not always make this distinction clear. In citation of sources the place and date of publication, when available, is given, but the name of the publisher is omitted in citation of books printed prior to 1800. Since these early imprints can quickly be identified in standard bibliographies, there is little point in attempting to divine whether printer or bookseller was the publisher.

Appointment as a Fellow of the Folger Library in Washington, D.C., made it possible to pursue a wide-ranging investigation of the British sources of American national self-consciousness. The kindness of Louis B. Wright, director of the Library, in providing this opportunity is gratefully acknowledged, as are the many courtesies of other members of the Folger staff.

Finally, I wish to express appreciation to the editors of *Daedalus* for permission to reprint portions of articles by Robert N. Bellah and Milton Himmelfarb; to Teachers College, Columbia University, for permission to use selections from Isaac B. Berkson's *Theories of Americanization;* to the University of Pennsylvania Press for permission to reprint a brief portion of Leo Pfeffer's discussion in Horace M. Kallen's *Cultural Pluralism and the American Idea;* and to Harper & Row for permission to reproduce several pages of Sidney E. Mead's *The Lively Experiment.*

Winthrop S. Hudson

Rochester, New York
January 1, 1970

CONTENTS

FOREWORD BY MARTIN E. MARTY, GENERAL EDITOR ix

PREFACE xi

INTRODUCTION xix

1. THE AMERICAN IDENTITY 1

THE MEMORY OF THE FATHERS 6

William Bradford, *Of Plymouth Plantation* 8

Nathaniel Morton, *New England's Memorial* (1669) 13

Cotton Mather, *Magnalia Christi Americana* (1702) 14

John Cushing, *A Discourse . . . July 4, 1796* 17

A COVENANTED PEOPLE 19

Robert Cushman, *A Sermon Preached at Plymouth in New England* (1622) 21

John Winthrop, *A Model of Christian Charity* (1630) 21

Thomas Hooker, *The Danger of Desertion* (1641) 24

Continental Congress: Fast Days and Thanksgiving Days 26

Peter Whitney, *American Independence Vindicated* (1777) 31

Samuel West, *A Sermon Preached, May 29, 1776* 32

A FREE PEOPLE 33
Samuel Danforth, *A Brief Recognition of New England's Errand into the Wilderness* (1671) 37
John Oxenbridge, *New England Freemen Warned and Warmed* (1673) 38
Urian Oakes, *New England Pleaded With* (1673) 40
Cotton Mather, *The Wonderful Works of God* (1690) 44
Revolution in New England Justified (1691) 45
Abraham Keteltas, *God Arising and Pleading His People's Cause* (1777) 48

2. MISSION AND DESTINY 54

THIS MIGHTY EMPIRE 59
Timothy Dwight, *A Valedictory Address* (1776) 59
David Ramsay, *An Oration on the Advantages of American Independence* (1778) 62
Ezra Stiles, *The United States Elevated to Glory and Honor* (1783) 63
Elhanan Winchester, *An Oration on the Discovery of America* (1792) 70

THE CIVIL WAR INTERPRETED 72
Horace Bushnell, *Reverses Needed* (1861) 75
Abraham Lincoln, "First Inaugural Address" (1861) 84
Abraham Lincoln, "Second Annual Message to Congress" (1862) 84
Abraham Lincoln, "Second Inaugural Address" (1865) 85

MINORITY APPROPRIATIONS 86
Seraphin Bandol, "A Thanksgiving Sermon" (1781) 86
John Ireland, *The Church and Modern Society* (1896) 88

Letter of Greeting to George Washington from the Hebrew Congregation in Newport (1790) 91
Emma Lazarus, "The New Colossus" (1883) 92

3. THE RENOVATION OF THE WORLD 93

MISSIONS, REVIVALS, AND REVOLUTIONS 94
Heman Humphrey, *The Promised Land* (1819) 96
Lyman Beecher, "The Memory of Our Fathers" (1827) 99
Lyman Beecher, "The Necessity of Revivals of Religion" (1831) 105

FROM CONTINENTALISM TO IMPERIALISM 109
Josiah Strong, *Our Country* (1885) 112
Albert J. Beveridge, *For the Greater Republic* (1899) 117
Charles S. Olcott, *The Life of William McKinley* (1916) 119
Editorial, *The Pittsburgh Catholic* (1898) 120
Henry Van Dyke, *The American Birthright and the Philippine Pottage* (1898) 120

4. THE ISSUE OF PLURALISM 124

THE MELTING POT 125
John Ireland, *The Church and Modern Society* (1896) 125
Israel Zangwill, *The Melting Pot: Drama in Four Acts* (1908) 126

A PLURALISTIC SOCIETY 128
Isaac B. Berkson, *Theories of Americanization* (1920) 129
Leo Pfeffer, "American Individualism and Horace Kallen's Idea" (1956) 134
Milton Himmelfarb, "Secular Society? A Jewish Perspective" (1967) 135

CIVIL RELIGION 138
William Penn, *England's Present Interest* (1675) 140
Sidney E. Mead, "Thomas Jefferson's 'Fair Experiment'—Religious Freedom" (1963) 142
Robert N. Bellah, "Civil Religion in America" (1967) 146

APPENDIX: THE ENGLISH HERITAGE 153
THE ELECT NATION 154
An abridgement of . . . [John Foxe's] *Acts and Monuments* (1589) 157
John Foxe, *Acts and Monuments* (1641) 159
John Aylmer, *An Harbor for Faithful and True Subjects* (1559) 162
The Bible and Holy Scriptures (Geneva Bible, 1560) 164

THE COVENANTED NATION 166
Cornelius Burges, *A Sermon . . . to the House of Commons* (1641) 168
Edmund Calamy, *England's Looking-Glass* (1642) 174
Edmund Calamy, *God's Free Mercy to England* (1642) 176
Edmund Calamy, *England's Antidote* (1645) 179
The Soldier's Pocket Bible (1643) 181

TRUE RELIGION AND SAXON LIBERTIES 182
John Goodwin, *Anti-Cavalierism* (1642) 185
Jeremiah Burroughes, *The Glorious Name of God* (1643) 188
Hugh Peters, *God's Doings and Man's Duty* (1646) 191
William Penn, *English Liberties* (1682) 194
William Penn, *The Excellent Privilege of Liberty and Property* (1687) 198

NOTES 201

INTRODUCTION

UNLIKE other nations which evolved from a dim and distant past, the American nation seemed to spring into existence almost overnight. Prior to the American Revolution, few believed that the colonies could ever be brought to unite. There was no territorial unity, no administrative unity, no unity of will or purpose. Benjamin Franklin noted in 1760 that the colonies "are not only under different governors, but have different forms of government, different laws, different interests, and some of them different religious persuasions and different manners." Moreover, "their jealousy of each other is so great that, however necessary a union of the colonies has long been for their common defense and security against their enemies . . . , yet they have never been able to effect such a union among themselves nor even to agree in requesting the mother country to establish it for them. . . . In short, there are so many causes that must operate to prevent it that, I will venture to say, a union amongst them for such a purpose is not merely improbable, it is impossible."[1] During the Revolution, the participants often were equally despairing. General Nathanael Greene spoke for many when he confessed the difficulty of making the Continental army an effective fighting unit because it seemed impossible to "unhinge" the separate loyalties and mutual antipathies of the troops.[2] After the Revolution, George Washington could only express his own sense of astonishment that the divisions had been bridged. "Who, that was not a witness, could imagine that the most violent local prejudices would cease so soon and men who came from different parts of the continent, strongly disposed by the habits of education to despise and quarrel with each other, would instantly become one patriotic band of brothers."[3] This, of course, was a charitable judgment after the event. The colonists had not "instantly become one patriotic band of brothers," but they had held together sufficiently for the war, with good luck and French assistance, to be won.

Small wonder that American nationalism should be a puzzling phenomenon. Superficially at least, the American experience seems to run counter to the process by which other peoples have emerged into self-conscious nationhood. The growth of national feeling, the sentiment which gives people a sense of belonging together and possessing a distinctive self-image or identity, ordinarily has covered a span of centuries. It has required sufficiently unlimited time and sufficiently circumscribed space for a common language to develop, for diverse groups to be assimilated to a common ancestry, and for shared experiences to become common memories that are transmuted into common traditions, customs, habits, convictions, expectations, and loyalties.

Looking back in 1644 on a thousand years of English history, Henry Parker was able to assert that "all our conquerors . . . did rather lose themselves and their customs and their laws to us than to assimilate us to themselves."[4] Parker may have oversimplified the process by which Celts, Saxons, Danes, Normans, and others became Englishmen, but he was correct in stressing that the consolidation of these diverse elements into one nation proceeded slowly. Only in the fourteenth century did the English language replace French in law courts and official life, and not until the latter part of the fifteenth century did English become dominant in legal documents. It was not until the accession of the Tudors in 1485 that centuries of endemic dynastic strife was brought to an end. And it was not until the time of Elizabeth I that common people began to feel that as Englishmen they had been assigned a role in history that could be decisive for all mankind.

In contrast to the lengthy antecedents of other nations, the historical existence of the American colonies was brief. And instead of the closely knit life of a tight little island, the settlements were widely dispersed and separately governed. Intercolonial trade was discouraged, and communication between the colonies was difficult and intermittent. Thus each settlement tended to become a little world by itself, physically isolated, with little opportunity for shared experiences with other settlements. For these separate colonies, with their disparate interests and mutual jealousies, to field an army that even resembled "one patriotic band of brothers" and to push the war to a successful conclusion was an outcome so surprising that it was almost universally interpreted by the colonists themselves as a miracle wrought by Divine Providence.

Even after independence had been won and a national government established, the diversity of American society continued to be a subject for comment and a source of wonder. "Picture to yourself . . . , if you can," Alexis de Tocqueville wrote to a friend, "a society which comprises all the nations of the world . . . , people differing from one another in language, in beliefs, in opinions; in a word, a society possessing no roots, no memories, no prejudices, no routine, no common ideas, no national character, yet with a happiness a hundred times greater than our own. . . . This, then, is our starting point! What is the connecting link between these so different elements? How are they welded into one people?"[5]

I

The answer to Tocqueville's question is that America was not as diverse as he believed. If he overstated the diversity, it was because the diversity was overplayed by almost every American. It was overplayed in part to magnify the achievement of the colonists in forging a new nation, but in a more important sense the divisions were emphasized to underscore and confirm the belief that independence was a design of Heaven, effected by God himself to further his own purposes for the world. Even Tocqueville recognized that there was unity within the diversity.

"What strikes me," he wrote, "is that the immense majority of spirits join together in certain common opinions."[6]

The colonists had common opinions, and even common memories and traditions, because they had common antecedents and common historical rootage. The vast majority had a common language, a common ancestry, and a common loyalty. While it is true that the colonists thought of themselves as Virginians, Pennsylvanians, and New Yorkers rather than as Americans, yet it is equally true that most of them thought of themselves as Englishmen. "It be the people that makes the land English, not the land the people," Richard Elburne had written of England in 1624,[7] and this contention was doubly pertinent when Englishmen occupied new land across the seas. Benjamin Franklin reflected this point of view when he asserted that there was little danger of the colonists "uniting against their own nation which protects and encourages them, with which they have so many connections and ties of blood, interest, and affection, and which, it is well known, they all love much more than they love one another."[8] Later, when they had united sufficiently to secure the repeal of the Stamp Act, William Smith, provost of the College of Philadelphia, praised the colonists for "asserting our pedigree and showing that we were worthy of having descended from the illustrious stock of Britons."[9]

William Smith's use of the word "Britons" is significant. During the century and a half preceding the American Revolution, Englishmen, Scots, Welshmen, and Protestants of northern Ireland (Scotch-Irish in America) were being assimilated to a common British nationality. Since 1603 they had had a single monarch, and since 1707 they had been bound together in a united kingdom. They had shared the trauma of civil war. The castles, bastions of localism, had been dismantled. And they had come to view themselves first of all as British, inheritors of ancient British and Saxon traditions and liberties, and only secondarily as English, Scottish, Welsh, or Irish. With this transition in mind, it is not without significance that the influential handbook *English Liberties* (1682) in its last revised edition was entitled *British Liberties* (1766).

At the time of the American Revolution, more than 80 per cent of the colonists stemmed from this British stock and the non-British elements were in process of being assimilated to it. English, with isolated exceptions, was the common language. The Dutch Reformed churches, for example, had adopted English even for their record books. Considerable intermarriage with colonists of Continental origin had occurred. Crèvecoeur, in his *Letters from an American Farmer,* reported that he could point out "a family whose grandfather was an Englishman, whose wife was Dutch, whose son married a French woman, and whose present four sons have now wives of different nations."[10] As a result of this process of assimilation, colonists of Dutch and German descent saw no incongruity in affirming their rights as Englishmen.

If the diversity of national origin of the colonists ought not to be overplayed, their religious diversity also ought not to be unduly magnified. They had "common opinions," not simply because of a common national origin, but also because most of them stood within a common religious tradition—the Puritan Protestantism of the British Isles. They were separated into different denominations only by what were acknowledged to be subordinate matters, not by what were called the fundamentals of faith. By and large the adherents of the different denominations believed the same things. Moreover, this common faith became progressively more uniform in the eighteenth century as the tide of evangelical religion swept through the colonies, penetrating and reshaping the life even of non-British denominations.

The Great Awakening, however, did more than foster common beliefs. It made a further contribution to national self-consciousness by emphasizing the bonds of sympathy and mutual affection which united God's people in America. What was involved was a union of hearts, not a mere meeting of minds. Unity was depicted by Jonathan Edwards as "one of the most beautiful and happy things on earth." And the "life and soul" of true unity, he continued, was purely inward, being grounded neither in common advantage nor mutual prosperity but in "love of the brethren." At the instigation of Edwards, this feeling or sentiment of brotherly attachment found expression in concerts of prayer which brought together Christians of all denominations, in South Carolina and Georgia as well as in New Jersey and New Hampshire, to pray at the same hour and on the same day for the coming of Christ's kingdom. Later this union of hearts was redefined and broadened by the clergy who "preached up" the Revolution to include all loyal Americans. The outward interests of the colonists may have been diverse but they were made brothers by an inward common devotion to freedom, both civil and religious. Small wonder that Washington and Jay and Madison in their efforts to consolidate the new nation were able to strike a responsive chord by reminding Americans that they were a "band of brothers" united by "brotherly affection" and "mutual sympathy." Again and again this union of hearts was to be emphasized, by Jefferson, Jackson, and Lincoln among others, as that which made Americans effectively one. Looking back in 1845, George Bancroft summarized the American experience by declaring that it demonstrated that a union "constituted by consent must be preserved by love."[11]

The Awakening also evoked national self-consciousness in more tangible ways. The gatherings for unison prayer, for example, became visible symbols and even instruments of intercolonial solidarity. More important, at a time when intercolonial contacts were few, was the activity of itinerant clergymen. Even before the revival, men such as Francis Makemie, George Keith, Abel Morgan, Henry Muhlenberg, and later Francis Asbury provided a link between the colonies by moving up and down the coast and into the hinterland, looking after their respective constituencies, gathering people into churches, and forming intercolonial synods, associations, and assemblies. Itinerant preachers also became bearers of the revival, carrying it from colony to colony, preaching in churches of all denominations and often in the open air to anyone who would listen. Three decades before George Washington, Benjamin Franklin, Thomas Jefferson, and Patrick Henry emerged into prominence, the names of such revivalists as George Whitefield, Jonathan Edwards, and Gilbert Tennant had become household words and the men themselves were rallying figures for a movement that cut across all colonial and denominational lines. At a time when political and commercial ties were mostly transatlantic, these itinerant preachers made a major contribution to the birth of an American national consciousness. It is perhaps significant that the "awakening" they helped to generate did not reach Nova Scotia until after the American Revolution, for Nova Scotia alone of the colonies on the Atlantic coast remained aloof from the struggle for independence.

In addition to a predominant national origin and a predominant religious faith, the American colonists were also characterized by a predominant political bias, by what Edmund Burke described as a "fierce spirit of liberty." Some Europeans, without firsthand knowledge of life in the "woods" and bemused by a romantic image of the noble savage, believed that a spirit of liberty was automatically generated by the free air of an empty continent. In 1774 the official *Gazette de France* reflected this point of view: "Our navigators who have studied the northern continent well assert that an innate taste for liberty is inseparable from the soil, the sky, the forests, and the lakes which keep this vast and still new country from resembling the other parts of the globe. They are persuaded that any European transported to those climes would contract this peculiar characteristic."[12] General John Burgoyne, for whom men in the woods were real persons and not legendary figures, knew that something more was involved than soil, sky, forests, and lakes. The French Canadians who joined the American rebels in 1776, he reported, did not follow "the cry of liberty, but the belief of strength." They had been subjects of France, "they were since so to England, they would be the same to the emperor of Morocco."[13] Far from being the product of the influence exerted by an empty continent, the fierce spirit of liberty of the British colonists, as Edmund Burke took care to point out in his *Speech on Conciliation with America,* had been brought by the colonists from England. Their devotion was to "liberty according to English ideas and on English principles." This fundamental rootage also was fully understood by Guillaume Raynal. In his *Histoire philosophique et politique des établissements et du commerce des Européens dans les deux Indes* (1770), Raynal painted a glowing picture of an America destined to bring about a new era of humanity in contrast to the moral decadence of Europe. But Raynal was sober-minded enough to warn the colonists of the danger of separating from Great Britain, reminding them that they owed their liberties to the English constitution and political tradition.[14]

II

When one speaks of the unity of the American colonies in terms of a common language, a common ancestry, and common opinions springing from a common faith and a common political bias, he is pointing to the fact that the colonies were outposts of Britain and to the fact that the colonists thought of themselves as an integral part of the British nation. Nor was it accidental that religious views and political convictions were closely intertwined in the colonists' sense of nationality, for the intermingling of these twin strands had given form and substance to British national self-consciousness.

While devotion to liberty as à characteristic trait of the British spirit had a long history, Sir Edward Coke did as much to establish it as a fundamental feature of the British constitution and thus of the British nation as anyone else. Following the death of Elizabeth in 1603, Coke took the lead in countering the absolutist claims of James I by asserting the constitutional prerogatives of the common law courts and parliament. In his *Institutes of the Laws of England,* Coke made use of medieval chronicles and the thirteenth-century *Mirroir des Justices* to fashion a legend of ancient British and Saxon liberties which stood in stark contrast to the bondage introduced by the Normans. The English, however, were not easily deprived of their heritage. Again and again the Norman monarchs and their successors were forced to confirm, and occasionally willingly acknowledged, the ancient liberties of the realm. Coke's version of England's constitutional heritage was especially persuasive because it was so easily harmonized with an account of the English past that had been assiduously promoted during Elizabeth's reign.

More than a half-century before Coke's *Institutes* were written, John Foxe had used the same chronicles to write a universal history, *Acts and Monuments of Matters Most Special and Memorable* (better known as the "Book of Martyrs"), which emphasized the special role of England and the English church in the story of mankind. Set within the context of the whole course of human history, Foxe's narrative was inspired by his identification of the English with the ancient Hebrew people in the age-long struggle between God and Satan. As the successive ages or dispensations into which history was divided moved toward their predetermined end, England had inherited the role of God's elect champion. Arrayed against her were the forces of Antichrist led by the proud prelates of Rome. To indicate that England had received the true faith directly from the apostles, Foxe reported the legendary accounts of the gospel being brought to England by Joseph of Arimathea, of the conversion of King Lucius, and of Emperor Constantine's birth in Britain of a British Christian mother. Foxe also recounted how native kings had combated corruption and resisted tyranny while native teachers kept true faith alive. With John Wyclif the first sign of the binding of Antichrist had appeared in England, and from England the gospel light was destined to shine to all nations for the recovery of apostolic faith and life.

Few books have been more influential than Foxe's "Book of Martyrs." Written with religious fervor and dramatic intensity, his contentions documented with what he believed to be the facts of history and the plain teaching of Scripture, Foxe's account of the course of human history became indelibly imprinted in the minds of all Englishmen, fostering pride in being English, and making them conscious of being a people set apart from all others.

Coke's interpretation of the English past was easily fused

with Foxe's account of the place of England within the total plan of God. For Foxe the Norman Conquest was as pivotal as it was for Coke. Foxe believed the conquest, the consequence of Harold's perfidy, to mark the beginning of the reign of Antichrist in England, and he equated it with the bondage of ancient Israel to the Egyptian oppressors as part of the age-old conflict between the forces of light and darkness. Also Foxe had viewed resistance to the Norman bondage as involving an effort to preserve ancient liberties as well as the indigenous apostolic faith. Thus it was easy to read Coke's reconstruction of England's constitutional history within the context of Foxe's overall interpretation of the English past.

The fusion of Foxe and Coke in the popular mind was cemented during the religious and constitutional crisis precipitated by the meeting of the Long Parliament in 1640, being facilitated by the common conviction that, while religious and constitutional concerns were not identical, neither were they incompatible. They were regarded as complementary, mutually reinforcing, closely intertwined, and of equal concern to God. When Oliver Cromwell referred to "religion" and "civil liberty" as "the two greatest concernments that God hath in the world," no parliamentary leader would have disagreed. "If anyone whatsoever think the interest of Christians and the interest of the nation inconsistent or two different things," Cromwell continued, "I wish my soul may never enter into their secrets." God's peculiar interest is with "his church, the communion of the faithful followers of Christ," and his general interest is with "living people, not as Christians, but as human creatures."[15]

The Puritan Revolution in many ways is crucial for an understanding of English and American nationalism. Hans Kohn, in *The Idea of Nationalism,* has called the Puritan Revolution "the first example of modern nationalism"—of "a people roused and stirred to its innermost depths, feeling upon its shoulders the mission of history," of being "chosen to do great things" with everyone called upon to participate. This sense of being engaged in a great task was not confined to the educated but became "a bond uniting the whole people," for its "vehicle" was the Bible, a book open and known to every Englishman.[16] There was some dissent, but the dissent was only at the point of the practical application of the major motifs of interpretation. The notion of Providence guiding and directing the affairs of men to a predetermined end, the idea of a chosen and covenanted people, the expectation of a messianic fulfillment, were shared by everyone.

This nationalism of the Puritan Revolution was a peculiarly open-ended nationalism, since "the community or nation for which they cherished this feeling [of full devotion] was a community decided not by blood but by faith." England was a nation by adoption and by grace after the manner of the Old Testament, and the faith from which it derived its vocation was a faith destined for all mankind. Thus the nationalism of the Puritan Revolution could run easily and naturally into internationalism. As Ernest Barker phrased it: "The chosen people of one nation, and the whole of that people through them, have a community and a fellowship with the chosen people of other nations, and with other nations through them."[17]

This nationalism was open-ended in another respect. The appeal to an ancient British and Saxon past, which incorporated the legendary King Arthur of the Celts, made the transition easy from the concept of an English to that of a British nation, for the ancient liberties were a common inheritance of the British Isles as a whole. And hand-in-hand with this went the conviction that it was Britain's privilege, by the grace of God, to be the home of liberties that were in no way meant for Great Britain alone. The ancient restraints incorporated in common law and constitutional arrangement were designed to protect rights which belonged to the whole of mankind, and no nation would be entirely happy until it possessed the blessing of British liberties.

While the Puritan movement suffered military and political defeat in 1660, its concepts and understandings continued to inform the minds of most Englishmen. Its principles continued to be voiced with unabated fervor in religious dissent and opposition politics, most notably in the parliamentary election of 1679 and in the events which culminated, first, in Monmouth's rebellion and, then, in the Glorious Revolution of 1688. And the tradition lived on, not only in the apologists for the constitutional arrangements which followed the expulsion of James II, but in the dissenting and opposition interpreters of the tradition in the eighteenth century.

In the colonies the tradition also lived on. From the beginning there had been those among the colonists who identified themselves with ancient Israel and described their perilous migration to the New World as an "exodus." And as members of what were dissenting churches in England, most of the colonists were also predisposed to accept an account of the past which incorporated Saxon liberties as falling within the scope of a biblical understanding of history. This predisposition was strengthened by a situation in which they were both forced and permitted to be independent, self-reliant, and resourceful. In the course of time, as threats to ancient liberties appeared to mount both in England and in America, they were prepared to identify their transatlantic venture, not only with the exodus of the Hebrews, but also with the exodus of the Saxon ancestors who had left their home on the Continent and crossed the English Channel to establish a firm base of liberty in a new land.

Nor was the messianic expectation nourished by Foxe's "Book of Martyrs" diminished in America. To the contrary, the very name "New World" was calculated to recall the biblical promise of "a new heaven and a new earth" and to cultivate the hope of a new beginning. This sense of expectancy was further heightened by the "holy experiments" undertaken in several of the colonies. And finally, the religious awakening which swept through the colonies after 1730 persuaded many that the renovation of the world was to begin in America.

III

While it is true that the colonists were widely dispersed with no administrative or territorial unity and with no unity of will or purpose of their own, yet, as has been noted, they were linked by a common language, a common ancestry, a common faith, a common devotion to liberty, and a common understanding of history. They also were bound together by a common loyalty to Great Britain. They regarded themselves as part of the British nation, sharing the memories, traditions, and rights of the British people. Admiration for the British constitution was never more clearly expressed than by Richard Bland of Virginia in *An Inquiry into the Rights of the British Colonies* (1766): "It is a fact as certain as history can make it that the present civil constitution of England derives its original from those Saxons who . . . established [in Britain] a form of government similar to that they had been accustomed to live under in their native country. . . . This government, like that from which they came, was founded upon principles of the most perfect liberty." Two years earlier, James Otis of Massachusetts in *The Rights of the British Colonies Asserted* (1764), declared: "Liberty was better understood and more fully enjoyed by our ancestors before the coming in of the first Normans than ever after, till it was found necessary for the salvation of the kingdom to combat the arbitrary and wicked proceedings of the Stuarts."[18]

Curiously but understandably, the colonists believed that the struggle to preserve their liberties was a struggle to preserve the liberties of Great Britain. This fact has been made abundantly evident by Bernard Bailyn's analysis of the pamphlet literature produced on the eve of the American Revolution.[19] By preserving "our liberties," Jonathan Mayhew contended, we may "have the great felicity and honor to . . . keep Britain herself from ruin."[20]

For more than a decade prior to the Declaration of Independence, there was a widespread conviction both in Britain and in America that political freedom was far from secure in Great Britain. Cause for alarm was found in the manipulation of parliamentary elections, the abuse of patronage and executive power, the misuse of libel laws, the continuing disabilities of dissenters, and the treatment meted out to John Wilkes, who was denied the seat in parliament to which he repeatedly had been elected. As early as 1760, Charles Carroll of Maryland reported from London that in England "our dear-bought liberty stands upon the brink of destruction."[21]

Within this context, the colonists viewed almost every action of the British government with suspicion. The Stamp Act, the Townshend Duties, the interference with the judiciary and the jury system, the stationing of troops in Boston—all were viewed as part of a surreptitious plot to destroy their liberties. Deeply involved in the conspiracy, it was thought, were Anglican ecclesiastics who were determined to bring all British subjects into conformity with the Church of England. The immediate objective was the reduction of the colonists to docility, but the ultimate aim was the destruction of all the rights and privileges embedded in the British constitution. First the colonists were to be reduced, and then Britain herself. John Adams later recalled that Oxenbridge Thacher reflected common opinion when he spoke of the determination of the British government

> to new-model the colonies from the foundation, to annul all their charters, to constitute them royal governments, to raise a revenue in America by parliamentary taxation, to apply that revenue to pay the salaries of governors, judges, and all other crown officers . . . , and further to establish bishops and the whole system of the Church of England, tithes and all, throughout all British America. This system, he said, if it were suffered to prevail, would extinguish the flame of liberty all over the world, that America would be employed as an engine to batter down all the miserable remains of liberty in Great Britain and Ireland, where only any semblance of it was left in the world.[22]

The colonists increasingly believed that America had become, by default, the heir of England as the trustee of liberty for all mankind. And they believed that, by God's intention, America was destined to be a purer and freer England, strong, healthy, undefiled, and more firmly devoted to freedom. The American continent and the American people became blended in a universally accepted myth of great symbolic significance. The continent was the Promised Land. The people were Israel, escaping from Egyptian bondage, crossing a forbidding sea, living a wilderness life, until, by God's grace and their own faithfulness, the wilderness became a new Canaan. Their pilgrimage was part and parcel of God's scheme of redemption for the whole human race. Viewed from this perspective, as Perry Miller put it, the American Revolution was a religious revival which had "the astounding good fortune to succeed."[23]

HARPER FORUM BOOKS

Martin E. Marty, General Editor

NATIONALISM AND RELIGION IN AMERICA

Concepts of American Identity and Mission

I

THE AMERICAN IDENTITY

"WHAT do we mean by the American Revolution?" John Adams wrote Hezekiah Niles in 1818. "Do we mean the American War? The Revolution was effected before the war commenced. The Revolution was in the minds and hearts of the people. . . . The radical change in the principles, opinions, sentiments, and affections of the people was the real American Revolution." It was no easy enterprise, he observed, to unite "the people of thirteen colonies, all distinct, unconnected, and independent of each other" and "compose them into an independent nation." Seldom, if ever, in history had a people been welded together in so short a time. "Thirteen clocks were made to strike together—a perfect mechanism which no artist had ever before effected." And yet, while the difficulties were great, Adams knew that the change was not quite so radical and not quite so quickly accomplished as he intimated, for he immediately suggested that the "principles and feelings" which united them should be "traced back for two hundred years and sought in the history of the country from the first plantations in America."[1]

The colonies did have a history, an even longer history than that dating from the first settler. The principles and feelings that united them were supplied to them out of a past that they believed ran back to Hebrew and Saxon times. Their love of liberty bound them together, and this was no newborn affection. This was their Saxon heritage. Their understanding of the ways of God with men and nations also united them. Derived from the Bible and Foxe's "Book of Martyrs," this understanding had informed the mind and heart of almost every Englishman since the reign of Elizabeth I. But national self-consciousness, an awareness of a separate national identity, requires a history of its own in which the common feelings, loyalties, and convictions have found expression. This need for a meaningful and significant American past was supplied largely by the writings of New Englanders.

The precedence given Plymouth over Jamestown in American mythology may be chronologically inaccurate but symbolically it is correct. The story of the Pilgrim fathers became the epic account of American beginnings because, until after World War I at least, Americans understood their own identity within concepts and categories that were most characteristic of early New England. The priority of New England in the American self-image was attested by almost everyone. Senator Albert J. Beveridge said that as "a son of Virginia" he "gladly" acknowledged "Forefathers' Day" as the birthday of American citizenship: "We have no 'Columbus Day' because the Santa Maria carried no principle necessary to our national welfare now, no 'Cavaliers' Day' because from Jamestown shines no light for our pathway as the century's evening darkens into night. But 'Forefathers' Day' will dawn as long as the Republic lives because the Puritan principle is to the Republic the very breath of life."

Matthew Simpson, Bishop of the Methodist Church in Indiana and born and reared in the Presbyterian country of southwestern Pennsylvania and southeastern Ohio, was equally euphoric in his view of early New England, saying that it was not without reason that Plymouth alone of all the early settlements flourished. John Ireland, Roman Catholic Archbishop of St. Paul, explained to a French audience that "the first colonists in the New England or northeastern states have, more than any other element of our population, contributed to the present American type. They have, beyond doubt, given to our whole population an impress which is ineffaceable, communicated to it a spirit which remains unchanged in the American despite our varied aggregations of types from other countries."

And Philip Schaff, a Swiss by birth, a German by education, a Reformed church minister in Pennsylvania by calling, and a perceptive interpreter of America, called New England "the garden of America," the seedbed of influences which shaped "the religious, social, and political life of the whole nation."[2]

There are several reasons why New England should have become pre-eminent and predominant in American self-understanding.

First of all, New England had a coherent understanding of itself, a sense of communal purpose, an awareness of being engaged in a venture of more than ordinary significance, a feeling of self-esteem. The New England migration was undertaken at the initiative of the settlers themselves, most of whom paid their own way. And it was a communal enterprise. They moved to the New World in family groups, sometimes in whole congregations. All the middle ranks of society were represented, both sexes, and people of all ages. No fewer than 130 university graduates came to New England before 1640, 92 of them ministers. A college was quickly established, and strenuous efforts were exerted to make sure that everyone could read. And New Englanders shared a common religious conviction that they had been impelled by God himself to forsake the corruptions of old England that "one small candle" might be kindled in the American wilderness from which a thousand others would be lighted.

New England had no real counterpart in any of these respects. Pennsylvania was somewhat similar in conception, but was established late, promoted as a commercial venture, lacked homogeneity of population, and had its initial vision eroded by the competing interests of its polyglot inhabitants. Elsewhere commercial considerations bulked large. There was a sharp distinction between "adventurers" who put up the money and "planters" who were sent out as settlers. The adventurers mostly stayed home, and the planters or colonists tended to come as individuals, usually as young indentured servants. The preferred age was from fifteen to twenty-four. Some were "pressed," forcibly placed on shipboard by those eager to receive bounty payments. Others were recruited by emptying jails. Many were illiterate. There were few women; and of the few, not many came willingly. These early colonists shared no common religious ideal, no sense of destiny, no compelling conviction of responding to a godly summons.[3]

New England became central to the American self-image, in the second place, partly by default. The New Englanders saw their own history as a revelation of God's providential dealings with his people and they became inveterate history writers. They felt under compulsion to record both the remarkable demonstrations of God's providence and the heroic deeds and witness of their fathers lest they be forgotten by their children. They had a story to tell. They told it repeatedly, and they told it well.

The story of the founding of the other colonies, in the absence of a "thumping ideological purpose," was less susceptible to treatment as the unfolding plot of a drama. Nor did the materials at hand lend themselves so readily to fashioning a noble epic. Most accounts that were produced were written to satisfy the curiosity of people in England rather than to instruct the colonists on the meaning of their common existence. No one attempted large-scale histories. Captain John Smith was the most celebrated of the Virginia annalists and he wrote to glorify his own exploits. He pictured Virginia as a natural paradise, spoiled by the settlers, and saved only by his own personal intervention. The significant point is that Smith was never more than a temporary colonist. The colony was incidental to his purpose. The narrative was designed to confirm his own self-image as a masterful and heroic figure. New York and Maryland, like Pennsylvania, had no consistent focus. The remaining colonies were founded when colonizing had become less novel, and thus were denied even the exuberant reporting typified by John Smith.[4]

Lastly, from New York to Georgia, there were many colonists who found the themes enunciated in the New England story familiar and congenial. This was partly because the New England themes were representative of traditional English views. The other colonies may have lacked sufficient awareness of communal purpose to produce histories of their own, but the colonists themselves retained their sense of British nationality. Other themes of the New England story were familiar and congenial because they reflected the religious convictions of a growing number of colonists elsewhere. The colonists outside New England, for the most part, may have come as individuals, but throughout the colonial period they were being gathered into churches. The churches were part of the broad current of English Puritanism. Baptists, Presbyterians, Quakers, and many Anglicans were no less Puritan in their views than the New Englanders. The College of New Jersey at Princeton, founded by Presbyterians, had New Englanders for its early presidents. The Princeton satellites to the west and south felt equally at home with New England theology. As for the Quakers, the exhortation of Thomas Budd could easily be ascribed to someone at Plymouth, Salem, or Boston.

> I am also sensible of the many exercises and inward combats that many of you met withal after you felt an inclination in your hearts of transplanting yourselves into America. O the breathings and fervent prayers and earnest desires that were in your hearts to the Lord that you might not go, except it was his good pleasure to remove you for a purpose of his own. . . . The Lord heard your prayers and answered your desires inasmuch as that his fatherly care was over you and his loving presence did accompany you over the great deep, so that you saw his wonderful deliverance and in a sense thereof praised his name for the same.
>
> The Lord having thus far answered our souls' desire as to bring us to our desired port in safety and to remain with us to be a counselor of good things unto us, let us now answer this kindness unto us by a righteous conversation and a pure, holy, and innocent life, that others beholding the same may be convinced thereby and may glorify our heavenly father.
>
> The eyes of many are on us, some for good and some for evil. Therefore my earnest prayers are to the Lord that he would preserve us and give us wisdom that we may be governed aright before him.[5]

With a common outlook so widely prevalent, no *tour de force* was required to cause other colonists to make the account of the

New England past their own. William Bradford, not John Smith, was the historian who recapitulated their understanding of the meaning and significance of the American experience.

THE MEMORY OF THE FATHERS

In 1641 Stephen Marshall, in a Thanksgiving Day sermon before the House of Commons, spoke to the question what should people do to testify to their thankfulness, saying:

> If you will go and ring bells, make bonfires, feast one another, and send portions to the poor for whom nothing is provided, I have nothing to say against it. I think you shall do well. But this I beseech you do: Go home and . . . write down a catalogue of all the great things which God hath this year done for us, and let your children know them. And the Lord put it into the heart of some wise observer of the times so to write them that the present and future generation may be blessed with a true narration of these wonderful mercies.[6]

The insistence upon recording God's mercies and preserving the memory of those valiant in the Lord's service was a consistent theme of Puritan preaching in both England and America. Urian Oakes spoke of it as "our great duty to be the Lord's remembrancers or recorders." Thomas Shepard suggested that just as there were "court books of record" so a "Book of Records" of "God's dealings with his church and people" should be kept. "O that it might be said concerning . . . the mercies, judgments, and great acts of the Lord, never to be forgotten by us, 'as it is written in the Book of the Chronicles of the Governors of Massachusetts.' "[7]

The recording of New England's history began with the story of the Pilgrims at Plymouth. The first account was Mourt's *A Relation or Journal of . . . the English Plantation Settled at Plymouth* (London, 1622). Two years later, Edward Winslow published *Good News from New England* (London, 1624), covering the events of the second and third years of the colony. Then the full history of the first twenty-seven years was given by William Bradford in *Of Plymouth Plantation*. John Winthrop chronicled the much larger migration to Massachusetts Bay in his "Journal," and Edward Johnson contributed an ecstatic account with his *Wonder-Working Providence of Zion's Savior in New England* (London, 1654). Later the dramatic sequence of events of King Philip's War was vividly depicted in complementary narratives by Increase Mather and William Hubbard.

The first historical work published in America was Nathaniel Morton's *New England's Memorial; or, A Brief Relation of the Most Memorable and Remarkable Passages of the Providence of God Manifested to the Planters of New England* (Cambridge, Mass., 1669). Morton was William Bradford's nephew, and *New England's Memorial* was a condensation of his uncle's unpublished manuscript, with the addition of some material dealing with Massachusetts Bay and Morton's own account of the years from 1647 to 1668. While Morton's work became the standard public history, direct use of the Bradford manuscript was made by William Hubbard for his *General History of New England,* by Cotton Mather for his *Magnalia Christi Americana; or, The Ecclesiastical History of New England* (London, 1702), by Thomas Prince, *A Chronological History of New England* (Boston, 1736), and by Thomas Hutchinson, *The History of the Colony and Province of Massachusetts Bay* (Boston, 1764–1767). Bradford's story also was reflected at secondhand in Daniel Neal's *The History of New England* (London, 1720).[8]

There were several conspicuous features of these accounts of New England. First, the New England story was viewed as a continuation of John Foxe's narrative of the pitched battles between Christ and Antichrist that had marked the course of human history from the beginning. Second, the biblical analogies were prominent. The leave-taking from England was compared to the departure of the Israelites out of Egypt. Bradford was "our Moses," and Winthrop "our New-English Nehemiah." When Bradford died, God raised up a "Joshua" to lead "our Israel" in its further pilgrimage. Third, the accounts rivaled *Pilgrim's Progress* for excitement, with a small band in the midst of winter being thrust into "a hideous and desolate wilderness, full of wild beasts and wild men." There were fights with Indians in thick forests and treacherous swamps, but also the friendship and kindness of Squanto and Massasoit. There was sickness and near starvation, but also the good harvest and the first thanksgiving. Fourth, it was an open-ended story, a drama of movement with a future as well as a past. From the beginning New England was viewed as a society in flux, with alternative possibilities before it. While events were always in the hands of God, they were ministered in proportion to New England's faithfulness or unfaithfulness. Cotton Mather appeared somewhat despondent in his *Magnalia Christi,* but this was partly a technique to emphasize the constant need for repentance and reform. His true sentiments were probably expressed in his dedicatory epistle to his uncle, Nathaniel Mather, where he affirmed that New Englanders "are the best people under heaven, there being among them, not only less open profaneness and less of lewdness, but also more of the serious profession [of Christ] . . . than is among any other people upon the face of the whole earth." Here was what seemed to be a boastful and almost strident claim to identity—"the best people under heaven." But the claim was tempered by the knowledge, ever present in the Puritan mind, that the best was far from perfection and that God demands a stricter accounting from those whom he has brought into a special relationship to himself.

John Cushing's discourse of 1796 is included as an early example of the Fourth of July oration which gives a clear definition of the Fourth of July as an annual American Passover observance.

William Bradford, *Of Plymouth Plantation*[9]

CHAPTER I

It is well known unto the godly and judicious how ever since the first breaking out of the light of the gospel in our honorable nation of England (which was the first of nations whom the Lord adorned therewith after that gross darkness of popery which had covered and overspred the world), what wars and oppositions . . . Satan hath raised, maintained, and continued against the saints from time to time in one sort or other. . . . But when he could not prevail by these means against the main truths of the gospel but that they began to take rooting in many places, being watered with the blood of the martyrs and blessed from heaven with a gracious increase, he then began to take him to his ancient stratagem, used of old against the first Christians, . . . he then began to sow errors, heresies, and wonderful dissensions amongst the professors themselves. . . .

Mr. [John] Foxe recordeth how . . . began that bitter war of contention and persecution about the ceremonies and service book, and other popish and antichristian stuff, the plague of England to this day. . . .

But that I may come more near my intendment, when . . . by the travail and diligence of some godly and zealous preachers and God's blessing on their labors (as in other places of the land, so in the north parts) many became enlightened by the Word of God and had their ignorance and sins discovered unto them . . . , the work of God was no sooner manifest in them but presently they were both scoffed and scorned by the profane multitude. . . . They could not long continue in any peaceable condition but were hunted and persecuted on every side. . . . Some were taken and clapped into prison, others had their houses beset and watched night and day. . . . Seeing themselves thus molested . . . by a joint consent they resolved to go into the Low Countries where they heard was freedom of religion for all men. . . .

Chapter IV

After they had lived in this city [Leyden] about some eleven or twelve years (which is the more observable being the whole time of that famous truce between that state and the Spaniards), . . . those prudent governors with sundry of the sagest members began both to apprehend their present dangers and wisely to foresee the future and think of timely remedy. . . . At length they began to incline to . . . removal to some other place. . . . The place they had thoughts on was some of those vast and unpeopled countries of America. . . . It was granted the dangers were great, but not desperate; the difficulties were many, but not invincible. For though there were many of them likely, yet they . . . by provident care and the use of good means might in a great measure be prevented, and all of them, through the help of God, by fortitude and patience might either be borne or overcome. . . . Their ends were good and honorable, their calling lawful and urgent, and therefore they might expect the blessing of God in their proceeding. Yea, though they should lose their lives in this action, yet might they have comfort in the same. . . . They lived here but as men in exile and in a poor condition, and as great miseries might possibly befall them in this place for the twelve years of truce [between the Dutch and the Spaniards] were now out and there was nothing but beating of drums and preparing for war, the events whereof are always uncertain. The Spaniard might prove as cruel as the savages of America, and the famine and pestilence as sore here as there, and their liberty less to look out for remedy. . . .

CHAPTER VII

At length, after much travail and these debates, all things were got ready and prepared. . . . And the time being come that they must depart, they were accompanied with most of their brethren out of the city unto . . . Delfshaven where the ship lay ready to receive them. So they left that good and pleasant city which had been their resting place near twelve years, but they knew they were pilgrims and looked not much on those things but lifted up their eyes to the heavens, their dearest country, and quieted their spirits. . . . The next day, the wind being fair, they went aboard, and their friends with them, where truly doleful was the sight of that sad and mournful parting, to see what sighs and sobs and prayers did sound amongst them, what tears did gush from every eye, and pithy speeches pierced each heart. . . . But the tide (which stays for no man) calling them away that were loath to depart, their reverend pastor falling down on his knees (and they all with him) with watery cheeks commended them with most fervent prayers to the Lord and his blessing. And then with mutual embraces and many tears, they took their leaves one of another, which proved to be the last leave to many of them. . . .

CHAPTER IX

Being thus arrived in a good harbor and brought safe to land, they fell upon their knees and blessed the God of heaven who had brought them over the vast and furious ocean, and delivered them from all the perils and miseries thereof again to set their feet on the firm and stable earth, their proper element. . . .

But here I cannot but stay and make a pause and stand half amazed at this poor people's present condition. And so I think will the reader too when he well considers the same. Being thus passed the vast ocean, and a sea of troubles before in their preparation . . . , they had now no friends to welcome them, nor inns to entertain or refresh their weatherbeaten bodies, no houses or much less towns to repair to, to seek for succor. . . . Besides, what could they see but a hideous and desolate wilderness, full of wild beasts and wild men? . . . Neither could they, as it were, go up to the top of Pisgah to view from this wilderness a more godly country to feed their hopes [Deut. 3:27], for which way soever they turned their eyes (save upward to the heavens) they could have little solace or content in respect of any outward objects. . . . What could now sustain them but the Spirit of God and his grace?

May not and ought not the children of these fathers rightly say: "Our fathers were Englishmen which came over this great ocean and were ready to perish in this wilderness, but they cried unto the Lord, and he heard their voice, and looked upon their adversity, etc. (Deut. 26:5, 7). Let them, therefore, praise the Lord because he is good and his mercies endure for ever. Yea, let them which have been redeemed of the Lord show how he hath delivered them out of the hand of the oppressor when they wandered in the desert wilderness out of the way and found no city to dwell in, both hungry and thirsty, their soul was overwhelmed in them. Let them confess before the Lord his loving kindness, and his wonderful works before the sons of men (Ps. 107:1–2, 4–5, 8)." . . .

The Second Book

The rest of this history . . . I shall, for brevity's sake, handle by way of annals. . . .

THE REMAINDER OF *Anno Dom.* 1620

I shall a little return back and begin with a combination made by them before they came ashore, being the first foundation of their government in this place. . . . The form was as followth:

In the name of God, Amen. We whose names are underwritten, the loyal subjects of our dread sovereign lord, King James, by the grace of God, of Great Britain, France, and Ireland, king, defender of the faith, etc., having undertaken for the glory of God and advancement of the Christian faith, and honor of our king and country, a voyage to plant the first colony in the northern parts of Virginia, do by these presents solemnly and mutually, in the presence of God and one of another, covenant and combine ourselves together into a civil body politic for our better ordering and preservation and furtherance of the ends aforesaid; and by virtue hereof to enact, constitute, and frame such just and equal laws, ordinances, acts, constitutions, and offices, from time to time, as shall be thought most mete and convenient for the general good of the colony, unto which we promise all due submission and obedience. In witness whereof we have hereunder subscribed our names at Cape Cod, the eleventh of November, in the year of the reign of our sovereign lord, King James of England, France, and Ireland the eighteenth, and of Scotland the fifty-fourth. *Anno Dom.* 1620. . . .

Anno Dom. 1629

Mr. Allerton, safely arriving in England and delivering his letters to their friends and acquainting them with his instructions, found . . . they were very forward and willing to . . . send over [more of] the Leyden people. . . . They had passage with the ships that came to Salem that brought over many godly persons to begin the plantations and churches of Christ there and in the Bay of Massachusetts. So their long stay and keeping back was recompensed by the Lord to their friends here with a double blessing, in that they not only enjoyed them now beyond their late expectation (when all their hopes seemed to be cut off) but with them many more godly friends and Christian brethren, as the beginning of a larger harvest unto the Lord, in the increase of his churches and people in these parts to the admiration of many and almost wonder of the world that of so small beginnings so great things should ensue, as time after manifested, and that here should be a resting place for so many of the Lord's people when so sharp a scourge came upon their own nation. But it was the Lord's doing, and it ought to be marvelous in our eyes [Ps. 118:23; Mt. 21:42; Mk. 12:11]. . . .

Anno Dom. 1630

Thus, out of small beginnings, greater things have been produced by his hand that made all things of nothing and gives being to all things that are. And, as one small candle may light a thousand, so the light here kindled hath shone to many, yea, in some sort to our whole nation. Let the glorious name of Jehovah have all the praise. . . .

Nathaniel Morton, *New England's Memorial; or, A Brief Relation of the Most Memorable and Remarkable Passages of the Providence of God Manifested to the Planters of New England* (Cambridge, Mass.: John Usher, 1669)

To the Christian Reader:

Gentle reader, I have for some length of time looked upon it as a duty incumbent, especially on the immediate successors of those that had so large experience of those many memorable and signal demonstrations of God's goodness (*viz.* the first beginners of this plantation in New England), to commit to writing his gracious dispensations on that behalf . . . , that so what we have seen and what our fathers have told us we may not hide from our children, showing to the generations to come the praises of the Lord (Ps. 78:3–4) that especially the seed of Abraham, his servant, and the children of Jacob, his chosen (Ps. 105:8–9), may remember his marvelous works in the beginning and progress of the planting of New England. . . .

The method I have observed is . . . a faithful commemorizing and declaration of God's wonderful works for, by, and to his people in preparing a place for them by driving out the heathen before them, bringing them through a sea of troubles, preserving and protecting them from and in those dangers that attended them in their low estate when they were strangers in the land, and making this howling wilderness [Deut. 32:10] a chamber of rest, safety, and pleasantness; . . . but especially in giving us . . . so great a freedom in our civil and religious enjoyments, and also in giving us hopes that we may be instruments in his hands. . . .

Let not the smallness of our beginnings nor weakness of instruments make the thing seem little or the work despicable. But, on the contrary, let the greater praise be rendered unto God who hath effected great things by small means. Let not the harshness of my style prejudice thy taste or appetite to the dish I present thee with. . . . Use it as a remembrance of the Lord's goodness to engage thee to true thankfulness and obedience. So may it be a help to thee in thy journey through the wilderness of this world . . . , which is the earnest desire of thy Christian friend,

NATHANIEL MORTON

Cotton Mather, *Magnalia Christi Americana; or, The Ecclesiastical History of New England* (London: Thomas Parkhurst, 1702)

[An Attestation to this Church History of New England.]

The first generation of our fathers that began this plantation of New England . . . are "gathered unto their fathers" [Judg. 2:10]. There hath been another generation succeeding the first . . . , but are apparently passing away as their fathers before them. There is also a third generation who are grown up and begin to stand thick upon the stage of action at this day. . . . Now, in respect of what the Lord hath done for these generations . . . , we have abundant cause of thanksgiving to the Lord our God, who hath so increased and blessed this people that from a "day of small things" [Zech. 4:10], he has brought us to be what we now are. We may set up an Ebenezer and say: "Hitherto the Lord hath helped us" [I Sam. 7:12]. Yet in respect of our present state we have need earnestly to pray as we are directed: "Let thy work further appear unto thy servants, and let thy beauty be upon us, and thy glory upon our children; establish thou the work of these our hands; yea, the works of our hands, establish thou them" [Ps. 90:16–17]. . . .

The Lord our God hath, in his infinite wisdom, grace, and holiness, contrived and established his covenant so as he will be the God of his people and of their seed with them and after them "in their generations" [Gen. 17:7, 9]. And in the ministerial dispensation of the covenant of grace in, with, and to his visible church, he hath promised covenant-mercies on the condition of covenant-duties. . . . That so the faithfulness of God may appear in all generations for ever [and] that if there be any breach between the Lord and his people it shall appear plainly to lie on his people's part . . . , he has taken care that his own dealings with his people in the course of his providence and their dealings with him in the ways of obedience and disobedience should be recorded, and so transmitted for the use and benefit of aftertimes, from generation to generation. . . . And this is one reason why the Lord commanded so great a part of the Holy Scriptures to be written in an historical way. . . . And after the Scripture-time, so far as the Lord in his wisdom hath seen mete, he hath stirred up some or other to write the Acts and Monuments of the church of God in all ages. . . . And therefore surely it hath been a duty incumbent upon the people of God in this our New England that there should be extant a true history of the wonderful works of God in the late plantation of this part of America. . . .

JOHN HIGGINSON

[General Introduction.] I write the wonders of the Christian religion flying from the depravations of Europe to the American strand. And, assisted by the Holy Author of that religion, I . . . report the wonderful displays of his infinite power, wisdom, goodness, and faithfulness wherewith his providence hath irradiated an Indian wilderness. . . .

The sum of the matter is that from the very beginning of the Reformation in the English nation there hath always been a generation of godly men desirous to pursue the reformation of religion "according to the Word of God and the example of the best reformed churches." . . . And there hath been another generation of men who have still employed the power which they have generally still had in their hands not only to stop the progress of the desired reformation but also with innumerable vexations to persecute those that heartily wished well unto it. There were many who joined with the reverend John Foxe in the complaints which he then entered in his Martyrology about the baits of popery yet left in the church. . . . But after a fruitless expectation . . . to have . . . the design of the first Reformers followed, as it should have been, a party very unjustly arrogating to themselves the venerable name of the Church of England by numberless oppressions grievously smote those their fellow servants. . . .

It is the history of these Protestants that is here attempted: Protestants . . . , by the mistake of a few powerful brethren, driven to seek a place for the exercise of the Protestant religion according to the light of their consciences in the deserts of America. . . . It may be 'tis not possible for me to do a greater service unto the churches on the best island in the universe than to give a distinct relation of those great examples which have been occurring among churches of exiles that were driven out of that island into an horrible wilderness for their being well-willers unto the Reformation. . . . 'Tis possible that our Lord Jesus Christ carried some thousands of reformers into the retirements of an American desert on purpose that . . . he might there (*to* them first, and then *by* them) give a specimen of many good things which he would have his churches elsewhere aspire and arise unto. . . . Behold, ye European churches, there are gold candlesticks [Rev. 1:12–13, 20], more than twice seven times seven, in the midst of this outer darkness. . . . And let us humbly speak it, it shall be profitable for you to consider the light which from the midst of this outer darkness is now to be darted over unto the other side of the Atlantic Ocean. . . .

As for such inaccuracies as the critical may discover . . . , I appeal to the courteous for a favorable construction of them. . . . Our English martyrologist [John Foxe] counted it a sufficient apology for what meanness might be found in the first edition of his *Acts and Monuments* that it was "hastily rashed up [put together] in about fourteen months." And I may apologize for this collection of our "Acts and Monuments" that I should have been glad . . . if I could have had one half of "about fourteen months" to have entirely devoted thereunto. . . .

COTTON MATHER

John Cushing, *A Discourse Delivered at Ashburnham, July 4, 1796* (Leominster, Mass.: Charles Prentiss, 1796)[10]

We are met to celebrate the fourth of July, the most important day when these United States were declared free, sovereign, and independent. . . . This day completes twenty years since that important declaration was made which, through God's goodness, has been maintained. It is a day to be remembered throughout all generations. Since that memorable era a generation has risen up . . . who ought to be told of the goodness of God to their fathers and to them. . . .

No people ever experienced such a series of wonders as the Israelites, and their deliverance from the tyrant Pharaoh was so marvelous that, by God's particular order, the day was to be observed throughout all generations [Exod. 12:14, 26–27; 13:8–10]. And it was given in commandment to them to make known his wonderful works to his children and they to theirs [Ps. 78:4–7]. . . . The design of annually commemorating his wonderful works was that they might set their hopes in God, keep his commandments and forget not his works, which they would be like to do if there had not been a special rite instituted and a feast to be kept in remembrance when their minds were to be refreshed with a recital of the deeds done in their favor.

God dealt with no people as with Israel. But in the history of the United States, particularly New England, there is as great similarity perhaps in the conduct of Providence to that of the Israelites as is to be found in the history of any people. Truly, God has done wonderful things. His works have been great. And it must afford pleasure to search them out and to speak of them to one another and to our children. It is what we ought to do to preserve a sense of gratitude, to encourage us to hope in God in future times of trouble, and to excite us to holy obedience. . . .

Our fathers were few in number and feeble when they first landed in this American wilderness and would easily have fallen prey to the savages if God had not restrained them. But what led them into this howling wilderness? To enjoy liberty, civil and religious. . . . Rather than be deprived of the liberty of worshipping God according to the dictates of their conscience, they chose to sacrifice all the delights of their native land and cross the wide Atlantic. . . .

When we think of it, it is a matter of wonder that our ancestors should be so adventurous. The march out of Egypt and through the wilderness was ever esteemed a wonderful thing, but they had Moses and Aaron to lead them. They had the cloud to direct their course and bread from heaven in plenty. Our fathers had no miracles wrought for them, but they experienced many mercies. . . . They trusted in Providence, and God preserved and fed them. . . .

With a great sum we bought our liberty. Independence has cost much blood and immense treasure. . . . When we take retrospect of our situation at the commencement of the war, we are ready to shudder at the dangers which are past. The interposition of Providence in our favor was wonderful. . . . It is evident that we have much to remember with gratitude. . . . God's works towards us . . . encourage us to set our hope in him. And we should tell them to our children, and give it in charge to them to tell their children [Joel 1:3]. . . . God's goodness in making us a free people ought to unite our hearts to fear before him all the days of our life. He has exalted us and given us a rank amongst the nations.

A COVENANTED PEOPLE

The tradition of a people in covenant with God was fundamental to New England's self-understanding. William Stoughton reflected the common conviction when he declared that God had "singled out New England . . . above any nation or people in the world." Equally commonplace was his reminder that "whenever the Lord enters into a covenant with any people, this covenant of his is a covenant with conditions." In John Higginson's words, "covenant mercies" are promised on condition of "covenant duties." God's people are always on probation. "It will be a doleful thing," explained Stoughton, "to be of broken credit with the Lord, and for the Lord to pronounce us bankrupts. If we frustrate the Lord's expectations, he will cut off ours." This warning was a constant theme. If those who are the Lord's, said Thomas Shepard, "shake off his government . . . , after so many smiles and tokens of his being New England's God . . . , we may then expect that the Lord [will] turn this fruitful land into a wilderness again."[11]

The way of God with his people, however, was not to abandon them forthwith. He weaned them from apostasy by bringing judgments to bear upon them; by awakening, rousing, and quickening them with the rod of correction; by refining them in the furnace of his wrath. Perry Miller noted how Increase Mather (much as Abraham Lincoln was to do two centuries later) used the concept of measured wrath as a basic interpretative motif in his *Brief History of the War with the Indians in New England:* "The logic of the narrative is controlled by a precise calculation: defeat must be measured out until the amount of present distress becomes equal to past transgression. In the swamp fight of July 19, 1675, had they pressed the attack, the colonists might have destroyed Philip, 'but God saw we were not yet fit for deliverance, nor could health be restored unto us except a great deal more blood be first taken from us.' "[12] Still God was not tied irrevocably to any people, and the possibility that he might cast them off could not be ruled out.

From the Mayflower Compact and Robert Cushman's early sermon at Plymouth through all succeeding documents, the notion of being a people in covenant with God was a concept which gave to New England a sense of being a people with an identity of their own. And it served the same purpose for all the colonies when they were brought together in a common struggle against Great Britain. The pattern of the Puritan Revolution in England was duplicated when, on June 12, 1775, the first Continental Congress issued a call for the observance of "a day of public humiliation, fasting, and prayer." Two years later the fast days were supplemented by recurrent days of thanksgiving. A confession of sin and unworthiness, rather than claims to righteousness, may seem a curious way to nerve men for conflict and to solicit divine aid, but the incongruity disappears when viewed within the context of the notion of a covenanted society.

Fast days and days of thanksgiving, of course, represented a highly stylized way of thinking and demanded a highly stylized language if violence to basic theological doctrines was to be avoided. It is interesting and significant, therefore, that the resolutions of the Continental Congress recommending the observance of such days were drafted by men from New York, New Jersey, Pennsylvania, Maryland, Virginia, North Carolina, and South Carolina, as well as by men from New England.[13] What testimony could be more eloquent of the pervasiveness of this pattern of understanding? Equally interesting is the fact that the committees drafting the resolutions, with only one or two exceptions, were composed of laymen—lawyers, merchants, physicians, planters. It is also worthy of note that the only time a resolution for a fast day or thanksgiving day was amended was on November 17, 1778, when the resolution had been drafted by the chaplains of the Congress.

Selections from two sermons are included to show how the doctrine was interpreted by the preachers during the Revolution.

The doctrine stated:

[Robert Cushman], *A Sermon preached at Plymouth in New England, December 9, 1621* ([London], 1622)[14]

If it should please God to punish his people in the Christian countries of Europe for their coldness, carnality, wanton abuse of the gospel, contention, etc. either by Turkish slavery or by popish tyranny, which God forbid, yet if the time be come or shall come (as who knoweth) when Satan shall be let loose to cast out his floods against them (Rev. 12:14–15), here is a way opened for such as have wings to fly into this wilderness. And as by the dispersion of the Jewish church through persecution, the Lord brought in the fulness of the Gentiles (Acts 11:20–21), so who knoweth whether now by tyranny and affliction which he suffereth to come upon them, he will not by little and little chase them even amongst the heathens that so a light may rise up in the dark (Luke 2:32) and the kingdom of heaven be taken from them which now have it, and given to a people that shall bring forth the fruit of it (Matt. 21:43). This I leave to the judgment of the godly wise, being neither prophet nor son of a prophet (Amos 7:14), but considering God's dealing of old (II Kgs. 17:23) and seeing the name of Christian to be very great but the true nature thereof almost quite lost in all degrees and sects, I cannot think but that there is some judgment not far off and that God will shortly, even of stones, raise up children unto Abraham (Matt. 3:5).

John Winthrop, *A Model of Christian Charity, written on board the Arbella on the Atlantic Ocean* (1630)[15]

It rests now to make some application of this discourse. . . . Herein are four things to be propounded: first, the persons; secondly, the work; thirdly, the end; fourthly, the means.

First, for the persons: We are a company professing ourselves fellow members of Christ, . . . knit together by this bond of love. . . .

Secondly, for the work we have in hand: It is by a mutual consent . . . to seek out a place of cohabitation and consortship under a due form of government both civil and ecclesiastical. In such cases as this, the care of the public must oversway all private respects by which not only conscience but mere civil policy doth bind us. For it is a true rule that particular estates cannot subsist in the ruin of the public.

Thirdly, the end is to improve our lives to do more service to the Lord, the comfort and increase of the body of Christ whereof we are members, that ourselves and posterity may be the better preserved from the common corruptions of this evil world to serve the Lord and work out our salvation under the power and purity of his holy ordinances.

Fourthly, for the means whereby this must be effected: They are twofold, a conformity with the work and end we aim at. These we see are extraordinary, therefore we must not content ourselves with ordinary means. Whatsoever we did or ought to have done when we lived in England, the same must we do and more also where we go. That which the most in their churches maintain as truth in profession only, we must bring into familiar and constant practice; as in this duty of love, we must love brotherly without dissimulation. We must love one another with a pure heart fervently. We must bear one another's burdens. We must not look only on our own things, but also on the things of our brethren.

Neither must we think that the Lord will bear with such failings at our hands as he doth from those among whom we have lived, and that for these three reasons: 1. In regard of the more near bond of marriage between him and us wherein he hath taken us to be his after a most strict and peculiar manner, which will make him the more jealous of our love and obedience. So he tells the people of Israel: "You only have I known of all the families of the earth, therefore will I punish you for your transgressions" [Amos 3:2]. 2. Because "the Lord will be sanctified in them that come near him" [Lev. 10:3]. 3. When

God gives a special commission, he looks to have it strictly observed in every article. When he gave Saul a commission to destroy Amaleck, he indented with him on certain articles, and because he failed in one of the least and that upon a fair pretence, it lost him the kingdom which should have been his reward if he had observed his commission.

Thus stands the cause between God and us. We are entered into a covenant with him for this work. We have taken out a commission. The Lord hath given us leave to draw our own articles. We have professed to enterprise these and those accounts upon these and those ends. We have hereupon besought him of favor and blessing. Now if the Lord shall please to hear us and bring us in peace to the place we desire, then hath he ratified this covenant and sealed our commission and will expect a strict performance of the articles contained in it. But if we shall neglect the observation of these articles which are the ends we have propounded . . . , seeking great things for ourselves and our posterity, the Lord will surely break out in wrath against us. . . .

Now the only way to avoid this shipwreck and to provide for our posterity is to follow the counsel of Micah "to do justly, to love mercy, to walk humbly with our God" [Mic. 6:8]. For this end we must be knit together in this work as one man. We must entertain each other in brotherly affection. We must be willing to abridge ourselves of our superfluities for the supply of other's necessities. . . . We must delight in each other; make other's conditions our own; rejoice together, mourn together, labor and suffer together, always having before our eyes our commission and community in the work as members of the same body. . . . The Lord will be our God and delight to dwell among us as his people and will command a blessing upon us in all our ways. . . . We shall find that the God of Israel is among us when ten of us shall be able to resist a thousand of our enemies, when he shall make us a praise and glory that men shall say of succeeding plantations: "The Lord make it like that of New England." For we must consider that we shall be as a city upon a hill. The eyes of all people are upon us. So that if we shall deal falsely with our God in this work we have undertaken, and so cause him to withdraw his present help from us, we shall be made a story and a by-word through the world. We shall open the mouths of enemies to speak evil of the ways of God and all professors for God's sake. We shall shame the faces of many of God's worthy servants, and cause their prayers to be turned into curses upon us till we be consumed out of the good land whither we are a going.

Thomas Hooker, *The Danger of Desertion, a farewell sermon preached immediately before his departure* [1633] *out of old England* (London, 1641)[16]

Now we will meddle only with the latter clause, "leave us not" [Jer. 14:9]. God might leave them, but they beg that he would not.

Doctrine: That God may justly leave off a people and unchurch a nation.

Israel suspected it and feared it. It is that that they prayed against, that God would not leave them. . . . Brethren, cast your thoughts afar off. What is become of those famous churches, Pergamus, and Thyatira, and the rest? Who would have thought that Jerusalem should have been made a heap of stones and a vagabond people? . . . "She is not my people nor my beloved. Let her cast away her fornications and idolatry lest I make her as at the first" (Hos. 2:2), that is, in Egypt, poor and miserable; as if he should say to England: "Plead with England, my ministers in the way of my truth, and say unto them, let them cast away their rebellions lest I make her as I found her in captivity in the days of bondage." . . .

England's sins have been great, yea, and their mercies great. England hath been a mirror of mercy, yet God may leave us and make us a mirror of his justice. . . . Learn, therefore, to hear and fear. God can be a God without England. Do not say there are many Christians in it. Can God be beholden to you for your religion? No, surely, for rather than . . . maintain such as profess his name and hate him, "he will raise up of these stones children unto Abraham" [Matt. 3:9]. He will rather go to the

Turks and say: "You are my people, and I will be your God." But will you let God go, England? Why are you so content to let him go? O, lay hold on him, yea, hang on him, and say thou shalt not go. . . . O England, plead with your God and let him not depart. . . .

I deal plainly with you, and tell you what God hath told me. . . . I, poor ambassador of God, am sent to do this message unto you. . . . Suppose God hath told me this night that he will destroy England and lay it waste, what say you brethren to it? It is my message that God bade me do. He expects your answer. What sayest thou, O England? I must return an answer to my Master that sent me tonight. Why speak you not an answer? I must have one. Do you like well of it? Would you have England destroyed? Would you put the old men to trouble and the young men to the sword? Would you have your women widows and your maids defiled? Would you have your children, your dear ones, to be thrown upon the pikes and dashed against the walls? . . . Will you see England laid waste without inhabitants? Are you willing to it? Are you content? God bade me ask. Why do you not answer me? I must not stir without it. I must have it. . . . Send me not away sad. Speak comfortably and cheerfully unto me. Are you willing to have God with you still? You are, are you not? I am glad of it. But you must not only say so, but use the means, plead with God. . . .

This is our misery: If that we have quietness and commodity, we are well enough. Thus we play mock holy-day with God. The gospel we make it our packhorse. God is going, his glory is departing, England hath seen her best days, and now evil days are befalling us. God is packing up his gospel because nobody will buy his wares nor come to his price. O, lay hands on God, and let him not go out of your coasts. He is a going. Stop him, and let not thy God depart. . . .

But how may we keep the Lord? . . . If you will come to the price, you shall have him. The means are these:

1. You must prepare room for him, for he is a king and a king sends an harbinger before him to prepare room for him

against he comes to any place. So must you do by cleansing yourselves from every evil course. . . .

2. As you must prepare room for God, so you must give him content, let him have his will. Where the king comes, there he will have all according to his mind. So it is with God. . . .

3. As we give him his mind, so we must give him welcome and entertainment. If you look lowering towards him and grudge at him and his truth, no wonder but he go away. This is the sin of England. . . . What are we? I will tell you, we are a burden to God. . . .

4. You must be importunate with him to stay and to continue, and count it a great favor that he will yet be entreated. . . . You that live under the means and will not walk in them, what great condemnation will be to you over them that have not the means. As it is of Capernaum (Matthew 18), so I say to England: Thou England, which wast lifted up to heaven with means, shalt be abased and brought down to hell, for if the mighty works which have been done in thee had been done in India or Turkey, they would have repented ere this. Therefore Capernaum's place is England's place. . . . And mark what I say, the poor native Turks and infidels shall have a cooler summer parlor in hell than you, for we stand at a high rate. We were highly exalted, therefore our torments shall be the more to bear. The Lord write these things in our hearts with the finger of his own Spirit for Christ's sake.

Continental Congress: Fast Days and Thanksgiving Days

Resolution of June 12, 1775, drafted by William Hooper, John Adams, and Robert Treat Paine, recommending July 20, 1775, as a fast day[17]

As the Great Governor of the World by his supreme and universal providence not only conducts the course of nature with unerring wisdom and rectitude but frequently influences the minds of men to serve the wise and gracious purposes of his providential government, and it being at all times our indispensable duty to acknowledge his superintending providence, especially in times of impending danger and public calamity, to reverence and adore his immutable justice, as well as to implore his merciful interposition for our deliverance:

This Congress, therefore, considering the present, critical, alarming, and calamitous state of these colonies, do earnestly recommend that Thursday, the twentieth day of July next, be observed by the inhabitants of all the English colonies on this continent as a day of public humiliation, fasting, and prayer, that we may, with united hearts and voices, unfeignedly confess and deplore our many sins and offer up our joint supplications to the all-wise, omnipotent, and merciful Disposer of All Events, humbly beseeching him to forgive our iniquities, to remove our present calamities, to avert those desolating judgments with which we are threatened, and to bless our rightful sovereign, King George III, and to inspire him with wisdom to discern and pursue the true interest of his subjects that a speedy end may be put to the civil discord between Great Britain and the American colonies without further effusion of blood. And that . . . the divine blessing may descend and rest upon all our civil rulers . . . that they may be directed to wise and effectual measures for preserving the union and securing the just rights and privileges of the colonies, that virtue and true religion may revive and flourish throughout our land, and that all America may soon behold a gracious interposition of Heaven for the redress of her many grievances, the restoration of her invaded rights, a reconciliation with the parent country on terms constitutional and honorable to both, and that her civil and religious privileges may be secured to the latest posterity. . . .

Resolution of March 16, 1776, drafted by William Livingston, appointing May 17, 1776, as a fast day[18]

In times of impending calamity and distress when the liberties of America are immediately endangered . . . , it becomes the indispensable duty of these hitherto free and happy colonies, with true penitence of heart and most reverent devotion, publicly to acknowledge the over-ruling providence of God, to confess and deplore our offenses against him, and to supplicate his interposition for averting the threatened danger and prospering our strenuous efforts in the cause of freedom, virtue, and posterity:

This Congress, therefore, considering the warlike preparations of the British ministry to subvert our invaluable rights and privileges and to reduce us by fire and sword . . . to the most abject bondage . . . do earnestly recommend that Friday, the seventeenth day of May next, be observed by the said colonies as a day of humiliation, fasting, and prayer, that we may with united hearts confess and bewail our manifold sins and transgressions, and by a sincere repentance and amendment of life appease his righteous displeasure, and through the merits and mediation of Jesus Christ obtain pardon and forgiveness, humbly imploring his assistance to frustrate the cruel purposes of our unnatural enemies, and by inclining their hearts to justice and benevolence prevent the further effusion of kindred blood. But if, continuing deaf to the voice of reason and humanity, and inflexibly bent on desolation and war, they constrain us to repel their hostile invasions by open resistance, that it may please the Lord of Hosts, the God of America, to animate our officers and soldiers with invincible fortitude, to guard and protect them in the day of battle, and to crown the continental arms by sea and land with victory and success; earnestly beseeching him to . . . grant that a spirit of incorruptible patriotism and of pure undefiled religion may universally prevail, and this continent be speedily restored to the blessings of peace and liberty. . . .

RESOLUTION OF NOVEMBER 1, 1777, DRAFTED BY SAMUEL ADAMS, RICHARD HENRY LEE, AND DANIEL ROBERDEAU, RECOMMENDING DECEMBER 18 AS A DAY OF THANKSGIVING[19]

Forasmuch as it is the indispensable duty of all men to adore the superintending providence of Almighty God, to acknowledge with gratitude their obligations to him for benefits received, and to implore such further blessings as they stand in need of, and it having pleased him to . . . smile upon us in the prosecution of a just and necessary war for the defense of our unalienable rights and liberties . . . and to crown our arms with most signal success;

It is, therefore, recommended to . . . these United States to set apart Thursday, the eighteenth day of December next, for solemn thanksgiving and praise . . . , and that, together with their sincere acknowledgements and offerings, they may join the penitent confession of their manifold sins whereby they had forfeited every favor, and their humble and earnest supplication that it may please God, through the merits of Jesus Christ, mercifully to forgive and blot out them from remembrance, that it may please him graciously . . . to secure for these United States the greatest of all blessings, independence and peace . . . , and to prosper the means of religion for the promotion and enlargement of that kingdom which consisteth in righteousness, peace, and joy in the Holy Ghost.

Resolution of March 7, 1778, drafted by Daniel Roberdeau, Samuel Huntington, and Nathaniel Scudder, recommending that April 22 be observed as a fast day[20]

Whereas Almighty God in the righteous dispensation of his providence hath permitted the continuation of a cruel and desolating war in our land, and it being at all times the duty of a people to acknowledge God in all his ways and more especially to humble themselves before him when evident tokens of his displeasure are manifested . . . :

Resolved that it be recommended to the United States of America to set apart Wednesday, the twenty-second day of April next, to be observed as a day of fasting, humiliation, and prayer, that at one time and with one voice the inhabitants may acknowledge the righteous dispensations of Divine Providence and confess their iniquities and transgressions for which the land mourneth, that they may implore the mercy and forgiveness of God and beseech him that vice, profaneness, extortion, and every evil may be done away and that we may be a reformed and happy people, that they may unite in humble and earnest supplication that it may please Almighty God to guard and defend us against our enemies and give vigor and success to our military operations by sea and land, that it may please him to . . . strengthen and perpetuate our union and in his own good time establish us in the peaceable enjoyment of our rights and liberties. . . .

Resolution of March 20, 1779, drafted by Gouverneur Morris, William Drayton, and William Paca, recommending that May 6 be observed as a fast day[21]

Whereas, in just punishment of our manifold transgressions, it hath pleased the Supreme Disposer of Events to visit these United States with a calamitous war, through which his divine providence hath hitherto in a wonderful manner conducted us so that we might acknowledge that the race is not to the swift nor the battle to the strong; and whereas, notwithstanding the chastisements received and the benefits bestowed, too few have been sufficiently awakened to a sense of their guilt or warmed with gratitude or taught to amend their lives and turn from their sins that so he might turn from his wrath; and whereas, from a consciousness of what we have merited at his hands . . . , there is reason to fear that he may permit much of our land to become the prey of the spoiler . . . :

Resolved that it be recommended to the several states to appoint the first Thursday in May next to be a day of fasting, humiliation, and prayer to Almighty God that he will be pleased to avert those impending calamities which we have but too well deserved, that he will grant us his grace to repent of our sins and amend our lives according to his Holy Word, that he will continue that wonderful protection which hath led us through the paths of danger and distress . . . , that he will give wisdom to our councils, firmness to our resolutions, and victory to our arms. . . .

Resolution of October 18, 1780 recommending that December 7 be observed as a day of thanksgiving[22]

Whereas, it hath pleased the Almighty God, the Father of All Mercies, amidst the vicissitudes and calamities of war, to bestow blessings on the people of these states which call for their devout and thankful acknowledgements . . . :

It is therefore recommended to the several states to set apart

Thursday, the seventh day of December next, to be observed as a day of public thanksgiving and prayer, that all the people may assemble on that day to celebrate the praises of our Divine Benefactor, to confess our unworthiness of the least of his favors, and to offer our fervent supplications to the God of all grace that it may please him to pardon our heinous transgressions and incline our hearts for the future to keep all his laws. . . .

Revolutionary sermons:

Peter Whitney, *American Independence Vindicated, a sermon at a special lecture, September 12, 1776* (Boston, 1777)[23]

Since we are become independent on an earthly power, we eminently need the divine favor, smiles, protection, and blessing, and should be concerned therefore to conduct in such a manner as to secure the same. As our revolt is undoubtedly of God, he is saying to us this day, as he said to Jeroboam and the tribes of Israel: "It shall be, if you will hearken unto all that I command you, and will walk in my ways and do what is right in my sight, to keep my statutes and commandments, that I will be with you and build you up" [I Kings 11:38]. To establish ourselves in independency let us not take the ways and measures that are sinful as Jeroboam and the ten tribes of Israel did. Let us be careful to profess, maintain, encourage, and promote the Protestant religion as far as in us lieth, in opposition to all heathenism, all idolatry. . . . God has ever been the friend and patron of the American Israel, and he will continue so if we act up to our character and obligation. "The Lord is with you while ye be with him; and if ye seek him, he will be found of you; but if ye forsake him, he will forsake you" [II Chron. 15:2]. . . . It is of more importance for us to keep in covenant with God and to be on good terms with Heaven than to be in league and friendship with the most potent states. . . .

We are ready to anticipate those happy times when these days of tribulation shall be at an end, when our brethren shall return from the high places of the field, when we with them shall sit under our own vines and fig trees [I Kings 4:25; Zech. 3:10] quietly enjoying the inheritance our ancestors have left us. . . . Here shall arts and sciences, the companions of tranquility and liberty, flourish. . . . "Truth shall spring out of the earth and righteousness shall look down from heaven. Yea, the Lord shall give us that which is good; righteousness shall go before him and shall set us in the way of his steps" [Ps. 85:12–13. Here we shall become great among the powers of the earth. . . . Here we shall enjoy the most perfect freedom and liberty . . . , and transmit the same to our children, and they to theirs . . . , for "the mercy of the Lord is from everlasting to everlasting upon them that fear him, and his righteousness unto children's children to such as keep his covenant and to them who remember his commandments and do them" [Ps. 103:17–18].

Samuel West, *A Sermon Preached . . . May 29, 1776* (Boston, 1776)[24]

Our fathers fled from the rage of prelatical tyranny and persecution and came into this land in order to enjoy liberty of conscience, and they have increased to a great people. Many have been the interpositions of Divine Providence on our behalf, both in our fathers' days and ours. And though we are now engaged in a war with Great Britain, yet we have been prospered in a most wonderful manner. And can we think that he who has thus far helped us will give us up into the hands of our enemies? Certainly he that has begun to deliver us will continue to show his mercy towards us in saving us from the hands of our enemies. He will not forsake us if we do not forsake him. Our cause is so just and good that nothing can prevent our success but only our sins. Could I see a spirit of repentance and reformation prevail through the land, I should not have the least apprehension or fear of being brought under the iron rod of slavery even though all the powers of the globe were combined against us. And though I confess that the irreligion and profaneness which are so common among us gives something of a damp to my spirits, yet I cannot help hoping and even believing that Providence has designed this continent to be the asylum of liberty and true religion. For can we suppose that that God who created us free agents, and designed that we should glorify and serve him in this world that we might enjoy him forever hereafter, will suffer liberty and true religion to be banished from off the face of the earth? But do we not find that both religion and liberty seem to be expiring and gasping for life in the other continent? Where, then, can they find an harbor or place of refuge but in this?

A FREE PEOPLE

In his Second Inaugural Address, Thomas Jefferson acknowledged that he would need "the favor of that Being in whose hands we are, who led our forefathers, as Israel of old, from their native land and planted them in a country flowing with all the necessaries and comforts of life, who has covered our infancy with his providence and our riper years with his wisdom and power." Jefferson, like his compatriots, identified Americans with ancient Israel as a people favored beyond measure by God. But Jefferson also knew that Americans were heirs of a dual tradition.

On July 4, 1776, the Continental Congress appointed a committee to devise a seal for the United States. According to John Adams, Jefferson proposed that on one side of the seal should be "the children of Israel in the wilderness led by a cloud by day and a pillar by night" and on the other side "Hengist and Horsa, the Saxon chiefs, from whom we claim the honor of being descended and whose political principles and form of government we have assumed."[25] While Jefferson's suggestion was not easily susceptible to pictorial representation and was not adopted, it does aptly symbolize the dual strands of American self-understanding.

Throughout the colonial experience, it had been commonplace to speak of "our English Israel," "our British Israel," "our New-English Israel," and finally "our American Israel." They were a chosen and covenanted people, successors to Israel of old. They were also a free people, English, British, American, heirs of ancient Saxon liberties. In terms of the normative New England account, they had come to the New World in the interest of true religion. Their "errand into the wilderness" had been motivated by a desire to pursue a thorough reformation of God's worship. They sought freedom to pursue that reformation and they had no thought of surrendering any of their liberties as Englishmen. Because they succeeded in their enterprise, Nathaniel Morton was able to rejoice that in 1657 "we sit under our vines and fig trees in peace, enjoying both civil and religious liberties. For which goodness of the Lord, let his holy name be praised."[26]

Devotion to ancient Saxon liberties posed no problem to the colonists. They were eagerly appropriated, defended, and maintained. The colonists were instructed in their liberties by Coke and Penn, and then by Sidney and many others. "In no country perhaps in the world," Edmund Burke was to remark, "is the law so general a study. . . . I hear that they have sold nearly as many of Blackstone's *Commentaries* in America as in England."[27] But when Morton referred to "both civil *and religious* liberties," it was quite another matter.

While men of Plymouth and Massachusetts Bay from the beginning had spoken of their quest for religious freedom, they were thinking primarily of freedom for themselves. The right to dissent was circumscribed, and the liberty they claimed for themselves stood in marked contrast to the broad toleration granted in such havens for dissent as Rhode Island, Maryland, and Pennsylvania. New Jersey, under Quaker influence, also had early extended a welcome to people representing a broad spectrum of differing religious views. New York, in more halting fashion, moved in this direction as a result of its inherited religious diversity and of pressures exerted first by the Dutch Reformed and then by the Presbyterians. The adjustment of the New England Congregationalists, on the other hand, was long and tortuous, but gradually they became more and more committed to a broader understanding of the meaning and implications of the slogan that had been so long upon their lips.

The early New England Congregationalists were in no mood to permit dissenters to undermine their attempt to fashion a new Zion in the American wilderness. Having sacrificed much to leave their homes in pursuit of an opportunity to "bring into familiar and constant practice" that which they previously had been able to "maintain as truth in profession only," they saw no reason why their endeavor should be compromised by dissidence. Others, they contended, had full liberty to stay away. They reminded those who differed from them that they had equal freedom to establish settlements of their own in the American wilderness. As early as 1635 the first of a long series of banishments was imposed. Banishment, John Cotton explained, was not so much "a confinement as an enlargement," in view of the "large and fruitful" country "round about."

The attempt to suppress dissent in Massachusetts was never wholly successful for several reasons. The mere fact of space, even in Massachusetts, made policing difficult. The policy of banishment created centers just beyond its boundaries (most notably in Rhode Island but also on Long Island) from which the contagion of dissent filtered back into the older settlements. Moreover, orthodox New Englanders had been taught from childhood that faith was a gift of grace and that forced worship was an abomination to the Lord. Augmenting the problem of suppressing dissent was the fact that every orthodox New Englander made at least a formal acknowledgment of his own fallibility, of the chance that he might be mistaken, of the possibility that the Lord may have "more light yet to break forth out of his Holy Word." In view of this fundamental principle, it is not surprising that Congregationalism was forever spawning its own dissidents—men and women who defended themselves by appealing to the truth that had been made known to them from "the written Word of God." Nor were Congregationalist consciences eased by the constant needling received from fellow Congregationalists in England, who sought to persuade them to adopt a more liberal policy.

Of decisive importance in the change of front in Massachusetts was the prospect of the colony's charter being revoked.

This would cost the colony its relatively independent status. The defense of the charter demanded a vigorous assertion of the colonists' liberties, both civil and ecclesiastical. The election sermons exhibit the tortured twistings involved in asserting one's own liberties while not granting too much to others. Later, when the charter was revoked and the English Act of Toleration of 1689 was adopted, the right to freedom under the Act of Toleration became a chief defense of the Congregational establishment in New England, and an effort was made to develop a united front of sorts to provide a broader base to counter Anglican intrusions. The New England Congregationalists also increasingly made common cause with the Dissenters in England among whom "liberty, both civil and religious" had long been firmly established as twin facets of the liberties of all Englishmen. Still later the pretensions and aggressiveness of Anglican missionaries in New England, backed by their prestige as representatives of the established church in England, pushed the Congregationalists to defend their own rights even more strongly on the basis of rights which belonged to all.

While the practice of New England Congregationalists left something to be desired even after Independence, as early as 1700 the New England story had been recast to make "liberty, both civil and religious," a chief end of the "errand into the wilderness." The election sermons of the 1670's give evidence of the halting and ambiguous adjustment, and they indicate how the notion of ancient liberties was becoming firmly wedded to the concept of a covenanted people. The revolution of 1689 in Massachusetts was of decisive importance in this process but the literary remains are meager. Sensitive negotiations were involved and presumably there was much more talking than publishing. The two selections provided, however, do give some indication of the further adjustment that was being made. Finally, a selection from a sermon is presented as illustrative of how the clergy interpreted the American Revolution as a struggle for liberties, both civil and religious, which God had designed for all mankind.

It was not only the clergy who interpreted the American

Revolution as a cause of God in defense of civil and religious freedom. Almost every patriot spoke in these terms. When the Continental Congress convened on September 5, 1774, a communication was received from Massachusetts urging the importance of the colonies uniting to recover "their just rights and liberties, civil and religious." Twelve days later the Congress was reminded by the Suffolk (Mass.) Resolves of the "indispensable duty which we owe to God, our country, ourselves, and posterity . . . to maintain, defend, and preserve those civil and religious rights for which many of our fathers fought, bled, and died, and to hand them down entire to future generations." On October 21, 1774, an address by the Congress to the inhabitants of the colonies spoke of the intrigues which "have been wholly exercised in sapping the foundations of civil and religious liberty." The following summer, on July 6, 1775, a declaration of Congress affirmed: "Our forefathers, inhabitants of the island of Great Britain, left their native land to seek on these shores a residence for civil and religious freedom. At the expense of their blood, at the hazard of their fortunes, without the least charge to the country from which they removed, by unceasing labor and unconquerable spirit, they erected settlements in the distant and inhospitable wilds of America."[28] The revision of the epic account of American beginnings and of the meaning of the American experience had been completed and had received official imprimatur.

ELECTION SERMONS:

Samuel Danforth, *A Brief Recognition of New England's Errand into the Wilderness . . . , made in the audience of the General Assembly of Massachusetts Colony . . . 1670* (Cambridge, Mass., 1671)[29]

Of solemn and serious inquiry to us all in this general assembly [is] whether we have not in a great measure forgotten our errand into the wilderness. You have solemnly professed before God, angels, and men that the cause of your leaving your country, kindred, and fathers' houses and transporting yourselves with your wives, little ones, and substance over the vast ocean into this waste and howling wilderness [Deut. 32:10] was your liberty to walk in the faith of the gospel with all good conscience according to the order of the gospel, and your enjoyment of the pure worship of God according to his institution, without human mixtures and impositions. . . .

The times were such that we could not enjoy it in our own land and therefore, having obtained liberty and a gracious patent from our sovereign, we left our country . . . and came into these wild woods and deserts where the Lord hath planted us. . . . What is it that distinguisheth New England from other colonies and plantations in America? Not transportation over the Atlantic Ocean but the ministry of God's faithful prophets and the fruition of his holy ordinances. . . . The hardships, difficulties, and sufferings which you have exposed yourselves unto, that you might dwell in the house of the Lord and leave your little ones under the shadow of the wings of the God of Israel, have not been few nor small. . . .

John Oxenbridge, *New England Freemen Warned and Warmed to Be Free Indeed . . . in a sermon preached before the court of election . . . 1671* (Printed in the year 1673)[30]

Magistratical power is of great weight and worth, especially among God's people, therefore with great consideration to be made over and managed by them that have it. . . . Pericles, being often chosen Praetor of Athens, every year when he put on his robe would bespeak himself: Remember thou rulest over freemen, thou rulest over Athenians. Yet Christ bespeaks you that rule here: Have a care what you do for ye rule over my children (Jn. 19:8). . . . It is spoken to magistrates: Ye may willingly and cheerfully serve the Lord in that capacity of doing good to his people, but tremble lest ye miscarry; if ye do them wrong, ye are sure to hear of it (Ps. 105:4,15). . . . If you touch his people harmfully or put power into the hands of such as will touch them, you touch the apple of God's eye (Zech. 2:8). . . .

Mind faithfully and diligently your liberties that ye may be free to act for and according to God in the constitution and manage[ment] of your magistracy. Quit once your liberties and ye must have such a magistracy and manage[ment] of it as will please not God nor yourselves, but other men will be your masters. For servants, yea, slaves, must you be to somebody when ye have let go your liberties. . . .

It is the trust and favor of God that ye have such liberties. . . . This your day of election is preferable before all your own days if we mar it not. . . . The liberty of choosing their own magistrates the Lord gave to his own people (Deut. 1:13,15). . . . This people of Israel were still free to choose when scarce any were free to be chosen. . . .

Your trust, by and for men, bespeaks your care and vigilance about your liberties. This honorable assembly consists of the trustees of all the freemen of the land. . . . We should have cause to complain of any that is chosen, if he should use this trust against our liberties. . . . Ye are also trusted for men, for many; all inhabitants have their liberties, women, children, servants, yea, and strangers too. Let me beseech this honorable assembly, in the name of all the freemen . . . , not to part with any of our liberties by force or fraud. . . . Your expressing agreement binds you. No man can choose or be chosen but he hath taken the oath for our liberties. . . . You have every one sweared by the great name of the Everliving God truly to endeavor to maintain and preserve the liberties and privileges of this commonwealth and government. . . .

Your civil and your religious liberties are so coupled . . . that if the one be lost, the other cannot be kept. . . .

Observe those neuters in Judges 8:6–7 who refused to owe any relief to their brethren in a needful time but (till they saw which would be the stronger side) would not meddle so they might sleep in a whole skin. . . . If this our wilderness breed any such lukewarm politicians in a needful time, it is to be hoped that it will also bring forth thorns enough to teach them [that] you have beautiful and precious liberties beyond other colonies. . . . If you so root in your present and particular profits and interests as to neglect your golden liberties, what will

England, what will all the world, say of you—that you are not new English but no English men. . . . Be ye now as hearty for your true and just liberties as ye were 40 years since. . . .

Urian Oakes, *New England Pleaded with and Pressed to Consider Those Things which Concern Her Peace, . . . delivered. . . . May 7, 1673, being the day of election* (Cambridge, Mass., 1673)[31]

Doctrine: That it is the great wisdom of a people that have been conducted by the mighty hand of God to a place of rest and liberty and settled in the possession of singular privileges and enjoyments to understand and consider, or understandingly to consider, what will be the latter end of their sinful ways, their unsuitable and unworthy deportments before the Lord. . . .

As the words of my text [Deut. 32:29] respect the body of a nation, even Israel, that were sometimes the peculiar people of God, so give me leave to direct my exhortation to the people of New England . . . and to persuade the New England Israel to . . . "consider what will be the latter end of your sinful ways and unworthy deportments before the Lord." . . . You have been conducted to a place of rest and liberty, and settled in the possession of very choice and singular privileges and enjoyments. . . . Many and wonderful are the favors and privileges which the Lord your God hath conferred on you.

1. As to your civil government you have had Moses, men I mean of the same spirit, to lead and go before you. The Lord hath not given children to be your leaders and babes to rule over you which is threatened as a great judgment (Is. 3:4, 8) . . . , but pious, faithful, prudent magistrates. He hath not set taskmasters and oppressors over us . . . as he threatens (Lev. 26:17). . . . God hath not given us rulers that would fleece us, that would pull the bread out of our mouths, that would grind our faces or break our bones, that would undermine and rob us of our liberties, civil and religious, to the enslaving of this people and their children after them. . . . Nor hath the Lord in displeasure left us to be Levellers and Libertines to do every man what seems good in his own eyes [Judg. 17:6]. Thus

far he hath delivered us from anarchy and confusion as well as from tyranny. . . .

2. As to your sundry mercies. God hath sequestered you from the rest of the world, allured you into this wilderness, and brought you into these parts of the earth (out of the streets of Rome, as some conceive . . .) that you might set up this way and worship in the purity and gospel-glory of it. . . .

If we cast up the account and sum up all our mercies and lay all things together, this our commonwealth seems to exhibit to us a specimen or a little model of the kingdom of Christ upon earth. . . . This work of God set on foot and advanced to a good degree here, being spread over the face of the earth and perfected as to greater degrees of light and grace and gospel-glory, will be (as I conceive) the kingdom of Jesus Christ so much spoken of. When this is accomplished, you may then say . . . [that] you have been as a city upon an hill [Matt. 5:14], though in a remote and obscure wilderness, as a candle upon a candlestick that gives light to the whole house [Matt. 5:15]. You have to a considerable degree enlightened the whole house (world, I mean). . . .

I would not have the ministers of Christ needlessly to tamper or intermeddle with state affairs or direct and dictate to rulers and intrude themselves into such things as are out of their sphere and foreign to their calling and profession, unless upon insuperable occasions. . . . However having this opportunity, unsought and undesired by me, nay, thrust upon me, I shall adventure, as God shall assist, to speak something to the present case and condition of the country. . . .

8. Consider what will be the latter end of contempt of, weariness under, or disaffection to the civil government established among us. . . . When God hath so graciously settled us upon so good foundation, now to kick and spurn at our corner stones, to be given to change and ready for innovations and alterations is great ingratitude to God and a very irreligious thing. For here, according to the design of our founders and the frame of things laid by them, the interest of righteousness in the commonwealth and holiness in the churches are inseparable. The prosperity of

church and commonwealth are twisted together. Break one cord, you weaken and break the other also. . . . He is a mad man that will hope for the continuance of our spiritual liberties, if the wall of our civil government be once broken down. . . . The change in our civil government will inevitably introduce a sad change in our churches. To divide what God hath conjoined, *viz.* civil and ecclesiastical liberties, to deliver up civil and yet hope to keep spiritual liberties, is folly. . . .

I am no statesman nor politician. It is neither my profession nor ambition. . . . Therefore I shall only say further, it hath been very sage counsel that hath been often given you: Keep to your Patent. Your Patent was a royal grant indeed, befitting a great prince to make, and that which our worthies that are gone to rest have many a time blessed God for. And it is instrumentally your defense and security. Recede from that one way or another and you will expose yourselves, for ought I know, to the wrath of God and rage of man. Fix upon the Patent and stand for the liberties and immunities conferred upon you therein, and you have God and the king with you, both a good cause and a good interest, and may with good conscience set your foot against any foot of pride and violence that shall come against you. . . .

9. Consider what will be the latter end of an inordinate affectation of liberty. I am far from speaking against due care to maintain our liberties. It is the property of Englishmen, and should be most of all of religious New Englishmen, to be tenacious and tender of their liberties. . . . Religious people . . . are wont to be as stout asserters of their liberties as any men. I am far from condemning . . . men of piety and principles that are sober and moderate and conscientious asserters of their liberties, but I would dissuade from an extreme and undue affectation of liberty. . . . Outcries for liberty are popular and plausible and make a pleasant sound in the ears of injudicious and unexperienced persons, but to those that have been abroad in the world and observed or acquainted themselves with the histories of states and kingdoms nothing is more suspected. Commonly they that raise the loudest outcry against

governors for robbing the people of their liberties, either design or eventually prove to be the greatest oppressors of them when they have come to be masters. . . .

10. Consider what will be the latter end of a licentious toleration of all opinions and religions among us. I profess I am heartily for all due moderation. I have real compassion towards the infirmities of the minds of men, the ignorance and weakness and errors of their understandings as well as the passions and other distempers of their wills and affections. . . . A tender consideration of the weakness of men and due moderation in this case is the duty of those that cannot but be conscious to themselves of their own infirmities. Nevertheless, I must add . . . that I look upon an unbounded toleration as the first-born of all abominations. . . . It is excellently determined by that judicious and blessed man, Mr. [John] Norton that "unity in judgment is to be endeavored because truth is one and indivisible, yet some difference touching the truth must be endured because of the weakness of man. To tolerate everything and to tolerate nothing are both intolerable." . . . I doubt not but it is the duty of the civil magistrate to tolerate what is tolerable. . . . [But] it is most unreasonable . . . in those that unchurch us, that deny our churches to be true churches, that antichristianize our magistrates, ministers, churches, and ordinances . . . to demand or expect a free toleration. They may as well ask liberty to destroy us. . . .

O you dear people of God in New England . . . , hear and give ear unto the word of the Lord. . . . Consider . . . what is like to be the latter end of your sinful deportments before the Lord. . . . If the Lord give you hearing ears and obedient hearts that you consider and repent and turn to the Lord your God, then he will be with you as he hath been with your fathers and predecessors. . . . Whether there shall be secret plottings or open assaulting and running upon your civil and sacred liberties, God will either defeat the counsels and frustrate the attempts and hopes of adversaries, or turn all that may befall you in a way of affliction to your singular good. . . .

The Revolution of 1689 in New England:

Cotton Mather, *The Wonderful Works of God Commemorated . . . in a thanksgiving sermon . . . 1689* (Boston, 1690)[32]

There is a further matter for our praises which has followed hereupon and we, that are a country of Nonconformists, may not pass it unmentioned. It is THE REPEAL OF THOSE LAWS WHICH THE PROTESTANT DISSENTERS WERE LONG HARASSED WITH. It is well known that those whose consciences did not allow them to worship God in some ways and modes then by law established were not many years ago persecuted with a violence to be abhored by all sober men. It is well known that five and twenty hundred faithful ministers of the gospel were silenced in one BLACK day because they could not comply with some things by them justly counted sinful but by the imposers confessed indifferent. And it is affirmed that . . . this persecution procured the untimely death of three thousand Nonconformists by imprisonment in noisesome jails, and the ruin of threescore thousand families within five and twenty years. . . .

The Dissenters are far from charging their sufferings upon all that the Church of England . . . acknowledges for her sons, for we have seen the most learned and worthy members of that church make their public pleas for the Nonconformists . . . and advance this assertion that "for every man to worship God according to his conviction is an essential right of human nature." . . . The late persecutors were mostly a knot of ill men who professed that they had rather be Papists than Presbyterians, and that they would as soon be Turks as Papists. . . . [They] thought to grow great by the ruin of both the parties whom they so set by the ears. So I hope the Dissenters will now forgive and forget the most inhumane injuries that they have ever yet sustained.

The severity of that persecution . . . caused the Dissenters to accept of liberty [from James II], though upon some terms which they approved not. You are not ignorant that we then told you there would quickly come an earthquake that should carry on that liberty to more perfection.[33] And behold, it is now done in a parliamentary way. Blessed be God. . . . O what hath God wrought? My brethren, it looks as if God hath begun the resurrection of his dead people. . . .

The late revolutions among ourselves have also been attended with some excellent things. . . . Indeed, nothing in the world could more exactly imitate and resemble the late circumstances of our mother England than the revolutions here. . . . And this though we understood not one another. This was from the excellent operations of that God who turns a wheel in a wheel. . . . Our charters were taken from us. And our land strangers devoured in our presence. . . . There were denied unto us the common rights which all Englishmen justly reckon themselves born unto. . . . All that was dear unto us was entirely given up to the arbitrary disposals of four or five men that . . . made no stick to tell us we were but slaves. . . .

Remember, O New England, how often that cry went up from thee to the Lord: Return, we beseech thee, O God of Hosts! Look down from heaven and visit this place. And now, behold, he is returned. . . .

And there are several excellent things that have been done for us by our God while he has been effecting our deliverance. . . . In the tumult of our action there was not the loss of a drop of blood nor such plunder and outrage as would have been a disgrace to our profession. . . . Our sovereign has declared he took it very well what we had done for him and for ourselves in the revolution. . . . We have been comfortably carried through the difficulties of a whole summer while we could not say that any law was of any force with us. Every week erected a new Ebenezer [I Sam. 7:12] for us. . . .

Revolution in New England Justified and the People There Vindicated (Boston, 1691)[34]

No man does really approve the Revolution in England but must justify that in New England also, for the latter was effected in compliance with the former. . . . They considered that the men then usurping government in New England were King James's creatures who had invaded both the liberty and property of English Protestants after such a manner as perhaps the like was never known in any part of the world where the English nation has any government. And the commission which they had obtained from the late King James was more illegal and arbitrary than . . . ever before given to any by King James himself or by anyone that ever swayed the English sceptre, which was a grievance intolerable. And yet they desired not to make themselves judges in a case which so nearly concerned them, but . . . declared . . . that they would leave it to the king and parliament of England to inflict what punishment they should think meet for such criminals. Their seizing and securing the governor was no more than was done in England. . . .

That Sir Edmund Andros, etc. did make laws destructive to the liberty of the subjects is notoriously known, for they made what laws they pleased without any consent of the people either by themselves or representatives, which is indeed to destroy the fundamentals of the English and to erect a French government. We cannot learn that the like was ever practiced in any place where the English are planters, but only where Sir E. A. hath been governor. For whereas in New England, by constant usage under their charter government, the inhabitants of each town did assemble as occasion offered to consider of what might conduce to the welfare of their respective towns . . . , Sir E. A. with a few of his council made a law prohibiting any town meeting except once a year. . . . But besides all this, they made laws for the levying moneys without the consent of the people either by themselves or by an assembly. . . . They did not only act according to these illegal taxes, but they did inflict severe punishment on those true Englishmen who did oppose their arbitrary proceedings. . . . They were committed to jail . . . , denied an *habeas corpus,* . . . and that they might be sure to be found guilty jurors were picked of such as were no freeholders, nay, of strangers. The prisoners pleading the privileges of Englishmen not to be taxed without their own consent, they were told that the laws of England would not follow them to the end of the earth (they meant the privileges of the English law, for the penalties they resolved should follow them). . . . And why should they insist on and talk of the privileges of Englishmen when it had been declared in the governor's council that the king's subjects in New England did not differ much from slaves, and that the only difference was that they were not bought and sold. . . . Inasmuch as the prisoners mentioned had asserted their English liberties, they were severely handled, not only imprisoned for several weeks, but fined and bound to their good behavior. . . . Those who were in confederacy with Sir E. A. for the enriching of themselves on the ruins of New England did invade the property as well as liberty of subjects. . . . What people that had the spirits of Englishmen could endure this? . . . When they had at vast charges of their own conquered a wilderness . . . [and] now a parcel of strangers . . . must come and inherit all that the people now in New England and their fathers before had labored for, let the whole nation judge whether these men were not driving on a French design and had not fairly erected a French government. . . .

What Englishmen in their right wits will venture their lives over the seas to enlarge the king's dominions and to enrich and greaten the English nation, if all the reward they shall have for their cost and adventures shall be their being deprived of English liberties and in the same condition with the slaves in France or in Turkey? . . .

Thus did Sir E. A. and his creatures, who were deeply concerned in the illegal actions of the late unhappy reigns, contrary to the laws of God and men commit a rape on a whole colony. For which violence, it is hoped, they may account and make reparation (if possible) to those whose many properties as well as liberties have been invaded by them.

Captain [John] Palmer in the close of his partial account of New England [*The Present State of New England Impartially Considered* (Boston, 1689)] entertains his readers with an harangue about the sin of rebellion and misapplies several Scriptures that so he might make the world believe that the people of New England have been guilty of wicked rebellion by their casting off the arbitrary power of those ill men who invaded liberty and property. . . . How or by whose authority our lawyer comes to play the divine we know not. But since he hath thought it meet to take a spiritual weapon into his hand, let him know that the Scripture speaks of a lawful and good rebellion as well as that which is unlawful. It is said of good Hezekiah that he rebelled against the king of Assyria and served him not (II Kgs. 18:7). . . . Hezekiah's predecessors had basely given away the liberties of the people . . . , and therefore Hezekiah did like a worthy prince in casting off a tyrannical government and asserting the liberty of them that were the Lord's people, and God did signally own and prosper him in what he did. . . . The like, we hope, may be the happy case of New England. . . .

The cause of liberty is the cause of God:

Abraham Keteltas, *God Arising and Pleading His People's Cause . . . , a sermon preached October 5, 1777 in . . . Newburyport* (Newburyport, Mass., 1777)[35]

"Arise, O God! Plead thine own cause" (Ps. 74:22).

. . . God pleads his own and his people's cause by his providence. The whole history of it, from the creation of the world, is a series of wonderful interpositions in behalf of his elect. . . . For them he dried up the Red Sea to make a passage and drowned Pharaoh and his host in a watery grave. He went before them with a pillar of cloud by day and a pillar of fire by night. He fed them with manna and quails in the wilderness, and brought them water out of the flinty rock. To promote the cause of truth and righteousness, he has performed the most surprising prodigies. . . . For them he stopped the mouths of lions, quenched the violence of fire, turned aside the edge of the sword, of weak made them strong and valiant in battle, and put to flight and destroyed whole armies of their enemies [Heb. 11:33–34]. . . .

I might easily show from profane, as well as from sacred history, that God has pled his own and his people's cause, the cause of religion, liberty, and virtue. I will only mention two instances in modern history. . . . The revolt of the seven United Provinces of the Netherlands, . . . [now] free and independent states. . . . The Swiss cantons, long oppressed by the mighty house of Austria, . . . now the freest people upon earth. . . .

From the preceding discourse, I think we have reason to conclude that the cause of this American continent against the measures of a cruel, bloody, and vindictive [British] ministry is the cause of God. We are contending for the rights of mankind, for the welfare of millions now living, and for the happiness of millions yet unborn. If it is the undisputed duty of mankind to do good to all as they have opportunity, especially to those who are of the household of faith [Gal. 6:10], if they are bound by the commandments of the Supreme Lawgiver to love their neighbors as themselves [Luke 10:27], and do to others as they would that others should unto them [Matt. 7:12], then the war carried on against us is unjust and unwarrantable, and our cause is not only righteous but, most important, it is God's own cause. It is the grand cause of the whole human race. . . . If the principles on which the present civil war is carried on by the American colonies against the British arms were universally adopted and practiced upon by mankind, they would turn a vale of tears into a paradise of God; whereas opposite principles, and conduct founded upon them, has filled the world with blood and slaughter, with rapine and violence, with cruelty and injustice, with wretchedness, poverty, horror, desolation, and despair. We cannot therefore doubt that the cause of liberty, united with that of truth and righteousness, is the cause of God.

This is the glorious cause in which Great Britain herself has frequently and strenuously contended against tyrants and oppressors. Not to mention preceding struggles for liberty, when Charles I invaded the rights of his people, the Lords and Commons aided by their adherents rose up in arms and waged a war against him which terminated in the loss of his crown and life. And when his infatuated son, James II, imitating his father's fatal example, endeavored to introduce popery and arbitrary power into his kingdom, the people of England invited the Prince of Orange to vindicate their liberties, who expelled the tyrant from his throne and was placed on it himself by the votes of a free parliament. . . .

Great Britain cannot in justice blame us for imitating her in those noble struggles for liberty which have been her greatest glory. She cannot condemn us without condemning the conduct of her greatest patriots and heroes, virtually denying her king's right to his crown, and acting in manifest opposition to the spirit and interest of her own excellent constitution. I am bold to affirm that all the surpassing glory by which she has eclipsed other nations has been owing to this admirable form of government so favorable to the rights of mankind. . . . England, I am bold to say, has prospered as her liberty prospered, and declined as despotism has prevailed. When principles of liberty, and a ministry and parliament under their influence, have governed Great Britain, how happy have her subjects been! How formidable to her enemies! But when opposite principles and rulers have been predominant, what misery has overwhelmed her inhabitants! And what a contemptible appearance did she make in the sight of other nations! How has she been torn to pieces by civil broils and been covered with her own blood! How evident is this from the present unnatural war waged against her own children to establish arbitrary power! . . . O England, thou once beloved, happy, and glorious country, thou land of freedom and delight, how is thy gold become dim and thy fine gold changed. . . . Thy rulers are companions of thieves. Everyone loveth gifts and followeth after rewards. They judge not the fatherless, neither doth the cause of the widow come unto them [Isa. 1:23].

You see, my brethren, from the preceding observations the unspeakable advantages of liberty to Great Britain, and how fatal to her have been the invasion and decline of this inestimable blessing. How absurd then, how inglorious, how cruel and unjust is her conduct in carrying on this bloody war to ruin and enslave us. . . .

But if liberty is thus friendly to the happiness of mankind and is the cause of the kind Parent of the Universe, certainly tyranny and oppression are the cause of the devil, the cause which God's soul hates. The Holy Scriptures abound with instances and prophecies of his judgments on tyrants and oppressors, and not only sacred but profane history prove the fulfilment of those prophecies. . . . How signal was the divine vengeance against King Ahab and his queen for falsely accusing Naboth, murdering him upon groundless pretences, and unjustly seizing upon his property. . . . "Arise," said the Lord to Elijah the Tishite. "Go down and meet Ahab, king of Israel, . . . speak unto him saying: Thus saith the Lord. In the place where dogs licked the blood of Naboth shall dogs lick thy blood, even thine. Behold, I will bring evil upon thee and will take away thy posterity." . . . And of Jezebel . . . spake the Lord also, saying: "The dogs shall eat Jezebel by the wall of Jezreel" [I Kings 21:18–23]. . . . This curse was awfully and punctually executed, and stands recorded in the Bible as a tremendous warning against tyranny and oppression. . . .

And now are there any who call themselves Christians who dare avow, espouse, and support the invasion of liberty and the murder of those who rise up in its vindication? Yes, to the disgrace of human nature be it spoken. There are such inveterate foes to mankind. And who are they? They are the ministry and parliament of Great Britain with their adherents and abettors. The groundwork of their present destructive measures is this most iniquitous decree, that the parliament of Great Britain hath power, and of right ought to have power, to make laws and statutes to bind these colonies in all cases whatsoever. This decree is contrary to the laws of God and man, to the British constitution, *Magna Charta,* the Bill of Rights, the charters of the colonies, and the express stipulations of preceding kings and their representatives. . . .

Ye cruel and bloody authors of this unjust, unnatural war! What desolation, what misery have ye not brought on this once happy land. . . .

Against whom doth Great Britain wage war? Against those

who once were her most affectionate children, . . . and who still, notwithstanding the unparalleled injuries . . . , pray for her peace and prosperity. But once more! Whom doth Great Britain destroy, whose blood does she shed, whose houses doth she burn, . . . whose ruin doth she seek? Why, of those who have rejoiced in her happiness, bewailed her calamities, earnestly prayed for her welfare . . . , who have rendered her the most signal and important services, enabled her to make the most glorious and extensive conquests . . . , fought and bled at her side and assisted her in the last war with so liberal a generosity that she frankly acknowledged that we had gone vastly beyond the bare line of duty. . . .

Besides all this, the principles of liberty upon which we act are the same which expelled James II from the British throne and seated his present majesty and his royal ancestors upon it. And if those principles and measures, according to which the present ministry conduct themselves had prevailed at the time of the [Glorious] Revolution, they would have effectually prevented their accession to it. How hard, how cruel, how painful the thought that the best friends to the principles upon which this throne was erected and established should suffer from it all the horrors of war at the instigation of its worst enemies. . . .

We have this further consolation to support us under our present affiiction, that all our assembles . . . have endeavored . . . to prevent the fatal war which now rages and desolates our land. . . . Our cause therefore, my dear brethren, is not only good but it has been prudently conducted. Be, therefore, of good courage. It is a glorious cause. It is the cause of truth against error and falsehood, the cause of righteousness against iniquity, the cause of the oppressed against the oppressor, the cause of pure and undefiled religion against bigotry, superstition, and human invention. It is the cause of reformation against popery, of liberty against arbitrary power, of benevolence against barbarity, of virtue against vice. . . . In short, it is the cause of heaven against hell. . . . It is the cause for which heroes have fought, patriots bled, prophets, apostles, martyrs, confessors, and righteous men have died. Nay, it is a cause for which the Son of God came down from his celestial throne and expired on a cross. It is a cause, for the sake of which, your pious ancestors forsook all the delights and enjoyments of England . . . and came to this once howling wilderness [Deut. 32:10], destitute of houses, cultivated fields, the comforts and conveniences of life. . . . Therefore do not despond, my dear brethren, at the present gloomy prospects.

The cause of God, his own cause, must prosper in spite of earth and hell. God will effectually plead it by his almighty Word, his all-conquering Spirit, and his over-ruling Providence. No weapon formed against Zion shall prosper. . . . God is in the midst of her, she shall not be moved. God will help her, and that right early [Ps. 46:5]. . . .

Eminent divines, celebrated poets, have given it as their opinion that America will be a glorious land of freedom, knowledge, and religion; an asylum for distressed, oppressed, and persecuted virtue. Let this exhilarating thought fire your souls, and give new ardor and encouragement to your hopes. You contend not only for your own happiness, for your dear relations, for the happiness of the present inhabitants of America; but you contend for the happiness of millions yet unborn. Exert therefore your utmost efforts, strain every nerve, do all you can to promote this cause . . . by continual prayer and supplication, by repentance and reformation, by forsaking every vice and the practice of universal virtue. Be ready to fight for it and maintain it to the last drop of your blood. . . . Pray for the happy period when tyranny, oppression, and wretchedness shall be banished from the earth, when universal love and liberty, peace and righteousness shall prevail, when angry contentions shall be no more and war shall cease, even unto the ends of the earth, . . . when the celestial court and the heaven of heavens shall resound with joyful acclamations, because the kingdoms of this world are become the kingdoms of our Lord and his Christ [Rev. 11:15]. Hasten this blessed, this long-wished for period, O Father of Mercies, for thy dear Son's sake. Amen.

2

MISSION AND DESTINY

NATIONAL identity and mission are closely intertwined. The mission of America embraced the two major strands of its identity—spiritual religion and constitutional liberties. Samuel K. Lathrop, a Boston Unitarian, viewed history as the unfolding of God's purpose, and he reflected the common conviction that the hand of God could be seen in the discovery of America, which was "so wonderfully opportune in time that we no longer ask why the Western Hemisphere was kept concealed for so many ages."

> Had the discovery been made a few centuries earlier, the semi-barbarous institutions and feudalism of the Old World would have been transplanted in their vigor to the New. . . . Had the discovery been delayed a few centuries, the new ideas and principles in regard to religious and civil liberty, government, society, man, the gospel in all its applications, which the Reformation called forth, would in all human probability have had but a short-lived, struggling existence. Confined to Europe, they would have been strangled, crushed, put down, and kept down by those influences of habit and custom . . . , which . . . so long prevented their legitimate results—the enfranchisement and elevation of humanity. . . .
>
> If ever civil and religious liberty . . . , if ever that great, intelligent, responsible freedom, which through the gospel and the Spirit of the Lord comes to the soul of man, is to prevail over the earth . . . , it will be because at the hour of its utmost need God gave it opportunity to plant itself on this new continent.[1]

But there were more specific facets to the mission of America.

When Congress appointed December 11, 1783, as a day of public thanksgiving for the treaty of peace with Great Britain, the Reverend John Rodgers at the observance in New York City exulted: "What great things has the God of Providence done for our race! By the revolution we this day celebrate, he has provided an asylum for the oppressed in all the nations of the earth." In Philadelphia the Reverend George Duffield stressed the same point: "Here has our God . . . prepared an asylum for the oppressed in every part of the earth."[2]

America had developed a language or vocabulary, almost a litany, of its own. Like the slogan "liberty, civil and religious," the term "asylum for the oppressed" was a standard item in any listing of the role of America. From the earliest settlements this had been a self-image of America; it was a basic theme of Daniel Neal's *History of New England;* it was given prominence in the sermons which hailed the Declaration of Independence; it was echoed in the writings of John Adams, Benjamin Franklin, and Thomas Paine; and this was a primary image of America reported by Crèvecoeur and the Marquis de Condorcet to their European readers. Furthermore, throughout the nineteenth century the notion of America as a refuge or haven for the oppressed continued to be a conspicuous feature of patriotic oratory.[3]

"The eyes of the world are upon you" was an equally common phrase used to delineate the American self-image. From John Winthrop to Woodrow Wilson these words were used to emphasize America's role as an "experiment" and an "example" to the nations.[4] Closely related to this imagery was America's role as the "guardian" of liberty, a role Americans believed to have been confirmed by Charles Fox's acknowledgment before the British parliament that "the resistance of the Americans to the oppressions of the mother country has undoubtedly preserved the liberties of mankind." In 1837 Andrew Jackson reminded the American people in his Farewell Address: "You have the highest of human trusts committed to your care. Providence has showered on this favored land blessings without number, and has chosen you as the guardians of freedom, to preserve it for the benefit of the human race."[5] It was widely believed that by the contagion of her example America would provoke revolutions throughout the earth until the whole world was free. It was in this sense that America constituted, in Abraham Lincoln's words, "the last best hope of earth."

A third feature of the American self-image was a vision of the destiny that God held in store for America. It was a vision of future greatness born of expectations bred by a contemplation of a vast continent to be settled and nourished by the millennial hopes of evangelical religion. America was to be the seat of a new empire. The vision had surfaced from time to time in the colonial period, with the shift of empire westward throughout history being duly noted,[6] but it was the victory of American arms in the struggle for independence that gave the vision its full luster. Coupled with the vision of future greatness was a doctrine of expansionism which later was defined as "manifest destiny" or "continentalism."

At first, attention was focused on natural boundaries. As early as 1709 William Penn had observed: "I should be glad if our north bounds [of English territory] might be expressed and allowed to the south side of St. Lawrence's river that feeds Canada eastward and comes from the lakes westward, which will make a glorious country; and from those lakes due west to the river Mississippi and traverse that river to the extreme bounds of the continent westward; whereby we may secure one thousand miles of that river down to the bay of Mexico."

By the time of the American Revolution, what Penn believed desirable had come to be considered by many as inevitable, even as a design of Heaven. John Adams was convinced that the new nation was "destined to spread over the northern part of that whole quarter of the globe." Three decades later Representative David Trimble denounced the Spanish treaty of 1819 with a ringing affirmation: "The Father of the Universe in his peculiar providence has given natural boundaries to every continent and kingdom—permanent, physical, imperishable barriers to every nation to shield it from invasion." God "fixed the natural limits of our country" at the Rio Grande to the south and the great mountain ranges to the west, "and man cannot change them."[7]

Expansionism was justified, as the earliest settlements had been justified,[8] by a doctrine of "regenerating the soil" based on God's command to Adam and repeated to Noah to "be fruitful and multiply and replenish the earth, and subdue it" (Gen. 1:28; 9:1). Untilled acres by God's intention should be reduced to tillage. When the issue of California arose in 1846, every reader knew that the *Illinois State Register* had but one answer in mind to the question: "Shall this garden of beauty be suffered to lie dormant in its wild and useless luxuriance?" Prior occupation posed a problem which Andrew Jackson sought to meet with his phrase "extending the area of freedom." Implicit in this phrase was the notion of "regenerating the people" as well as the soil. But the major purpose of "extending the area of freedom" was to counter the threat to American liberties presented when European despotisms established sovereignty or influence in adjacent territory. Thus expansion could be viewed as a purely defensive move to make the citadel of freedom secure.[9]

Expansion by attraction, with neighboring territories voluntarily seeking admission to the federal union, was generally favored as against expansion by force. Samuel Cooper had voiced this view in 1780 in a sermon at the inauguration of the new government of Massachusetts. "Conquest is not the aim of these rising states. Sound policy must even forbid it. We have before us an object more truly great and honorable." Accretions of territory will occur in the same fashion as "the injured and the oppressed, the worthy and the good," are drawn to these shores, by making this portion of the globe "a seat of knowledge and liberty, of agriculture, commerce, and the arts, and, what is more important than all, of Christian piety and virtue." John Howard Pugh explained the principle with clarity in an 1865 Fourth of July oration at Burlington, New Jersey. "The day is coming, I do not doubt, when Canada and Mexico and the states of Central America will join the federal union, not by conquest . . . but by the attractive power of a political system that combines all the freedom of independent states with the strength and solidity of a consolidated government."[10]

Expansion with freedom intact, as Pugh intimated, was made possible by the principle of federalism, a principle which Henry Clay, Daniel Webster, Edward Everett, and other eloquent orators hailed as the unique contribution of the American Constitution. By virtue of this constitutional arrangement, local liberties could be preserved in most matters affecting the daily life of people while bringing a widely dispersed population under one government in matters of over-all concern. When the nullification crisis arose, it is not surprising that Andrew Jackson should have informed the American people that "the eyes of all nations are fixed on our republic," for the outcome of "the existing crisis will be decisive in the opinion of mankind on the practicality of our federal system of government." After the Civil War, Andrew Johnson became so enamored with the principle of federalism that he believed it susceptible to unlimited extension. In his fourth annual message to Congress in 1868, he asserted that "comprehensive national policy would seem to sanction the acquisition and incorporation into our federal union of the several adjacent continental and insular communities as speedily as it can be done peacefully, lawfully, and without any violation of national justice, faith, or honor." He then continued:

> I am aware that upon the question of further extending our possessions it is apprehended by some that our political system cannot successfully be applied to an area more extended than our continent, but the conviction is rapidly gaining ground in the American mind that with the increased facilities for intercommunication between all portions of the earth the principles of free government, as embraced in our Constitution, if faithfully maintained and carried out, would prove of sufficient strength and breadth to comprehend within their sphere and influence the civilized nations of the world.

Although equally devoted to federalism, most Americans were more modest than Johnson in their expansionist objectives. There was a strong tendency to counter undue expansionist thrusts by stressing America's role as an example to the nations. "You have a Sparta, embellish it," was Daniel Webster's dictum. And Grover Cleveland's counsel was almost as succinct: "The mission of our nation is to build up and make a greater country out of what we have."[11]

THIS MIGHTY EMPIRE

The vision of America's future greatness had many eloquent spokesmen. It was voiced with youthful enthusiasm in a valedictory address at the Yale commencement of 1776 by Timothy Dwight, later to be president of the college (1785–1817). Ezra Stiles, Dwight's predecessor as president of Yale (1778–1785), presented an equally exalted vision of American destiny in his election sermon of 1783. The Fourth of July oration of David Ramsay, a South Carolina physician, in 1778 illustrates the pervasiveness of the millennial expectation. Elhanan Winchester, Baptist clergyman and a founding father of American Universalism, blended an account of the lessons to be learned from the new nation with his vision of American destiny in *An Oration on the Discovery of America* (1792). The influence of this oration was further extended by being reduced to catechetical form and widely distributed as *A Plain Political Catechism* (1806).[12]

Timothy Dwight, *A Valedictory Address . . . at Yale College, July 25, 1776* (New Haven, 1776)[13]

Give me leave to describe to you the nature and circumstances of the country which will probably be the scene of your future actions. . . . [The climate] is as healthy, serene, and delightful as any country of the same magnitude on earth. . . . Nor are its advantages of soil less conspicuous. . . . Heaven, resolving that all the circumstances of this continent should be of a piece, has blessed it with naval and commercial advantages superior to those of any state on earth. . . . The Most High has replenished it with every source of strength and greatness. Its present circumstances [of transatlantic conflict] . . . arise from events altogether political and accidental, . . . for a war like this cannot with any probability be a second time expected. . . . I cannot but observe that, if any kingdom should unwisely become our enemy, the immense distance between us and them . . . must blast their brightest prospects and whelm them in ignominy and ruin.

But the fairest part of the scene is yet to be unfolded. Not all the articles I have mentioned could spread happiness through the continent if the manners of the inhabitants were corrupted and luxurious or their civil government arbitrary and slavish. . . . The southern and western parts of North America [are] subject to the dominion of Spain, [yet] . . . a concise but very just account of them must necessarily convince us that the moment our interest demands it these extensive regions will be our own. . . . [Otherwise] this continent is inhabited by a people who have the same religion, the same manners, the same interests, the same language, and the same essential forms and principles of civil government. This is an event which, since the building of Babel [Gen. 11:9] till the present time, the sun never saw. That a vast continent, containing near three thousand million acres, should be inhabited by a people in all respects one is indeed a novelty upon the earth. . . . A sameness in these particulars cannot fail to produce the happiest effects. It wrought miracles in the minute microscopic states of Greece. What may we not expect from its benign influence on the vast regions of America. . . .

It is a very common and just remark that the progress of liberty, of science, and of empire has been with the sun from east to west since the beginning of time. It may as justly be observed that the glory of empire has been progressive, the last constantly outshining those which were before it. . . . From the first of these remarks, it is evident that the empire of North America will be the last on earth; from the second, that it will be the most glorious. Here the progress of temporal things towards perfection will undoubtedly be finished. Here human greatness will find a period. Here will be accomplished that remarkable Jewish tradition that the last thousand years of the reign of time would, in imitation of the conclusion of the first week [of creation], become a glorious Sabbath of peace, purity, and felicity. . . . This favorite region, by the hand of Heaven sequestered from the knowledge of mankind till that period when European greatness began to totter . . . , beholds a rapid progress toward the consummation of excellence already commenced. Never were the rights of men so generally, so thoroughly understood or more bravely defended. No country ever saw learning so largely diffused through every class of people, or could boast of so sensible, so discerning a commonalty. . . .

Allow me to proceed one step further, and I have done. From every deduction of reason as well as from innumerable declarations of inspired truth, we have the best foundation to believe that this continent will be the principal seat of that new, that peculiar kingdom, which shall be given to the saints of the Most High, that also was to be the last, the greatest, the happiest of all dominions. . . . This is emphatically that "uttermost part of the earth" whose songs and happiness so often inspired Isaiah with raptures [Isa. 24:16]. This with peculiar propriety is that "wilderness" which shall "rejoice and blossom as a rose," and to which shall be given the "glory of Lebanon," the "excellency of Carmel and Sharon" [Isa. 35:1–2]. Here shall a king reign in righteousness whose kingdom shall be everlasting and whose kingdom shall not be destroyed [Ps. 145:13; Dan. 2:44; 4:3; 7:14, 27]. . . .

This, young gentlemen, is the field in which you are to act. It is here described to you that you may not be ignorant . . . of that great whole of which each of you is a part, and perhaps an important one. The period in which your lot is cast is possibly the happiest in the role of time. It is true you will scarcely live to enjoy the summit of American glory, but you now see the foundations of that glory laid. . . . You should by no means consider yourselves as members of a small neighborhood, town, or colony only, but as being concerned in laying the foundations of American greatness. Your wishes, your designs, your labors are not to be confined by the narrow bounds of the present age, but are to comprehend succeeding generations and be pointed to immortality. You are to act, not like the inhabitants of a village nor like beings of an hour, but like citizens of a world and like candidates for a name that shall survive the conflagration. . . .

You may, especially at the present period, be called unto the active scenes of a military life. Should this be your honorable lot, I can say nothing which ought more to influence you than that you fight for the property, the freedom, the life, the glory, the religion of the inhabitants of this mighty empire; for the cause, for the honor, of mankind and your Maker. . . .

David Ramsay, *An Oration on the Advantages of American Independence* (Charleston, S.C., 1778)[14]

It is difficult to compute the number of advantages arising from our present glorious struggle. . . . It has attracted the attention of all Europe to the nature of civil liberty and the rights of the people. Our constitutions, pregnant with the seeds of liberty and happiness, have been translated into a variety of languages and spread far and wide. Who can tell what great events, now concealed in the womb of time, may be brought into existence by the nations of the Old World emulating our successful efforts in the cause of liberty? The thrones of tyranny and despotism will totter when their subjects shall learn and know by our example that the happiness of the people is the end and object of all government. The wondering world has beheld the smiles of Heaven on the numerous sons of America resolving to die or be free. Perhaps this noble example, like a widespreading conflagration, may catch from breast to breast and extend from nation to nation till tyranny and oppression are utterly extirpated from the face of the earth. . . .

As at the conflagration of Corinth the various melted metals running together formed a new one called Corinthian brass which was superior to any of its component parts, in like manner perhaps it is the will of Heaven that a new empire should be here formed of the different nations of the Old World which will rise superior to all that have gone before it and extend human happiness to its utmost possible limits. . . . We bid fair to be the happiest and freest people in the world for ages yet to come.

When I anticipate in imagination the future glory of my country and the illustrious figure it will soon make on the theater of the world, my heart distends with generous pride for being an American. . . . We have laid the foundations of a new empire which promises to enlarge itself to vast dimensions and to give happiness to a great continent. . . . Liberty, both civil and religious, in her noontide blaze shines forth with unclouded luster on all ranks and denominations of men.

Ever since the Flood, true religion, literature, arts, empire, and riches have taken a slow and gradual rise from east to west, and are now about fixing their long and favorite abode in this new western world. Our sun of political happiness is already risen and hath lifted his head over the mountains, illuminating our hemisphere with liberty, light, and polished life. Our independence will redeem one quarter of the globe from tyranny and oppression, and consecrate it the chosen seat of truth, justice, freedom, learning, and religion. . . . Generations yet unborn will bless us for the blood-bought inheritance we are about to bequeath to them. O happy times! O glorious days! O kind, indulgent, bountiful Providence, that we live in this highly favored period, and have the honor of helping forward these great events, and of suffering in a cause of such infinite importance!

Ezra Stiles, *The United States Elevated to Glory and Honor, a sermon . . . at the anniversary election, May 8, 1783* (New Haven, 1783)[15]

However it may be doubted whether . . . the prosperity and decline of other empires have corresponded with their moral state as to virtue and vice, yet the history of the Hebrew theocracy shows that the secular welfare of God's ancient people depended upon their virtue, their religion, their observance of that holy covenant which Israel entered into with God on the plains at the foot of Nebo on the other side [of] Jordan. Here Moses, the man of God, assembled three million of people (the number of the United States), recapitulated and gave them a second publication of the sacred jural institute delivered thirty-eight years before with the most awful solemnity at Mount

Sinai. A law dictated with sovereign authority by the Most High . . . becomes of invincible force and obligation without any reference to the consent of the governed. . . . But in the case of Israel he condescended to a mutual covenant, and by the hand of Moses led his people to avouch the Lord Jehovah to be their God and in the most public and explicit manner voluntarily to engage and covenant with God to keep and obey his law. Thereupon this great prophet . . . declared, in the name of the Lord, that the Most High . . . took them for a peculiar people to himself, promising to be their God and protector, and upon their obedience to make them prosperous and happy (Deut. 29:10, 14; 30:9, 19). He foresaw, indeed, their rejection of God and predicted the judicial chastisement of apostasy. . . . But, as well to comfort and support the righteous in every age and under every calamity as to make his power known among all nations, God determined that a remnant should be saved. Whence Moses and the prophets, by divine direction, interspersed their writings with promises that when the ends of God's moral government should be answered . . . , he would, by his irresistible power and sovereign grace, subdue the hearts of his people to a free, willing, joyful obedience. . . . Then the words of Moses, hitherto accomplished but in part, will be literally fulfilled when this branch of the posterity of Abraham shall be nationally collected and become a very distinguished and glorious people under the great messiah, the Prince of Peace. He will then "make them high above all nations which he hath made in praise, and in name, and in honor, and they shall become a holy people unto the Lord their God" [Deut. 26:19].

I shall enlarge no further upon the primary sense and literal accomplishment of this and other prophecies respecting both Jews and Gentiles in the latter-day glory of the church, for I have assumed the text only as introductory to a discourse upon the political welfare of God's American Israel and as allusively prophetic of the future prosperity and splendor of the United States. We may then consider . . . what reason we have to expect that, by the blessing of God, these states may prosper and flourish into a great American republic and ascend into high and distinguished honor among the nations of the earth. "To make thee high above all nations which he hath made in praise, and in name, and in honor." . . .

Heaven hath provided this country, not indeed derelict but only partially settled, and consequently open for the reception of a new enlargement of Japheth [son of Noah, Gen. 5:32]. Europe was settled by Japheth. America is settling from Europe. And perhaps this second enlargement bids fair to surpass the first. . . . Already for ages has Europe arrived to a plenary, if not declining, population of one hundred millions. In two or three hundred years this second enlargement may cover America with three times that number if the present increase continues with the enterprising spirit of Americans for colonization and removing out into the wilderness and settling new countries. . . . Can we contemplate their present and anticipate their future increase and not be struck with astonishment to find ourselves in the midst of the fulfilment of the prophecy of Noah [Gen. 9:24–27; 10:1–5]? May we not see that we are the object which the Holy Ghost had in view four thousand years ago when he inspired the venerable patriarch with the visions respecting his posterity? While the principal increase was first in Europe westward from Scythia (the residence of the family of Japheth), a branch of the original enlargement extending eastward into Asia and spreading round to the southward of the Caspian became the ancient kingdoms of Media and Persia. . . . And now the other part of the prophecy is fulfilling in a new enlargement. . . .

The population of this land will probably become very great and Japheth become more numerous millions in America than in Europe and Asia, and the two or three millions of the United States may equal the population of the oriental empires which far surpasses that of Europe. . . .

But a multitude of people, even the two hundred million of the Chinese empire, cannot subsist without civil government. All the forms of civil polity have been tried by mankind except one, and that seems to have been reserved in providence to be realized in America. Most of the states of all ages in their originals, both as to policy and property, have been founded in rapacity, usurpation, and injustice, so that in the contests recorded in history the public right is a dubious question, it being rather certain that it belongs to neither of the contending parties. . . . All original right is confounded and lost. We can only say that there still remains in the body of the people at large, the body of mankind of any and every generation, a power (with which they are invested by the Author of their being) to wrest government out of the hands of reigning tyrants and originate new policies [forms of government] adapted to the conservation of liberty and promoting general welfare.

But what is the happiest form of civil government is the great question. Almost all the polities may be reduced to hereditary dominion in either a monarchy or aristocracy, and these supported by a standing army. . . . True liberty is preserved in the Belgic and Helvetic republics, and among the nobles in the elective monarchy of Poland. For the rest of the world, the civil dominion, though often wisely administered, is so modeled as to be beyond the control of those for whose end God instituted government. But a democratical polity for millions standing upon the broad basis of the people at large, amply charged with property, has not hitherto been exhibited. . . .

A well-ordered democratical aristocracy, standing upon the annual election of the people and revocable at pleasure, is the polity which combines the United States. And from the nature of man and the comparison of ages, I believe it will approve itself the most equitable, liberal, and perfect. . . . By the annual appeals to the public, a power is reserved to the people to remedy any corruptions or errors in government. And even if the people should sometimes err, yet each assembly of the states and the body of the people always embosom wisdom sufficient to correct themselves so that a political mischief cannot be durable. Herein we far surpass any states on earth. We can correct ourselves if in the wrong. . . .

Already does the new constellation of the United States begin to realize this glory. . . . And we have reason to hope and, I believe, to expect that God has still greater blessings in store for this vine which his own right hand hath planted to make us "high among the nations in praise, and in name, and in honor." The reasons are numerous, weighty, and conclusive. . . .

Liberty, civil and religious, has sweet and attractive charms. The enjoyment of this, with property, has filled the English settlers in America with a most amazing spirit which has operated, and still will operate, with great energy. Never before has the experiment been so effectually tried of every man's reaping the fruits of his labor and feeling his share in the aggregate system of power. . . .

Our degree of population is such as to give us reason to expect that this will become a great people. It is probable that within a century of our independence the sun will shine on fifty millions of inhabitants in the United States. This will be a great, a very great nation, nearly equal to half Europe. . . . An accelerated multiplication will attend our general propagation and overspread the whole territory westward for ages, so that before the millennium the English settlements in America may become more numerous millions than that greatest dominion on earth, the Chinese empire. . . .

I am sensible some will consider these as visionary, utopian ideas. And so they would have judged had they lived in the apostolic age and been told that by the time of Constantine the [Roman] empire would become Christian. As visionary that the twenty thousand souls which first settled New England should be multiplied to near a million in a century and a half. . . . As utopian would it have been to the loyalists at the battle of Lexington that in less than eight years the independence and sovereignty of the United States should be acknowledged. . . . How wonderful the revolutions, the events of Providence! We live in an age of wonders. We have lived an age in a few years. We have seen more wonders accomplished in eight years than are usually unfolded in a century.

God be thanked that we have lived to see peace restored to this bleeding land. . . . Does it not become us to reflect how wonderful, how gracious, how glorious has been the good hand of our God upon us in carrying us through so tremendous a warfare? We have sustained a force brought against us which might have made any empire on earth to tremble. And yet, . . . having obtained the help of God, we continue unto this day. Forced unto the last solemn appeal, America watched for the first blood. This was shed by Britons on the nineteenth of April, 1775, which instantly sprung an army of twenty thousand into spontaneous existence. . . . Whereupon Congress put at the head of this spirited army the only man on whom the eyes of all Israel were placed. Posterity, I apprehend, and the world itself, inconsiderate and incredulous as they may be of the dominion of Heaven, will yet do so much justice to the divine moral government as to acknowledge that this American Joshua was raised up by God . . . for the great work of leading the armies of this American Joseph (now separated from his brethren) and conducting this people through the severe, the arduous conflict, to liberty and independence. . . .

Great and extensive will be the happy effects of this warfare in which we have been called to fight out, not the liberties of America only, but the liberties of the world itself. The spirited and successful stand which we have made against tyranny will prove the salvation of England and Ireland. And by teaching all sovereigns the danger of irritating and trifling with the affections and loyalty of their subjects, introduce clemency, moderation, and justice into public government at large through Europe. . . .

This great American Revolution . . . will be attended to and contemplated by all nations. Navigation will carry the American flag around the globe itself, and display the thirteen stripes and new constellation at Bengal and Canton, on the Indus and Ganges, on the Whang-ho and the Yang-tse-kiang, and with commerce will import the wisdom and literature of the East. That prophecy of Daniel is now literally fulfilling: there shall be a universal traveling "to and fro, and knowledge shall be increased" [Dan. 12:4]. This knowledge will be brought home and treasured up in America, and being here digested and carried to the highest perfection may reblaze back from

America to Europe, Asia, and Africa and illumine the world with truth and liberty. . . .

Little would civilians have thought ages ago that the world should ever look to America for models of government and polity. Little did they think of finding this most perfect polity among the poor outcasts, the contemptible people of New England, and particularly in the long despised civil polity of Connecticut—a polity conceived by the sagacity and wisdom of a Winthrop, a Ludlow, Haynes, Hopkins, Hooker, and the other first settlers of Hartford in 1636.

And while Europe and Asia may hereafter learn that the most liberal principles of law and civil polity are to be found on this side of the Atlantic, they may also find the true religion here depurated [purified] from the rust and corruption of the ages, and learn from us to reform and restore the church to its primitive purity. . . . Here will be no bloody tribunals . . . forcibly to control the understanding and put out the light of reason, the candle of the Lord, in man. . . . Religion may here receive its last, most liberal, and impartial examination. Religious liberty is peculiarly friendly to fair and generous disquisition. Here Deism will have its full chance. Nor need libertines more to complain of being overcome by any weapons but the gentle, powerful ones of argument and truth. Revelation will be found to stand the test to the ten-thousandth examination. . . .

In this country (out of sight of mitres and the purple, and removed from systems of corruption confirmed for ages and supported by the spiritual janizaries of an ecclesiastical hierarchy aided and armed by the secular power) religion may be examined with the noble Berean freedom [Acts 17:11], the freedom of American-born minds. . . . Great things are to be effected in the world before the millennium . . . , and perhaps the liberal and candid disquisitions in America are to be rendered extensively subservient to some of the most glorious designs of Providence, and particularly in the propagation and diffusion of religion through the earth, in filling the whole earth with the knowledge of the glory of the Lord. A time will come when six hundred millions of the human race shall be ready to drop their idolatry and all false religion. . . . And when God in his providence shall convert the world, . . . should American missionaries be blessed to succeed in the work of Christianizing the heathen in which the Romanists and foreign Protestants have very much failed, it would be an unexpected wonder and a great honor to the United States. And thus the American republic, by illuminating the world with truth and liberty, would be exalted and made "high among the nations in praise, and in name, and in honor." I doubt not this is the honor reserved for us. . . .

Elhanan Winchester, *An Oration on the Discovery of America . . ., October 12, 1792* (London, [1792])[16]

The discovery of America by Columbus was situated in point of time between two great events. . . . I mean the art of printing, which was discovered about the year 1440 . . ., and the reformation from popery, which began about the year 1517. . . . These three events . . . followed each other in quick succession, and combined together have already produced much welfare and happiness to mankind and certainly will produce abundance more.

By the art of printing knowledge is far more generally diffused among mankind. . . . But what I esteem more than everything else is that by the noble art of printing, Bibles in barbarous languages are so multiplied that they will never more become scarce. . . .

By the discovery of America there was much room given to the inhabitants of the Old World. An asylum was prepared for the persecuted of all nations to fly for safety, and a grand theater was erected where liberty might safely lift up her standard and triumph over all the foes of freedom. America may be called the very birthplace of civil and religious liberty, which had never been known to mankind until since the discovery of that country.

By the Reformation, which so soon followed the discovery of

America, the minds of men began to emerge out of that darkness, ignorance, blindness, bondage, idolatry, and superstition in which they had grovelled for ages. . . .

I consider the discovery of America as of the greatest importance to mankind as it has pleased God to distinguish it from all other countries in causing it to be the first place upon the globe where equal civil and religious liberty has been established. . . . The United States of America have the happiness of teaching the world the following grand and important lessons.

1. That it is possible for a large and extensive country to be ruled by a republican form of government, without monarchy or aristocracy.

2. That religious worship may be well supported without any legal establishment. . . .

3. That to place all denominations on an exact equal footing is the ready way to destroy all animosity and strife, all bigotry, persecution, and intolerance; and tends to promote peace, harmony, and good will in the community.

4. That church and state may both subsist and flourish without being allied together. . . .

5. That changing the punishment of death for hard labor and confinement tends to prevent crimes far more than the penal code of laws which inflicts death as the punishment of almost every offense.

6. That the more mild and equitable government is, the more happy and contented the people will be; and that such a government . . . is really far stronger and is not in so much danger of being overturned.

7. America has also shown the world that to admit Jews to all the privileges of natural born subjects is far from being a dangerous experiment. . . . I cannot see . . . that God will be angry with the United States for giving to the Jews, in common with other nations, the equal blessings of protection, liberty, property, etc. I find threatenings in Scripture against those nations that have afflicted the Jews but none against those who afford them rest and peace. . . .

These are a few of the important lessons which the United

States of America have the honor and happiness of teaching the world at large both by precept and practice. . . .

The message which the Lord sent by St. John the Divine to the church of Philadelphia in Asia has been and will be remarkably fulfilled in Philadelphia in America: "Behold, I have set before thee an open door and no man shall shut it" [Rev. 2:8]. This is the door of civil and religious liberty which began to be opened in Philadelphia in North America, and no man has been able hitherto, or ever shall be able, to shut it. And it will spread throughout the world.

Thus it is plain that the discovery of America was not only a great event in itself but has been of great consequence to the world of mankind in general and to Europe in particular. But the importance of the discovery will appear greater and greater every year. . . . The prospect opens. It extends itself upon us. "The wilderness and the solitary place shall rejoice; the desert shall rejoice and blossom as the rose" [Isa. 35:1]. . . .

Behold the whole continent highly cultivated and fertilized, full of cities, towns, and villages, beautiful and lovely beyond expression. I hear the praises of my great Creator sung upon the banks of those rivers unknown so long. Behold the delightful prospect! See the silver and gold of America employed in the service of the Lord of the whole earth! See slavery, with all its train of attendant evils, forever abolished! . . . Behold the glory of God extending and the gospel spreading through the whole land!

THE CIVIL WAR INTERPRETED

Slavery was a cancer in the tissues of American nationhood, initially recognized as such by men both South and North. Noah Webster perhaps spoke for most Americans in 1785 when he declared: "Aside from the detestable principle of subjecting one man to the service of another which dishonors a free government, . . . slavery inspires other principles repugnant to the genius of our American constitutions. It cherishes a spirit of supercilious contempt, a haughty, unsocial, aristocratic temper inconsistent with that equality which is the basis of our governments and the happiness of human society."[17]

But with radical surgery rejected and temporizing measures adopted, a slow process of dissolution set in which was to culminate in the trauma of the Civil War. In spite of the damaging blow to American pretensions inflicted by fratricidal strife, the American self-image survived the conflict relatively unimpaired.

Americans had not forgotten the ways of God with his people. On July 3, 1776, John Adams had written his wife: "It may be the will of Heaven that America shall suffer calamities still more wasting and distresses yet more dreadful. . . . The furnace of affliction produces refinement in states as well as individuals, and the new governments we are assuming . . . will require a purification of our vices and an augmentation of our virtues or they will be no blessings."

In the midst of the new conflict people were reminded that afflictions could be redemptive judgments. George B. Phillips, in his Ohio pulpit, announced that the war was "a terrible remedy for a terrible disease." At a thanksgiving service in Brooklyn on November 28, 1861, Nathaniel West spoke of "our public humiliation on account of our transgressions" and thanked God that, "chastened by affliction," we have begun to learn that "there are such things as national righteousness, national sin, national guilt, and national reckoning." God's purpose is "to discipline us by national judgments into obedience to himself."[18]

All the old themes were used—wrath, judgment, and redemption; purging, refining, and purifying; death, sacrifice, and rebirth; baptism, regeneration, and renovation. Lincoln's assassination—"the just dying for the unjust," George Bancroft called it in his Memorial Address before Congress—became a symbol of the whole tragic cycle of death and sacrifice which yet ended in rebirth. "The assassination of Lincoln, who was so free from malice, has by some mysterious influence struck the country with solemn awe and hushed, instead of exciting, the passion for revenge." The only consolation, Bancroft continued, is "the established union of the regenerated nation."[19]

Bancroft had caught the mood of the nation and his words reflected the general interpretation of the war. In the autumn of 1865 Philip Schaff told German and Swiss audiences that the effect of the war, through the alchemy of God's providence, had been assimilation and consolidation, and that the assassination of Lincoln instead of dividing the nation had cemented it. In the South such leading churchmen as Stephen Elliott of Georgia and Richard H. Wilmer of Alabama, sharing Lincoln's conviction that "the judgments of the Lord are true and righteous altogether" (Ps. 19:9), expressed their gratitude to God for settling "the meaning of the Constitution," restoring to the American people "one undivided country," and making clear the true mission of the nation.[20]

While most Americans were sobered by the conflict and shared Lincoln's conviction that the war had come as the "woe" due an unworthy people that its offenses might be requited, few doubted that God's purpose in the war had been to forward America's national vocation. Even during the war George S. Phillips was probably not alone in still being able to give voice to the heady apocalyptic vision of America's worldwide mission. After rehearsing the "high trust" committed "to us as a nation and to no one else" to be "an asylum for the oppressed of other nations" and to demonstrate mankind's capacity for liberty and self-government, Phillips concluded: "Our mission . . . should only be accomplished when the last despot should be dethroned, the last chain of oppression broken, the dignity and equality of redeemed humanity everywhere acknowledged, republican government everywhere established, and the American flag . . . should wave over every land and encircle the world with its majestic folds. Then, and not till then, should the nation have accomplished the purpose for which it was established by the God of heaven."[21] Others would have stated the mission more modestly and with less undisciplined rhetoric, but few would have questioned the basic postulate that, having been purged of slavery, America would retain its God-given mission.

Horace Bushnell of Hartford, Connecticut, was one of those who sought, throughout the war, to find a deeper meaning to the conflict than a mere purging of slavery from national life. On the Sunday after the disaster at Bull Run he spoke on the subject "Reverses Needed" and told his people that only through a "bloody baptism" could Americans, having been "left to the luckless condition of being no nation at all," be formed into "a solid and compact nation such as God would have us." Out of the crucible would come a people tested, toughened, and united. Abraham Lincoln also was preoccupied with the meaning of the war, a meaning which came to him with deepening insight and growing clarity as the war progressed. Never was the basic theme of God effecting his own purposes in the conflict, purposes which perhaps were not those of either party, expressed with more compelling power than by Abraham Lincoln in his Second Inaugural Address.

Horace Bushnell, *Reverses Needed, a discourse delivered on the Sunday after the disaster at Bull Run* (Hartford: L. E. Hunt, 1861)[22]

Adversity kills only where there is weakness to be killed. Real vigor is at once tested and fed by it, seen to be great as the adversity mastered is great, and also to be made great by the mastering. . . .

The last Sabbath morning when you were assembled here in the sacred quiet of worship, the patriot soldiers of your army . . . were being joined in battle with its enemies. . . . The tidings of the evening came, and it was so far victory. . . . In the news of the morning, it was defeat and flight and carnage and loss. Our fine army was gone, our hopes were dashed, our hearts sunk down struggling as it were in an agony, and our fancy broke loose in the imagination of innumerable perils. . . .

These first apprehensions are already quieted in part. The loss turns out to be less than was feared. . . . And what is more . . . , we have the grand satisfaction of knowing that our soldiers fought the day out in prodigies of valor almost unexampled. Defeat is on us therefore, but not dishonor. Nothing has occurred to weaken us, but examples have been set to inspire us rather in all the future struggle. Let us thank God

. . . that we find ourselves beginning at once to meet our adversity with a steady and stout resolve. . . . Our adversity since we began to bear it is already increasing our strength. . . .

What I wish . . ., on the present occasion, is . . . to go over . . . the matter of the war itself, showing what it means and the great moral and religious ideas that are struggling to the birth in it. . . .

Our grand revolutionary fathers left us the legacy of this war in the ambiguities of thought and principle which they suffered in respect to the foundations of government itself. The real fact is that, without proposing it or being distinctly conscious of it, they organized a government, such as we at least have understood it to be, without moral or religious ideas, . . . a merely man-made compact that without something farther (which in fact was omitted or philosophically excluded) could never have more than a semblance of authority. More it has actually had because our nature itself has been wiser and deeper and closer to God than our political doctrines, but we have been gradually wearing our nature down to the level of our doctrines, breeding out, so to speak, the sentiments in it that took hold of authority till at last we have brought ourselves down as closely as may be to the dissolution of all nationality and all ties of order. Hence the war. It has come just as soon as we made it necessary, and not a day sooner. And it will stay on to the end of our history itself unless the mistake we have suffered is at least practically rectified. We have never been a properly loyal people. We are not so now save in the mere feeling or flame of the hour. Our habit has been too much a habit of disrespect, not to persons only, but to law. Government, we say or have been saying, is only what we make ourselves; therefore we are at least on a level with it. We too made the nationality, and can we not as well unmake it?

That we may duly understand this matter, go back a moment to the Revolution and trace two very distinct yet, in a certain superficial sense, agreeing elements that entered into it. First, there was what, for distinction's sake, we may call the historic element represented more especially by the New England people. The political ideas were shaped by religion, so far church ideas. The church, for example, was a brotherhood. Out of that grew historically the notions of political equality in the state. Government also was conceived to be for the governed just as the church was for the members. And both were God's institutes, ordinances of God. The major vote in both was only the way of designating rulers, not the source of their sovereignty or spring of authority. Their text for elective government was the same that our Hartford [Thomas] Hooker used when preaching in 1638 for the convention which framed our [Connecticut] constitution . . . : "Take you wise men, and understanding, and I will make them rulers over you" [Deut. 1:13]. God was to be the head of authority, and the rulers were to have their authority from him. Such was the historic training that preceded and prepared this wing of the Revolution.

The other wing was prepared by sentiments wholly different, such, for example, as one sufficiently well represented in . . . Mr. Jefferson, a man who taught abstractly, not religiously, and led the unreligious mind of the time by his abstractions. . . . He had no conception of any difficulty in making a complete government for the political state by mere human composition, following Rousseau's theory which discovers the foundation of all government in a "social compact." Going never higher than man or back of man, he supposed that man could somehow create authority over man, that a machine could be got up by the consent of the governed that would really oblige or bind their consent; not staying even to observe that the moment anything binds or takes hold of the moral nature, it rules by force of a moral idea and touches by the supposition some throne of order and law above the range of mere humanity. Covered in by this oversight, he falls back on the philosophic, abstractive contemplation of men, and finding them all so many original monads with nothing historic in them as yet, he says: Are they not all equal? Taking the men thus to be inherently equal in their natural prerogatives and rights, he asks their consent, makes the compact, and that is to be the grand political liberty of the world.

But the two great wings thus described can agree, you will see, in many things, only saying them always in a different sense: one in a historic, the other in an abstractive, theoretic sense; one in a religious and the other in an atheistic; both looking after consent and the major vote, both going for equality, both wanting articles of agreement, and finally both a constitution. And the result is that in the consent, in the major vote, in the equality, in the articles of agreement, in the constitution, Christianity in its solid and historic verity as embodied in the life of a people joins hands, so to speak, with what have been called . . . the "glittering generalities" of Mr. Jefferson. Thus, in drawing the Declaration of Independence, he puts in by courtesy the recognition of a Creator and creation, following on with "self-evident truths," such as that "all men are created equal" and that "governments derive their just powers from the consent of the governed," in which too the other wing of the Revolution can well enough agree, only they will take them not as abstractions but in the sense that is qualified and shaped by their history. They had nothing to do with some theoretic equality in man *before* government in which as a first truth of nature governments are grounded. They were born into government, and they even believed in a certain sacred equality under it as their personal right. They had also elected their rulers, and so far they could agree to the right of a government by consent. But they never had assumed that men are *ipso facto* exempt from obligation who have not consented, or that an autocratic and princely government is of necessity void and without "just power." Their "equality," their "consent," were the divine right of their history from the landing of the fathers downward, and before the French encyclopedists were born.

You will thus perceive that two distinct or widely different constitutional elements entered into our political order at the beginning; that, agreeing in form of words, they . . . have in fact been struggling in the womb of it, like Jacob and Esau, from the first day until now.

We have not always been conscious of the fact, yet so it has been. On the one side, we have had the sense of a historic and morally binding authority, freedom sanctified by law and law by God himself, living as it were in a common, all-dominating nationality. On the other, we have not so much been obeying as speculating, drawing out theories from points back of all history . . . till finally we have speculated almost everything away, and find that actually nothing is left to us but to fight out the question whether we shall have a nationality or not. . . . Proximately our whole difficulty is an issue forced by slavery. But if we go back to the deepest root of our trouble, we shall find that it comes of trying to maintain a government without moral ideas, and to concentrate a loyal feeling around institutions that, as many reason, are only human compacts, entitled of course, if that be all, to no feeling of authority or even of respect. . . .

Glance down the track of our history now and see how they have been letting us regularly down toward the present disruption of order, how the moral ideas that constitute the only real basis of government . . . are ignored, omitted, or quite frittered away. . . .

Our statesmen or politicians, not being generally religious men, take up with difficulty conceptions of government . . . that suppose the higher rule of God. . . . When they hear it affirmed that "the powers that be are ordained of God" [Rom. 13:1] . . ., [they have little notion that this means] that God, as certainly as there is a God, dominates all history, building all societies into forms of order and law, and that when constitutions are framed by men, they were as really framed by God . . ., and are nothing in fact but the issuing into form of a government that he before implanted in the social orders and historic ideas of the people, possible therefore to be framed and to hold the binding force of laws because God himself has prepared them and stamped them with his own providential sovereignty. Sometimes too the politicians are a little annoyed . . . by this foisting in of the claims of religion. What has religion to do with political matters? What has the church to do with the state? As if the state were really outside God's prerogatives and he had nothing to do with the state, nothing to do with the marshaling and well-ordering and protecting rule of society.

So they fall off easily into the "glittering generalities" and begin to theorize about compacts, consentings, and the like, building up our governmental order from below. First of all, they clear the ground by a sweeping denial, rejoicing in the discovery that all claims of divine right in government are preposterous. If they only meant by this that all claims to govern wrong by divine right are a baseless and dreadful hypocrisy, it would be well. But they really conceive that government is now to rule without any divine right at all. . . . They do not perceive that God is joined to all right and all defenses of right in society by the eternal necessity of his nature—stands by them, makes them his own, clothes them with his own everlasting authority. Hence [it is] that all law gets the binding force of law.

But the ground is clear. Religion is one thing, government is another. And now there is nothing to do but to find how man can make or does make a government without God or any divine sanction. . . . Man is the fact given, government the problem. And the man being a complete individual, independent and sole arbiter of his own actions and exactly equal . . . to every other, he may choose, if he please, never to have any government at all. But he consents, and there government begins. . . . The government is, of course, a compact. The major vote chooses the rulers, and the people are the sovereign head whence all law and authority emanate. To them only the rulers are responsible, being in fact their agents. . . . And this, it is conceived, is a true account of civil government, our own constitutional government.

These now are the saws of our current political philosophy. . . . They could, many of them, be true enough were they qualified so as to let in God and religion or so as to meet and duly recognize the moral ideas of history. But, taken as they are meant, they are about the shallowest, chaffiest fictions ever accepted by a people as the just account of their laws.

Let there be no misunderstanding here. I am not complaining of the laws or the constitutions. Better and more beneficent never existed. I am only complaining of the account that is made of them. . . .

There was never, in the first place, any such prior man or body of men to make a government. We are born into government as we are into the atmosphere. And when we assume to make a government or a constitution, we only draw out one that was providentially in us before. We could not have a king or nobility, for example, in this country, for there was no material given out of which to make either one or the other. The church life and order was democratic too. The whole English constitution also was in us before. In these facts, prepared in history by God, our institutions lie. We did not make them. We only sketched them, and God put them in us to be sketched. And when that is done they are his, clothed with his divine sanction. . . .

But the crowning mischief is yet to be named. Out of these baseless, unhistoric, merely speculative theories of the government, and the gradual demoralization of our habit under them, a doctrine of state rights is finally to emerge and organize the armed treason that explodes our nationality. Our political theories never gave us a real nationality but only a co-partnership, and the armed treason is only the consummated result of our speculations. Where nothing exists but a consent, what can be needed to end it but a dissent? And if the states are formed by the consent of individuals, was not the general government formed by the consent of the states? What then have we to do but give up the partnership of the states when we will? If a tariff act is passed displeasing to some states, they may rightfully nullify it. If a president is elected not in the interest of slavery, they may secede, i.e. withdraw their consent. . . . We are landed in the very strange predicament of being a people, the only one ever heard of in the world, without a nationality. Is the nationality in the states? No, that was never so much as thought of. Is it in the general government? No, that is philosophically denied. And so we are left to the luckless condition of being no nation at all, and having no nationality anywhere. . . .

And what is it now that is arming to assert and establish this broken nationality? Not religion, certainly. It does not appear that our people are consciously more given to religion than they have been. Yet, in another view, it is no other than the old historic religious element in which our nationality has been grounded from the first, that which has been smothered and kept under by the specious fictions we have contrived to account for the government without reference to God or to moral ideas. Yes, it is this old, implicitly if not formally, religious element that is struggling out again now, clad all over in arms, to maintain the falling nationality. . . . What a wonder is it even to ourselves to see the blaze that is kindled. We call it loyalty. We did not imagine that we had it. What a grand, rich sentiment it is! See what strength it has! See how it raises common men into heroes! See the bloody baptism wherewith it is able to be baptized! . . . What in fact is more priceless to a nation than great sentiments? So we bless ourselves in the loyalty of the hour, and the more, that there certainly is some latent heat of religion in the blaze of it.

But more is wanted, and God is pressing us on to the apprehending of that for which we are apprehended. Our passion must be stiffened and made a fixed sentiment as it can be only when it is penetrated and fastened by moral ideas. And this requires adversity. As the dyers use mordants to set in their colors, so adversity is the mordant for all sentiments of morality. The true loyalty is never reached till the laws and the nation are made to appear sacred or somewhat more than human. And that will not be done till we have made long, weary, terrible sacrifices for it. Without shedding of blood, there is no such grace prepared. There must be tears in houses as well as blood in the fields. . . . In these and all such terrible throes, the true loyalty is born. The nation emerges at last a true nation, consecrated and made great in our eyes by the sacrifices it has cost.

But this is war, we shall be told, and war is certainly no such moral affair. How then do we expect any such moral regeneration to come out of it? In one view, the objection is good. War is a great demoralizer, throwing back on society men who have been hardened and made desperate often by the vices and reckless violences of camp life. But the same is true of peace, that also has its dangers and corruptions, breeding finally all most selfish, unheroic, and meanest vices; untoning all noblest energies, making little men, . . . ignorant of sacrifice. . . . Peace will do for angels, but war is God's ordinance for sinners. And they want the schooling of it often. In a time of war, what a sense of discipline is forced. Here at last there must be and will be obedience. And the people outside get the sense of it about as truly as the army itself. . . . All the laxities of feeling and duty are drawn tight. Principles and moral convictions are toned to a practical supremacy. . . .

Neither is it any objection that ours is a civil war, however much we may seem to be horrified by the thought of it. Where a civil war is not a war of factions but of principles and practical ends, it is the very best and most fruitful of wars. The great civil war of Cromwell and Charles, for example, what was it in fact but a fighting out of all that is most valuable in the British constitution? And what was the result of it briefly stated but liberty enthroned and fortified by religion? And there was never a people more fortunate in the occasions of a civil war than we. Not one doubt is permitted us that we are fighting . . . to save the best government of the world and they to destroy it. Whence it follows that, as God is with all right and for it by the fixed necessity of his virtue, we may know that we are fighting up to God and not away from him. And the victory when it comes will even be a kind of religious crowning of our nationality. . . . What we have fought out by so many and bloody sacrifices will be hallowed by them in one feeling. Our loyalty will be entered into our conscience and the springs of our religious nature. Government now will govern and will be valued because it does, and the feeble platitudes we let in for a philosophy will be displaced by old historic habits and convictions that have been the real life of our institutions from the first. . . .

As to the great and frowning misery of slavery, I know not what to say or how the matter may be issued. . . . And yet . . . simply to be victorious . . . will . . . put a stop forever to the disgusting and barbarous propagandism of the past. . . .

Henceforth we [shall be] . . . a homogeneous, universally free people, a solid and compact nation such as God would have us. . . .

Abraham Lincoln, "First Inaugural Address," March 4, 1861[23]

Physically speaking, we cannot separate. We cannot remove our respective sections from each other, nor build an impassable wall between them. A husband and wife may be divorced, and go out of the presence and beyond the reach of each other; but the different parts of our country cannot do this. They cannot but remain face to face, and intercourse, either amicable or hostile, must continue between them. . . . Suppose you go to war, you cannot fight always. And when, after much loss on both sides, and no gain on either, you cease fighting, the identical old questions as to terms of intercourse are again upon you. . . .

Why should there not be a patient confidence in the ultimate justice of the people? Is there any better or equal hope in the world? In our present differences is either party without faith of being in the right? If the Almighty Ruler of Nations, with his eternal truth and justice, be on your side of the North or on yours of the South, that truth and that justice will surely prevail by the judgment of this great tribunal of the American people. . . . Intelligence, patriotism, Christianity, and a firm reliance on him who has never yet forsaken this favored land, are still competent to adjust in the best way all our present difficulty. . . .

Abraham Lincoln, "Second Annual Message to Congress," December 1, 1862[24]

Fellow citizens, we cannot escape history. We of this Congress and this administration will be remembered in spite of ourselves. . . . The fiery trial through which we pass will light us down, in honor or dishonor, to the latest generation. We say we are for the Union. The world will not forget that we say this. We know how to save the Union. The world knows we do know how to save it. We, even we here, hold the power and bear the responsibility. In giving freedom to the slave, we assure freedom to the free; honorable alike in what we give and in what we preserve. We shall nobly save or meanly lose the last best hope of earth. . . . The way is plain, peaceful, generous, just; a way which, if followed, the world will forever applaud and God must forever bless.

Abraham Lincoln, "Second Inaugural Address," March 4, 1865[25]

On the occasion corresponding to this four years ago, all thoughts were anxiously directed to an impending civil war. All dreaded it; all sought to avert it. . . . Both parties deprecated war; but one of them would make war rather than let the nation survive; and the other would accept war rather than let it perish. And the war came. . . .

Neither party expected for the war the magnitude or the duration which it has already attained. . . . Each looked for an easier triumph and a result less fundamental and astounding. Both read the same Bible and pray to the same God, and each invokes his aid against the other. It may seem strange that any men should dare to ask a just God's assistance in wringing their bread from the sweat of other men's faces, but let us judge not that we be not judged [Matt. 7:1]. The prayers of both could not be answered; that of neither has been answered fully. The Almighty has his own purposes. "Woe unto the world because of offenses, for it must needs be that offenses come; but woe to that man by whom the offense cometh" [Matt. 18:7]. If we shall suppose that American slavery is one of those offenses which, in the providence of God, must needs come but which, having continued through his appointed time, he now wills to remove, and that he gives to both North and South this terrible war as the woe due to those by whom the offense came, shall we discern therein any departure from those divine attributes which the believers in a living God always ascribe to him. Fondly do we hope, fervently do we pray, that this mighty scourge of war may speedily pass away. Yet, if God wills that it continue until all the wealth piled up by the bondmen's two hundred and fifty years of unrequited toil shall be sunk and until every drop of blood drawn with the lash shall be paid by another drawn with the sword, as was said three thousand years ago so still it must be said: "The judgments of the Lord are true and righteous altogether" [Ps. 19:9].

With malice toward none, with charity for all, with firmness in the right as God gives us to see the right, let us strive on to finish the work we are in, to bind up the nation's wounds, to care for him who shall have borne the battle, and for his widow, and his orphan—to do all which may achieve and cherish a just and a lasting peace, among ourselves and with all nations.

MINORITY APPROPRIATIONS

The dominant pattern of American self-understanding was Puritan-Protestant, but it was a self-understanding which both Roman Catholics and Jews found it possible largely to appropriate within the context of their own religious views. An early indication of Roman Catholic appropriation is represented by Father Seraphin Bandol's sermon delivered before members of Congress in Philadelphia on the occasion of Cornwallis's surrender. Later and more eloquent expression of Roman Catholic identification was supplied by numerous addresses of John Ireland, Archbishop of St. Paul. From the Jewish congregation in Newport, Rhode Island, on August 17, 1790, came words of heartfelt gratitude to "the work of the great God" in establishing the United States as a haven of "civil and religious liberty." A century later Emma Lazarus penned the words inscribed on the Statue of Liberty in New York harbor which have become a classic expression of American self-regard.

Seraphin Bandol, "A Thanksgiving Sermon, November 27, 1781"[26]

A numerous people assembled to render thanks to the Almighty for his mercies is one of the most affecting objects and worthy the attention of the Supreme Being. While camps resound with triumphal acclamations, while nations rejoice in victory and glory, the most honorable office a minister of the altar can fill is to be the organ by which public gratitude is conveyed to the Omnipotent.

Those miracles which he once wrought for his chosen people are renewed in our favor, and it would be equally ungrateful and impious not to acknowledge that the event which lately confounded our enemies and frustrated their designs was the wonderful work of that God who guards your liberties.

And who but he could so combine the circumstances which led to success? We have seen our enemies push forward . . . to the spot which was designed to witness their disgrace, yet they eagerly sought it as their theater of triumph. Blind as they were, they bore hunger, thirst, and inclement skies, poured their blood in battle against brave republicans, and crossed immense regions to confine themselves in another Jericho whose walls were fated to fall before another Joshua. It is he, whose voice commands the winds, the seas, and the seasons, who formed a junction, on the same day in the same hour, between a formidable fleet from the south and an army rushing from the north like an impetuous torrent. Who but he in whose hands are the hearts of men could inspire the allied troops with the friendships, the confidence, the tenderness of brothers? . . . Worldlings would say it is the wisdom, the virtue, and moderation of their chiefs . . . which has performed this prodigy. They will say that to the skill of the generals, to the courage of the troops, to the activity of the whole army, we must attribute this splendid success. Ah, they are ignorant that the combining of so many fortunate circumstances is an emanation from the all perfect mind. That courage, that skill, that activity bear the sacred impression of him who is divine.

For how many favors have we not to thank him during the course of the present year? Your union, which was at first supported by justice alone, has been consolidated by your courage, and the knot which ties you together is become indissoluble by the accession of all the states and the unanimous voice of all the confederates. You present to the universe the noble sight of a society which, founded in equality and justice, secures to the individuals who compose it the utmost happiness which can be derived from human institutions. This advantage, which so many other nations have been unable to procure even after ages of effort and misery, is granted by Divine Providence to the United States, and his adorable decrees have marked the present moment for the completion of that memorable happy revolution which has taken place in this extensive continent. . . .

John Ireland, *The Church and Modern Society* (Chicago: D. H. McBride and Co., 1896)[27]

[1889]. This is a providential nation. How youthful and yet how great. How rich in glorious promise. . . . A hundred years ago the states hardly exceeded the third million in population, today they approach the sixty-fifth million. . . . The world's throngs are drawn to us. The country must grow and prosper. In the solution of social and political problems, no less than in the development of industry and commerce, the influence of America will be dominant among the nations. . . . The spirit of American liberty wafts its spell across seas and oceans, and prepares distant continents for the implanting of American ideas and institutions. The influence will grow with the nation. . . . The center of human action . . . is rapidly shifting, and at no distant day America will lead the world. . . .

We cannot but believe that a singular mission is assigned to America, glorious for itself and beneficent to the whole race, the mission of . . . securing to the multitude of the people social happiness and equality of rights. With our hopes are bound up the hopes of millions of the earth. . . .

[1892]. Four hundred years ago today, America first unfolded to the eyes of civilized people her beauty and her wealth. Fraught, indeed, with solemn meaning for the whole world of men was the occurrence. Few words recorded in story were the signal of so great things to come as were the words, "Land! Land!" which rose in swelling chorus and rent the air above the decks of the weary and wave-beaten caravels of the admiral of the seas. A new land was in sight, fruitful in resources, pregnant in possibilities. A new world was being given to human longings, to human action. A new era was dawning for mankind, a marvelous epoch of human progress. Since the preaching of the Christian religion, nothing had happened of such import for the human race as the discovery of America. . . . For good reason do the nations of the world keep sacred this quadricentennial anniversary.

To the United States has been allotted the solemn commemoration of the discovery of America. To the first nation of the continent belonged of right the gracious task. She is the giant daughter of the progress of the age. She has the power to command the splendors which should mark the commemoration. Proper was it that, among the cities of the United States, Chicago be the chosen one within whose portals the Exposition be enthroned. Chicago, the prairie village of fifty years ago, the stupendous city of today, is the world's object lesson of progress. . . . Chicago typifies the mighty destiny of the United States—to rule among earth's nations, the admired queen, the arbitress of their destinies, marshaling with her sceptre of peace all peoples into one harmonious and indestructible brotherhood. . . .

In the course of history Providence selects now one nation, now another, to be the guide and the exemplar of humanity's progress. . . . A great era, the like of which has not been seen, is now dawning upon the horizon. Which will now be God's chosen nation to guide the destinies of mankind?

The chosen nation of the future! She is before my soul's vision. Giant in stature, comely in feature, buoyant in the freshness of morning youth, matronly in prudent stepping, the ethereal breezes of liberty carressing with loving touch her tresses, she is (no one seeing her can doubt it) the queen, the mistress, the teacher of coming ages. To her keeping the Creator has entrusted a mighty continent . . . which he had held in reserve for long centuries, awaiting the propitious moment in humanity's evolution to bestow it on men when men were worthy to possess it. . . . Of this nation it is the mission to give forth a new humanity. She embodies in her life and institutions the hopes, the ambitions, the dreamings of humanity's priests and prophets. . . . The nation of the future! Need I name it? . . . It is the United States of America.

[1894]. America, rising into the family of nations in these latter times, is the highest billow in humanity's evolution, the crowning effort of age in the aggrandizement of man. Unless we view her in this altitude we do not comprehend her. We belittle her towering stature and hide from ourselves the singular design of Providence in creating her. When the fathers of the republic declared "that all men are created equal, that they are endowed by their Creator with certain inalienable rights, that among these are life, liberty, and the pursuit of happiness," a principle was enunciated which in its truth was as old as the race but in practical realization was almost unknown. . . . Not until the Republic of the West was born, not until the star-spangled banner rose towards the skies, was liberty caught up in humanity's embrace and embodied in a great and abiding nation. . . . One republic only is liberty's native home—America.

The God-given mission of America is not confined to its own people alone. It extends to all the peoples of the earth to whom it is the symbol of human rights and of human liberty, and towards whom its flag flutters hopes of future happiness. . . .

Ceaseless and soul-rending was the anxiety of freedom's sons during the dreary years of America's Civil War. . . . Great were the sacrifices which the war in defense of the country demanded. But great also were the results. Today no one doubts that . . . a free people may be relied upon to defend their country. . . . The seal of finality has been set upon the Union, the God of battles ending our strife and decreeing that we are a nation, one and indestructible. Slavery has been blotted out and the escutcheon of America is free of blemish. Liberty is without peril in her chosen home, and from America's shores she sends inspiring messages across seas and oceans. The quickened spirit of republicanism and democracy, to be seen today in Europe and throughout the southern continent of America, goes out from the triumphant republic of the United States.

The sacrifices! Each of you . . . may say in truth: "Of

those a fair share was mine." . . . Of the results! They are yours, since yours were the sacrifices that purchased them. This great nation is yours in an especial manner. By the libation of your blood it was saved. By you, at the peril of your life, the star-spangled banner was guarded in its hour of trial.

The days of peace have come upon America. . . . What was saved in the days of war must be guarded in days of peace. . . . The destinies of many people are in the balance. Nations move towards liberty according as liberty is seen to reign undisturbed in America; they recede towards absolutism and hereditary regime according as dangers arise that threaten peace and order in the republic. . . .

Letter of Greeting to George Washington from the Hebrew Congregation in Newport, August 17, 1790[28]

Sir:

Permit the children of the stock of Abraham to approach you with the most cordial affection and esteem for your personal merits, and to join with our fellow citizens in welcoming you to Newport.

With pleasure we reflect on those days, those days of difficulty and dangers, when the God of Israel who delivered David from the peril of the sword shielded your head in the day of battle. And we rejoice to think that the same Spirit who rested in the bosom of the greatly beloved Daniel, enabling him to preside over the provinces of the Babylonish empire, rests and ever will rest upon you, enabling you to discharge the arduous duties of chief magistrate in these states.

Deprived as we heretofore have been of the invaluable rights of free citizens, we now with a deep sense of gratitude to the Almighty Disposer of All Events behold a government erected by the majesty of the people, a government which to bigotry gives no sanction, to persecution no assistance, but generously affording to all liberty of conscience and immunities of citizenship; deeming everyone, of whatever nation, tongue, or language, equal parts of the great governmental machine. This so ample and extensive federal union, whose basis is philanthropy, mutual confidence, and public virtue, we cannot but acknowledge to be the work of the great God who ruleth in the armies of heaven and among the inhabitants of the earth, doing whatsoever seemeth him good.

For all the blessings of civil and religious liberty which we enjoy under an equal and benign administration, we desire to send up our thanks to the Ancient of Days, the great preserver of men, beseeching him that the angel who conducted our forefathers through the wilderness into the promised land may graciously conduct you through all the difficulties and dangers of this mortal life. And when, like Joshua full of days and full of honor, you are gathered to your fathers may you be admitted into the heavenly paradise to partake of the water of life and the tree of immortality.

Done and signed by order of the Hebrew Congregation in Newport, Rhode Island, August 17, 1790.

MOSES SEIXAS

Emma Lazarus, "The New Colossus" (1883)[29]

Not like the brazen giant of Greek fame,
With conquering limbs astride from land to land;
Here at our sea-washed, sunset gates shall stand
A mighty woman with a torch, whose flame
Is the imprisoned lightning, and her name
Mother of Exiles. From her beacon-hand
Glows world-wide welcome; her mild eyes command
The air-bridged harbor that twin cities frame.

"Keep, ancient lands, your storied pomp!" cries she
With silent lips. "Give me your tired, your poor,
Your huddled masses yearning to breathe free,
The wretched refuse of your teeming shore.
Send these, the homeless, tempest-tost to me,
I lift my lamp beside the golden door!"

3

THE RENOVATION OF THE WORLD

JOHN AYLMER, returning to England in 1559, had reminded Queen Elizabeth that laws alone were not enough to secure ready obedience. "The heart, I say, must be framed and brought into the circle of obedience, and then will all the rest follow. . . . The heart being in order, the rest cannot be out of order." In 1646 Jeremiah Burroughes spoke in similar vein of the difficulty of seeking "to beat the nail in by the hammer of authority without making way [for it] by the wimble of instruction. . . . If you meet with sound wood, with heart of oak, though the hammer and the hand that strikes be strong, yet the nail will hardly go in. It will turn crooked or break, or at least if it enters it may split that it enters into, and if so it will not hold long." And then he added laconically: "You have to deal with English consciences. There is no country so famous for strong oaks as England. You will find English consciences to be so."[1] The heart must be prepared, even English and American hearts, or dissension, strife, and disorder will prevail.

It was this firmly grounded conviction which explains American preoccupation with the dual tradition of civil liberty and spiritual religion. The two emphases were viewed as closely intertwined and mutually supportive. Without civil and religious liberty, the voluntary obedience of spiritual religion would be compromised and America would repeat the folly of forced and external worship. And the obverse seemed equally true. Without the willing obedience and respect for the common good engendered by spiritual religion, civil liberty would end in chaos, anarchy, and despotism. "Remove it, destroy it, and liberty is dead; extend it through all the governments of earth, and the world is free."[2] Even the rationalists regarded religion as indispensable to domestic tranquillity and as the bond which held together a free society. Accepted by George Washington as axiomatic, this stanchly held conviction was voiced with greater fervor and urgency by those whose hearts had been more deeply touched by evangelical religion. It became one of the driving concerns motivating the great burst of revivalistic and home missionary activity in the early decades of the nineteenth century.

Religion in its Christian expression, particularly during periods of evangelistic ardor, always has had difficulty in adjusting the horizon of its concern to national boundaries. The churches in America were no exception, never really being content merely to serve the ends of domestic utility. The cosmopolitan interest had found expression in the stress upon America's vocation to redeem the world by high example. This passive role was supplemented in 1810 by a more active stance with the formation of the American Board of Commissioners for Foreign Missions. American interest in foreign missions had been aroused shortly after 1800 by news of English missionary activity and by firsthand reports of distant lands brought back by clipper ships engaged in the Pacific trade. At this moment when public attention was being focused upon faraway places, the second Great Awakening was kindling new religious fervor and devotion. Given these circumstances, it is not surprising that ardent and adventurous young Christians should have felt an insistent summons to carry the gospel to the storybook lands of the Pacific. Nor is it surprising that their venture should have introduced a new element into America's sense of national vocation.

MISSIONS, REVIVALS, AND REVOLUTIONS

Embarking upon foreign mission activity did not involve any slackening of home mission interest. To American churchmen the two concerns were interlocking, both part of a single enterprise. The conversion of the burgeoning population of mid-America to evangelical Christianity was regarded as a prerequisite to foreign missions. "To seek the conversion of the heathen without the conversion of our countrymen," an 1842 promotional brochure declared, "would be to seek the end without the means." Catharine Beecher put the need for a strong home base of operations even more succinctly when she said that if the West is lost, all is lost.[3]

The home and overseas thrusts were viewed as interlocking in a more fundamental sense than the mere necessity of a strong home base. The role to be performed by the contagion of American example in all facets of its common life was not forgotten.

Heman Humphrey, preaching in 1819 at the ordination of two young missionaries to the Sandwich Islands (Hawaii), presented the case for foreign missions. It was no narrowly conceived task that was envisioned. The mission being sent included, in addition to the two missionaries, an agriculturalist, a physician, a mechanic, a catechist, and a printer; the latter three to serve also as schoolmasters. They were to be aided by three Hawaiians who had been trained as teachers after having been brought to the United States by New England sea captains. "Your views are not to be limited to a low or narrow scale," ran the instructions of the Board, "but you are to open your hearts wide and set your mark high. You are to aim at nothing short of covering those islands with fruitful fields, and pleasant dwellings, and schools, and churches; of raising up the whole people to an elevated state of Christian civilization."[4]

The interlocking concerns, aimed at the renovation of the whole world, were explicated again and again by Lyman Beecher, a man who brought into focus in his own person most of the significant tendencies of the first half of the nineteenth century. In his *Plea for the West* of 1835 he spoke of "the rapid and universal extension of civil and religious liberty, introductory to the triumphs of universal Christianity," and he reminded his readers of Jonathan Edwards' opinion that "the millennium would commence in America" and that from America would "the renovating power go forth." We cannot believe, he continued, that God brought "our fathers to this goodly land to lay the foundations of religious liberty, and wrought such wonders in their preservation, and raised their descendents to such heights of civil and religious prosperity, only to reverse . . . his providence and abandon his work." Consequently, if we fail in "our great experiment of self-government," an experiment demanding "the education of the head and heart of the nation," we shall find that "our destruction will be as signal as the birth-right abandoned. . . . The descent of desolation will correspond with the past elevation. No punishments of Heaven are so severe as those for mercies abused, and no instrumentality employed in their infliction is so dreadful as the wrath of man."[5] The selections which follow Humphrey's sermon explicate Beecher's basic theme.

Heman Humphrey, *The Promised Land, a sermon delivered . . . at the ordination of . . . Hiram Bingham and Asa Thurston as missionaries to the Sandwich Islands, September 29, 1819* (Boston: S. T. Armstrong, 1819)[6]

God, as the supreme ruler and absolute proprietor of the world, thought fit to give all the land of Canaan to Abraham and his posterity for an everlasting inheritance. This grant was again and again renewed, and confirmed to Isaac and Jacob as heirs of the promise. But they were not to take immediate possession. While the Canaanites were filling up the measure of their iniquities, the children of Israel sojourned and were oppressed in Egypt; and it was not until the time of Moses that they were delivered from that terrible bondage and conducted by a series of miracles through the wilderness to the eastern border of the promised land. There upon the top of a mountain which overlooked the fertile plain of Jordan Moses yielded up at once his commission and his life, not however till he had by divine authority invested Joshua with the supreme command. . . .

Joshua proved himself in all respects worthy of the high trust reposed in him. . . . Had the Israelites . . . vigorously pushed their advantage with a humble trust in God, they might soon have completed the conquest of Canaan. But their courage seems to have failed them. . . . The people were inclined to sit down ingloriously content with present acquisitions. . . . "There remaineth yet very much land to be possessed" [Josh. 13:1] was a cutting reproof of their inactivity and unbelief. And that no more time might be lost, the aged Joshua was commanded to divide the remainder by lot among the tribes and require them immediately to . . . take possession for themselves and their children.

The text admits of an easy and I think a legitimate application. . . . As the nation of Israel was then militant, so is the church now. As the land of Canaan belonged to Israel in virtue of a divine grant, so does the world belong to the church. And as God's chosen people still had much to do before they could come into full and quiet possession of the land, so has the church a great work to accomplish in subduing the world "to the obedience of Christ." In this spiritual . . . sense "there remaineth yet very much of the land to be possessed." The plan of my discourse, therefore, will naturally embrace the following topics, *viz.*

that immense regions of the earth which belong to the church are still unsubdued;

that the ultimate conquest and possession of all these is certain;

that, although the excellency of the power is of God, this great work is to be accomplished by human instrumentality;

that, but for the lamentable and criminal apathy of the church, it might have been accomplished ages ago;

that, as Christendom now possesses ample resources and ability, she is solcmnly bound in the name of God and with the least possible delay to set up her banners in every heathen land; and,

that the aspects of Divine Providence are peculiarly auspicious to the missionary enterprises of the day. . . .

This great work . . . might be effected by a miracle in a single day. . . . But not so is the will of her King. As well might the Israelites have waited in the wilderness for the conquest of Canaan. God had promised to drive out the nations, but he thought fit to employ his people to effect it instead of doing it by his own immediate power. They had actually to go up and take possession. . . . In the same manner, by the use of means and instruments, is the whole world to be subdued and rendered fruitful. . . . Missionaries must be sent. . . .

As Christendom now possesses ample resources and ability, she is solemnly bound in the name of God and with the least possible delay to set up her banners in every heathen land. . . . If Great Britain alone could raise four hundred millions of dollars in a single year to carry on the war against her great Continental rival, how easily might she support an army of ten thousand missionaries. . . . The mere cost of powder and cannon balls for one battle would comfortably support all the missionaries now in service for ten years. But not to carry you too far from home nor detain you too long in foreign parts, how much more might be done by our American Israel than has ever yet been attempted. . . .

The question of ability then being decided in the affirmative, that of duty next presents itself. . . . Is the church bound with the least possible delay to give the gospel to the heathen? This, my brethren, is one of the few questions which will not bear argument. . . . The command of Christ is: "Go ye into all the world and preach the gospel to every creature" [Mark 16:15]. . . .

My dear Christian friends [turning to the assistants and teachers of the mission], you also have enlisted as soldiers in this important expedition. You have set your faces towards Hawaii as part of "the promised land" which remaineth "yet to be possessed." . . . It is not to enslave the free or circumvent the ignorant or stimulate rival chiefs to acts of hostility [that you go], but it is to "proclaim liberty to the captives and the opening of the prison doors to them that are bound" [Isa. 61:1]. . . . It is to save their children from the shark [human sacrifice] and to make them acquainted with the arts and improvements of civilized nations. It is . . . to multiply among them the sources of enjoyment in this life, and above all to prepare them for endless happiness in the world to come. . . .

Lyman Beecher, "The Memory of Our Fathers," a sermon delivered at Plymouth, Massachusetts, December 22, 1827[7]

The history of the world is the history of human nature in ruins. No state of society, which corresponds with the capacity of enjoyment possessed by man or with his conceptions and desires, has been permanent and universal. Small portions only of the human family have, at the same time, enjoyed a state of society in any considerable degree desirable, while much the greatest part of mankind have, in all ages, endured the evils of barbarism and despotism.

It is equally manifest that this unhappy condition of our race has not been the result of physical necessity but of moral causes. The earth is as capable of sustaining a happy as a miserable population, and it is the perversion of her resources and of the human faculties which has made the misery of man so great. . . .

From these experiments so long and so hopelessly made, it appears that in the conflict between the heart and the intellect of man victory has always declared on the side of the heart, which had led many to conclude that the condition of man, in respect to any universal abiding melioration, is hopeless. [But] the text throws light upon this dark destiny of our race. It is a voice from heaven announcing the approach of help from above: "He that sitteth upon the throne saith, Behold, I make all things new" [Rev. 21:5].

The renovation here announced is a moral renovation which shall change the character and condition of men. It will not be partial in its influence like the sun shining through clouds on favored spots but co-extensive with the ruin. Nor shall its results be national glory which gilds only the palace and cheers only the dwellings of the noble. It shall bring down the mountains and exalt the valleys [Isa. 40:4]. It shall send liberty and equality to all the dwellings of men. . . . It shall enter . . . the heart and there destroy the power which has blasted human hopes and baffled human efforts. Nor will the change be transient. It is the last dispensation of Heaven for the relief of this miserable world, and shall bring "glory to God in the highest, and upon earth peace and good will to men" [Luke 2:14]. . . .

For the accomplishment of this renovation, great changes are required in the civil and religious conditions of nations.

1. The monopoly of the soil must be abolished. Hitherto the majority of mankind who have tilled the earth have been slaves or tenants. The soil has been owned by kings and military chieftains and nobles, and by them rented to landlords, and by these to still smaller dealers, and by these again it has been divided and subdivided until the majority who paid the rent have sustained in the sweat of their brow, not only their own families, but three or four orders of society above them, while they themselves have been crushed beneath the weight and have lived on the borders of starvation. . . . This same monopoly of the soil has sent another large class of the community into manufacturing establishments to wear out their days in ignorance and hopeless poverty. . . .

The consequence of excluding such numbers from the possession and healthful cultivation of the soil has been ignorance, improvidence, reckless indifference, turbulence, and crime. Tortured by their oppressions and unrestrained by moral principle, they have been prepared for desperate deeds. Such a state of society cannot be made happy. . . .

2. To effect the moral renovation of the world a change is required in the prevailing forms of government. The monopoly of power must be superseded by the suffrages of free men. While the great body of the people are excluded from all voice and influence in legislation, it is impossible to constitute a state of society such as the faculties of man allow and the word of God predicts. While the few govern without responsibility, they will seek their own elevation and depress the multitude. . . .

3. Before the moral renovation of the world can be achieved, the rights of conscience must also be restored to man. Few of the millions that have peopled the earth have been qualified by knowledge or permitted by the governments under which they lived to read the Bible and judge for themselves. The nominal religions of this world have been supported by governments

who, of course, have prescribed the creed and modeled the worship and controlled the priesthood. From such a state of things what better results could be expected than that ambitious men should be exalted to the sacred office, while religion itself was despised and persecuted? . . .

To accomplish these changes in the civil and religious condition of the world, revolutions and convulsions are doubtless indispensable. The usurpation of the soil will not be relinquished spontaneously, nor the chains knocked off from the body and mind of man by the hands which for ages have been employed to rivet them. He that sitteth upon the throne must "overturn and overturn" [Ezek. 21:27] before his rights and the rights of man will be restored. Revolutions, of course, are predicted such as shall veil the sun, and turn the moon into blood [Joel 2:31], and shake the earth with the violence of nation dashing against nation, until every despotic government shall be thrown down and chaos resume its pristine reign, until the Spirit of God shall move again upon the face of the deep and bring out a new creation. . . .

But to the perfection of this work a great example is required of which the world may take knowledge, and which shall inspire hope and rouse and concentrate the energies of man. But where should such an experiment be made? . . . In Europe and Asia it would have required ages to dig up the foundations of despotism and remove the rubbish to prepare the way for such a state of society as we have described. . . . There was also such a mass of uninformed mind accustomed to crouch under burdens and so much was required to prepare it for civil liberty that little hope remained that the Old World, undirected and unstimulated by example, would ever disenthral itself. Some nation, itself free, was needed to blow the trumpet and hold up the light. . . .

But where could such a nation be found? It must be created for it had no existence upon the earth. Look now at the history of our fathers and behold what God hath wrought. They were such a race of men as never before laid the foundations of an empire. . . . But how should this portion of a nation's population be uprooted and driven into exile? They were not permitted to remain at home. In that age of darkness and land of bondage, they had formed some just conceptions of civil and religious liberty and . . . could not in all things conform and were not permitted to dissent. And thus they were driven into exile and compelled to lay the foundations of a new empire.

And now behold their institutions, such as the world needs and, attended as they have been by the power of God, able to enlighten and renovate the world. They recognize the equal rights of man. They give the soil to the cultivator, and self-government and the rights of conscience to the people. They enlighten the intellect, and form the conscience, and bring the entire influence of divine government to bear upon the heart. It was the great object of our fathers to govern men by the fear of the Lord; to exhibit the precepts, apply the motives, and realize the dispositions which the word of God inculcates and his Spirit inspires; to imbue families and schools and towns and states with the wisdom from above. They had no projects of human device, no theories of untried efficacy. They hung all their hopes of civil and religious prosperity upon the word of God and the efficacy of his Spirit. . . .

The great excellence of these institutions [of our fathers] is that they are practical and powerful. The people are not free in name and form merely but in deed and truth. . . . The governments are free governments from the foundation to the top stone, and of such practical efficacy as to make free men. The family, embodying instruction and government, was itself an embryo empire. In the school district the people were called upon to exercise their own discretion and rights. And in the ecclesiastical society to rear their place of worship, elect their pastor, and provide for his support. And all under the protection and guidance of law. The towns, in their popular assemblies, discussed their local interests and administered their own concerns. In these originated the legislature. . . . In the states, as they are now organized in our nation, all which is local and peculiar is superintended with a minuteness and efficacy which no consolidated government could possibly accomplish. . . .

It has been doubted whether a republic so extensive as ours can be held together and efficiently governed. But where there is this intellectual and moral influence, and the habitual exercise of civil and religious liberty from the family upward, we see not why a republic may not be extended indefinitely and still be the strongest and most effective government in the world.

The history of our nation is indicative of some great design to be accomplished by it. It is a history of perils and deliverances, and of strength ordained out of weakness. . . . No nation out of such weakness ever became so strong, or was guided through such perils to safety. . . . But in the whole history of the world God has not been accustomed to grant signal interpositions without ends of corresponding magnitude to be answered by them. Indeed, if it had been the design of heaven to establish a powerful nation in the full enjoyment of civil and religious liberty, where all the energies of man might find scope and excitement, on purpose to show the world by experiment of what man is capable and to shed light on the darkness which should awake the slumbering eye and rouse the torpid mind and nerve the palsied arm of millions, where could such an experiment have been made but in this country, and by whom so auspiciously as by our fathers, and by what means so well adapted to that end as by their institutions? . . .

For two hundred years the religious institutions of our land were secured by law. But as our numbers increased and liberty of conscience resulted in many denominations of Christians, it became impossible to secure by law the universal application of religious and moral influence. And yet without this mighty energy the whole system must fail. For physical power without religious and moral influence will not avail to sustain the institutions of civil liberty. . . . But at the very time when the civil law had become impotent for the support of religion and the prevention of immoralities, God began to pour out his Spirit upon the churches, and voluntary associations of Christians were raised up to apply and extend that influence which the law could no longer apply. And now we are blessed with societies to aid in the support of the gospel at home, to extend it to the new settlements and through the earth. We have Bible societies, and tract societies, and associations of individuals who make it their business to see that every family has a Bible, and every church a pastor, and every child a catechism. . . . And while these means of moral culture are supplied, this great nation from her eminence begins to look abroad with compassion upon a world sitting in darkness, and to put forth her mighty arm to disenthral the nations and elevate the family of man. Let it be remembered also that the means now relied on are precisely those which our fathers applied and which have secured their prosperity.

And when we contemplate the unexampled resources of this country, . . . is it too much to be hoped that God will accept our powerful instrumentality and make it effectual for the renovation of the world?

The revivals of religion which prevail in our land among Christians of all denominations furnish cheering evidence of the presence of evangelical doctrine and of the power of that Spirit by which the truth is to be made efficacious in the salvation of mankind. . . . They are without parallel in the history of the world and are constituting an era of moral power entirely new. . . . These revivals then, falling in with all these antecedent indications, seem to declare the purpose of God to employ this nation in the glorious work of renovating the earth.

If we look at our missionaries abroad and witness the smiles of Heaven upon their efforts, our confidence that it is the purpose of God to render our nation a blessing to the world will be increased. . . . If we consider also our friendly relations with the South American states and the close imitation they are disposed to make of our civil and literary institutions, who can doubt that the spark which our forefathers struck will yet enlighten this entire continent?

But when the light of such a hemisphere shall go up to the heavens it will throw its beams beyond the waves; it will shine into darkness there and be comprehended; it will awaken desire and hope and effort, and produce revolutions and overturnings, until the world is free.

From our revolutionary struggle proceeded the revolution in France and all of which has followed in Naples, Portugal, Spain, and Greece. And though the bolt of every chain has been again driven, they can no more hold the heaving mass than the chains of Xerxes could hold the Hellespont vexed with storms. Floods have been poured upon the rising flame, but they can no more extinguish it than they can extinguish the fires of Etna. Still it burns, and still the mountain heaves and murmurs. And soon it will explode with voices and thunderings and great earthquakes. Then will the trumpet of Jubilee sound, and earth's debased millions will leap from the dust, and shake off their chains, and cry, "Hosanna to the Son of David."

[Lyman Beecher], "The Necessity of Revivals of Religion to the Perpetuity of our Civil and Religious Institutions," *Spirit of the Pilgrims,* IV (Sept., 1831)[8]

The dangers which threaten these United States and the free institutions here established are numerous and appalling. They arise in part from our vast extent of territory, our numerous and increasing population, from diversity of local interests, the power of selfishness, and the fury of sectional jealousy and hate. All these are powerful causes of strife, and never were they in more powerful or terrific action.

These causes, alone sufficient to set on fire the course of nature, have . . . been welded, concentrated, and blown into fury by . . . the thirst for power and dominion [of] some of our leading politicians to whom the ordinary elements of strife seem tame and lazy in the work of ruin. . . . And there is a religious party spirit destroying the confidence of the great Christian denominations in one another, . . . and paralyzing their energy of action against a common foe for their common Lord. . . .

The dangers which threaten us . . . are not fictitious, nor are trifles magnified for rhetorical effect. . . . Unless some subduing, tranquilizing influence can be applied, superior to all which man can apply, our race as a nation is swift and our destruction is sure.

Let me then call the attention of my readers to our only remaining source of hope—God, and the interpositions of his Holy Spirit in great and general revivals of religion to reform the hearts of this people and make the nation good and happy.

There is for us assuredly but one remedy and that is such a state of the affections towards God and our neighbor as the Law and the Gospel require; not the ascendency of Christians over the world but the world in God's power becoming Christian. The influence which is necessary to save us is the influence of truth made effectual by the supernatural influence of God's Holy Spirit; not supernatural as revealing any new truth . . . but supernatural in this respect that God accomplishes by the truth that change in the affections which the interests of time and eternity alike require and which no human skill avails to achieve.

It is not to be supposed a thing beyond the power of God to effect such a change of human character as will reconcile liberty and boundless prosperity with their permanence and purity. Neither reason nor philosophy requires us to suppose that God has created a race whom he cannot, if it seems good to him, reclaim and govern in accordance with the highest degree of temporal prosperity.

The benevolence and mercy of God would lead us to infer from what he has done in providing redemption that he will do much more than he has done in its application. Everything shows that his purposes are tending to intellectual and civil and social results much beyond what has ever before existed. And this . . . would lead us to anticipate a more than corresponding moral and religious amelioration. . . . Every other cause has been tried and has completely failed. 1. Force has failed. It may intimidate and perpetuate ignorance, superstition, and hypocrisy, but it cannot compel benevolence, honesty, purity, and the graces of the Christian character. . . . 2. The cultivation of the intellect has failed. . . . 3. The insufficiency of creeds to preserve faith and holiness has long been determined. . . . 4. A faithful evangelical ministry is not alone sufficient to diffuse and perpetuate moral purity. . . .

There is no remedy for self-ruined man but regeneration. And there is no remedy for corrupt, agitated, threatened communities but revivals of religion. . . . The government of God is the only government which will hold society against depravity within and temptation without, and this it must do by the force of its own law written upon the heart. This is that unity of the Spirit and that bond of peace which alone can perpetuate national purity and tranquility, that law of universal and impartial love by which alone nations can be kept back from ruin. There is no safety for republics but in self-government under the influence of a holy heart swayed by the government of God.

But even these principles of national conservation to avail must become immensely more extensive and operative than they have been or are, for it is not the church which is to govern the world but the world must become Christian and govern itself. There is as much liberty in self-government according to the laws of Christ as in self-government according to the laws of the devil, as much free agency and republicanism in holiness as in vice and irreligion. The renovating power must then operate in greater masses of mind than it has ever done. It must move onward in the work of mercy more rapidly, more simultaneously, through towns and cities and states and nations. . . . The existing moral power of the gospel, with all its supernatural efficiency, is nothing to those tremendous causes of opposition which are every day developing their strength and concentrating their power. A few drops in the Mississippi might as well attempt to stop and turn back the descending flood as Christianity attempt in its present state to turn the public sentiment of the nation. The wicked will do wickedly . . . but as the hearts of men by the grace of God shall be radically changed. . . .

We have fallen on other times than the church of God ever saw before, times in which the same amount of religious and moral influence which once availed to advance the cause of Christ will not now enable it to hold its own. The intellect of man has waked up to a new activity . . . and with tenfold means of influence is going forth in its mightiness to agitate society. Old foundations are broken up, and old principles and maxims are undergoing a thorough and perilous revision. . . .

In our colonial state we were few and poor and feeble. Intercourse was difficult and rare, and moral causes insulated and local. What was said in one colony was not heard in another. . . . But now each colony is a state, and each state a nation, and intercourse is rapid and local causes tell in their results throughout the whole. . . . Since such new and increased action has commenced, for the moral energies of religion to be stationary is relatively to retrograde. . . .

Some who, reasoning from past analogies, think it most desirable that conversions should be dilatory and gradual rather than sudden and multitudinous forget that the revivals in the kingdom of darkness are moving with terrific haste and power. Millions are bursting into that kingdom while hundreds only are added to the kingdom of Christ. It is no time for ministers to think themselves faithful and successful without revivals. The seed cannot be long buried without being trodden down past coming up. . . . Nothing but speedy, extensive, and powerful revivals of religion can save our nation from impending ruin. . . . No influence but that of the wisdom from above . . . can unite the local, jarring interests of this great nation and constitute us benevolently one, so that if one member suffers all will sympathize and if one is honored all will rejoice. . . .

The political renovation of the world by revolutions will demand enterprise and treasure and blood. But the whole boundless sacrifice and victory will be a wanton waste . . . unless Christianity . . . bind up the wounds of a bleeding world. But to do this no accidental effort will suffice, no handfuls of charity occasionally dropped. . . . The world itself must be aroused (the redeemed and emancipated part) to enlighten and emancipate those that sit in darkness. . . . Revolution is to liberty and virtue only what the breaking up of winter is to a future harvest. It only removes obstacles and throws the field open to cultivation which must be desolate still unless the plow pass over it and the seed . . . be sown. . . .

I am aware that revivals of religion, so called, have been . . . abused. And so may civil liberty be abused. . . . What great change of human character and condition was ever accomplished without defect? . . . The defects of Luther and Calvin were spots on their sun, but still they were suns without whose blessed light the night of ages might still have brooded over the earth. . . . Our own blessed Revolution, was it marked by no excess and folly? . . . Why must the moral renovation of man alone be expected to move on unattended by the accidents of human imperfection? . . .

It hath been inquired whether a more gradual dispensation of the Spirit were not better than these sudden outpourings. But we have been accustomed to feel that God is the best judge of this matter and that man cannot make a revival either gradual or sudden. When he gives us drop by drop, we are thankful. And when the cloud of mercy bursts, . . . we dare not request him to stay his hand. . . . Nor can we perceive how it is possible that 800,000,000 of souls, or any considerable part of this number, can be washed from their sins . . . by single drops falling in such slow and deliberate succession as should not excite the fears and should satisfy the prudence of some very good men. We doubt not that greater revivals than have been are indispensable to save our nation and to save the world by giving universal and saving empire to the kingdom of Christ. . . .

FROM CONTINENTALISM TO IMPERIALISM

America's mission to humanity had been conceived as a witness to the world, the creation of a model republic which would win the admiration and emulation of mankind. But Americans also were expansionists, moving ever westward to occupy and claim new land for themselves. Until after the Civil War the expansionist horizon seldom extended beyond the boundaries of the continent. Men spoke of the "manifest destiny" (John L. O'Sullivan coined the term in 1845) of the United States to extend its limits to include all of North America. There was a flurry of excitement in the 1850's when covetous eyes were laid on Cuba, and later William H. Seward sought to add island possessions to the American domain. But it was only in the latter years of the nineteenth century that overseas expansion became a pressing issue.

Interest in the redemption of the islands of the Pacific and the lands of the Orient had marshaled the resources of the churches for foreign mission activity, and this in turn served to generate a wider interest in the role of the United States in world affairs. By the end of the nineteenth century this developing interest had led to a shift in expansionist thinking from "continentalism" to what was soon labeled "imperialism."

The new imperialism was born neither of necessity nor of self-interest. The objectives sought gave promise, when realistically appraised, of no economic gain to the nation, and they were not supported by the business class. The chief sponsors were ideologues—nationalist politicians, naval strategists, and loquacious scholars.[9] Frederick Merk has noted that expansionism has usually been the product of crusading ideologies. "In the case of Arab expansionism, it was Islam; in Spanish expansionism, Catholicism; in Napoleon's expansionism, revolutionary liberalism; in Russian and Chinese expansionism, Marxian communism."[10] This was equally true in the United States. Whether in terms of the earlier continentalism or the later imperialism, the ideology of American expansionism was a blend of many elements, including biblical concepts, millennial expectations, religious freedom, civil liberty, representative democracy, localism (federalism), and enlightened ("spiritual" and "nonsuperstitious") religious faith. Informing, shaping, correlating, and giving meaning to these several elements were understandings associated with the whole history of English-speaking people. No one set forth the late nineteenth-century version of American ideology more succinctly than Josiah Strong in his famous home missionary tract of 1886, *Our Country: Its Possible Future and Its Present Crisis*.

Strong, an Ohio clergyman serving as a secretary of the American Home Missionary Society, devoted a chapter of *Our Country* to "The Anglo-Saxon and the World's Future," a topic which he was to treat at greater length in *The New Era or the*

Coming Kingdom (1893) and *Expansion under New World Conditions* (1900). *Our Country* was an immediate popular success, approximately 150,000 copies having been sold by 1891 when a revised edition making use of the 1890 census statistics was issued.[11] Strong's thesis can easily be misinterpreted by modern readers as a mere glorification of race and nation. This was not his intention. He did accept current sociological analyses of population trends which seemed to indicate a growing predominance of Anglo-Saxons among the peoples of the world. But as a major proponent of the "social gospel" among Protestants, his was a humanitarian stress on the duty to share with others the blessings possessed by Anglo-Saxons in general and by the Americans in particular. Several points should be noted in this connection: (1) Strong regarded "mixed" races as the strongest. (2) He attributed Anglo-Saxon energy to climate rather than to blood. (3) He said that by Anglo-Saxon he meant English-speaking people. (4) He further defined Anglo-Saxons as the custodians and bearers of a cultural tradition—the two great ideas of spiritual religion and civil liberty. (5) He classified the immigrant population in the United States as Anglo-Saxon, believing that the temperate climate, the adoption of the English language, and the pervasive power of American sentiment quickly and effectively made them one with the rest of the population. There was a danger of immigrants arriving in such overwhelming numbers that the historic continuity would be broken, but generally "the strains of other bloods . . . may be expected to improve the stock and aid it to a higher destiny." Thus, to Strong, Anglo-Saxon was more a matter of faith and cultural convictions than of racial extraction. And the God-given mission of the Anglo-Saxon was cast in the servant rather than the master image. "This race," Strong was to write in *Expansion under New World Conditions,* "has been honored not for its own sake, but for the sake of the world. It has been made . . . powerful not to make subject, but to serve; . . . free not simply to exult in freedom, but to make free; exalted not to look down, but to lift up."[12]

In the crisis occasioned by the Spanish-American War, the servant image became badly strained in the pronouncements of such men as Senator Albert J. Beveridge and President McKinley. The older tradition of mission was better expressed by the *Pittsburgh Catholic* and by Henry Van Dyke, minister of the Brick Presbyterian Church in New York City.

It may seem curious that, on the whole, the defenders of racial superiority were opposed to imperial expansion.[13] They were fearful of the ultimate consequence of educating and freeing lesser breeds. Thus there were mixed motives in both the isolationist and the imperialist camps. Also of interest is the fact that the publication of Strong's book coincided with the establishment of the Student Volunteer Movement, which gave a new burst of enthusiasm to Protestant foreign missions.

Josiah Strong, *Our Country: Its Possible Future and Its Present Crisis* (New York: Baker and Taylor Co., 1885)[14]

Every race which has deeply impressed itself on the human family has been the representative of some great idea—one or more—which has given direction to the nation's life and form to its civilization. . . . The Anglo-Saxon is the representative of two great ideas which are closely related. One of them is that of civil liberty. . . . The other great idea of which the Anglo-Saxon is the exponent is that of a pure *spiritual* Christianity. . . . It was the fire of liberty burning in the Saxon heart that flamed up against the absolutism of the Pope. . . . But, with rare and beautiful exceptions, Protestantism on the Continent has degenerated into mere formalism. By confirmation at a certain age the state churches are filled with members who generally know nothing of a personal spiritual experience. . . .

It is not necessary to argue to those for whom I write that the two great needs of mankind . . . are, first, a pure spiritual Christianity, and, second, civil liberty. Without controversy, these are the forces which in the past have contributed most to the elevation of the human race and they must continue to be in the future the most efficient ministers to its progress. It follows then that the Anglo-Saxon as the great representative of these two ideas, the depositary of these two greatest blessings, sustains peculiar relations to the world's future, is divinely commissioned to be in a peculiar sense his brother's keeper. . . . Anglo-Saxons (I use the term somewhat broadly to include all English-speaking peoples) . . . occupy lands which invite almost unlimited expansion—the United States, Canada, Australia, and South Africa. [And] . . . emigration from Europe, which is certain to increase, is chiefly into [these] Anglo-Saxon countries. While these foreign elements exert a modifying influence on the Anglo-Saxon stock, their descendants are certain to be Anglo-Saxonized. . . . It is not unlikely that before the close of the next century this race will outnumber all the other civilized races of the world. Does it not look as if God were not only preparing in our Anglo-Saxon civilization the die with which to stamp the peoples of the earth, but as if he were also massing behind that die the mighty power with which to press it? . . .

There can be no reasonable doubt that North America is to be the great home of the Anglo-Saxon, the principal seat of his power, the center of his life and influence. Not only does it constitute seven-elevenths of his possessions but this empire is unsevered, while the remaining four-elevenths are fragmentary and scattered over the earth. . . . Our continent has room and resources and climate. It lies in the pathway of the nations, it belongs to the zone of power, and already among Anglo-Saxons do we lead in population and wealth. Of England, Franklin once wrote: "That pretty island which, compared to America, is but a stepping-stone in a brook, scarce enough of it above water to keep one's shoes dry." . . . Mr. Darwin . . . says: "There is apparently much truth in the belief that the wonderful progress of the United States as well as the character of the people are the results of natural selection, for the more energetic, restless, and courageous men from all parts of Europe have emigrated during the last ten or twelve generations to that great country, and have there succeeded best." . . . There is abundant reason to believe that the Anglo-Saxon race is to be . . . more effective here than in the mother country. The marked superiority of this race is due in large measure to its highly mixed origin. Says Rawlinson: "It is a general rule, now almost universally admitted by ethnologists, that the mixed races of mankind are superior to the pure ones." . . . The ancient Egyptians, the Greeks, and the Romans were all mixed races. Among modern races, the most conspicuous example is afforded by Anglo-Saxons. . . . Mr. Tennyson's poetic line,

"Saxon and Norman and Dane are we,"

must be supplemented with Celt and Gaul, Welshman and Irishman, Frisian and Flamand, French Huguenot and German Palatine. What took place a thousand years and more in England again transpires today in the United States. "History repeats itself." But, as the wheels of history are the chariot wheels of the Almighty, there is with every revolution an onward movement toward the goal of his eternal purposes. There is here a new commingling of races. And while the largest injections of foreign blood are substantially the same elements that constituted the original Anglo-Saxon admixture so that we may infer the general type will be preserved, there are strains of other bloods being added which . . . may be expected to improve the stock and aid it to a higher destiny. If the dangers of immigration . . . can be successfully met . . . , it may be expected to add value to the amalgam which will constitute the new Anglo-Saxon race of the New World. . . .

It may be easily shown . . . that the two great ideas of which the Anglo-Saxon is the exponent are having a fuller development in the United States than in Great Britain. There the union of church and state tends strongly to paralyze some of the members of the body of Christ. Here there is no such influence to destroy spiritual life and power. Here also has been evolved the form of government consistent with the largest possible civil liberty. . . . Another marked characteristic of the Anglo-Saxon is what may be called an instinct or genius for colonizing. His unequaled energy, his indomitable perseverance, and his personal independence made him a pioneer. . . . It was those in whom this tendency was strongest that came to

America. And this inherited tendency has been further developed by the westward sweep of successive generations across the continent. . . . Again, nothing more manifestly distinguishes the Anglo-Saxon than his intense and persistent energy, and he is developing in the United States an energy which in eager activity and effectiveness is peculiarly American. This is due partly . . . to our climate which acts as a constant stimulus. . . . Moreover, our social institutions are stimulating. In Europe the various ranks of society are . . . fixed and fossilized. . . . Here . . . everyone is free to become whatever he can make of himself. . . . Thus many causes operate to produce here the most forceful and tremendous energy in the world.

What is the significance of such facts? These tendencies unfold the future. They are the mighty alphabet with which God writes his prophecies. May we not by a careful laying together of the letters spell out something of his meaning? It seems to me that God with infinite wisdom and skill is training the Anglo-Saxon race for an hour sure to come in the world's future. Heretofore there has always been in the history of the world a comparatively unoccupied land westward into which the crowded countries of the East have poured their surplus populations. But the widening waves of migration . . . meet today on our Pacific coast. There are no more new worlds. The unoccupied arable lands of the earth are limited and will soon be taken. . . . Then will the world enter upon a new stage of its history—*the final competition of races, for which the Anglo-Saxon is being schooled*. . . . Then this race of unequaled energy, with all the majesty of numbers and the might of wealth behind it—the representative, let us hope, of the largest liberty, the purest Christianity, the highest civilization—having developed peculiarly aggressive traits calculated to impress its institutions upon mankind will spread itself over the earth. . . . Can anyone doubt that the result of this competition of races will be the "survival of the fittest"? . . . Nothing can save the inferior race but a ready and pliant assimilation. . . . The contest is not one of arms, but of vitality and civilization. . . .

Some of the stronger races doubtless may be able to preserve their integrity. But in order to compete with the Anglo-Saxon, they will probably be forced to adopt his methods and instruments, his civilization and his religion. Significant movements are now in progress among them. While the Christian religion was never more vital or its hold upon the Anglo-Saxon mind stronger, there is taking place among the nations a widespread revolt against traditional beliefs. . . . Old superstitions are loosening their grasp. The dead crust of fossil faiths is being shattered by the movements of life underneath. . . . Thus, while on this continent God is training the Anglo-Saxon race for its mission, a complemental work has been in progress in the great world beyond. God has two hands. Not only is he preparing in our civilization the die with which to stamp the nations but, by what Southey called the "timing of Providence," he is preparing mankind to receive our impress.

Is there room for reasonable doubt that this race . . . is destined to dispossess many weaker races, assimilate others, and mold the remainder, until in a very true and important sense it has Anglo-Saxonized mankind. Already "the English language, saturated with Christian ideas, gathering up into itself the best thought of all ages, is the great agent of Christian civilization throughout the world." . . . In my own mind, there is no doubt that the Anglo-Saxon is to exercise the commanding influence in the world's future, but the exact nature of that influence is as yet undetermined. [Every civilization has its destructive and preservative elements. The Anglo-Saxon race would speedily decay but for the salt of Christianity. Bring savages into contact with our civilization and its destructive forces become operative at once, while years are necessary to render effective the saving influences of Christian instruction.][15] . . .

How rapidly . . . [the Anglo-Saxon] will hasten the coming of the kingdom wherein dwelleth righteousness [II Pet. 3:13] or how many ages he may retard it is still uncertain, but *it is now being swiftly determined*. . . . When Napoleon drew up his troops . . . under the shadow of the Pyramids, pointing to the latter, he said to his soldiers: "Remember that from yonder heights forty centuries look down on you." Men of this generation, from the pyramid top of opportunity on which God has set us, *we look down on forty centuries!* We stretch our hand into the future with power to mold the destinies of unborn millions. . . . I believe it is fully in the hands of the Christians of the United States during the next fifteen or twenty years to hasten or retard the coming of Christ's kingdom in the world by hundreds and perhaps thousands of years. We of this generation and nation occupy the Gibraltar of the ages which commands the world's future.

Albert J. Beveridge, *For the Greater Republic, Not for Imperialism.* An address before the Union League Club of Philadelphia, February 15, 1899[16]

The Republic never retreats. . . . The Republic could not retreat if it would. Whatever its destiny, it must proceed. For the American Republic is a part of the movement of a race, the most masterful race of history, and race movements are not to be stayed by the hand of man. They are mighty answers to divine commands. Their leaders are not only statesmen of peoples, they are prophets of God. The inherent tendencies of a race are its highest law. They precede and survive all statutes, all constitutions. . . .

The sovereign tendencies of our race are organization and government. We govern so well that we govern ourselves. We organize by instinct. Under the flag of England our race builds an empire out of the ends of the earth. . . . In America it wove out of segregated settlements that complex and wonderful organization called the American Republic. Everywhere it builds. Everywhere it governs. Everywhere it administers order and law. Everywhere it is the spirit of regulated liberty. Everywhere it obeys that Voice not to be denied which bids us strive and rest not, makes of us our brothers' keeper and appoints us steward under God of the civilization of the world. . . .

God did not make the American people the mightiest human force of all time simply to feed and die. He did not give our race the brain of organization and heart of domination to no purpose and no end. No! He has given us a task equal to our talents. . . . He has made us the lords of civilization that we may administer civilization. Such administration is needed in Cuba. Such administration is needed in the Philippines. And Cuba and the Philippines are in our hands. . . .

The dominant notes in American history thus far have been self-government and internal improvement. But these were not ends only, they were means also. They were modes of preparation. . . . The dominant notes in American life henceforth will be not only self-government and internal improvement, but also administration and world improvement. It is the arduous but splendid mission of our race. It is ours to govern in the name of civilized liberty. It is ours to administer order and law in the name of human progress. It is ours to chasten that we may be kind. . . . It is ours to build that free institutions may finally enter and abide. . . . It is ours to reinforce that thin red line [the British empire] which constitutes the outposts of civilization all around the world. . . .

The frail of faith declare that . . . [Cubans and Filipinos] are not fitted for citizenship. It is not proposed to make them citizens. . . . Those who measure duty by dollars cry out at the expense. When did America ever count the cost of righteousness? And besides, this Republic must have a mighty navy in any event. . . .

Those who mutter words and call it wisdom deny the constitutional power of the Republic to govern Puerto Rico, Cuba, the Philippines. . . . The constitution is not to be interpreted by degrees of latitude or longitude. . . . There have always been those who have proclaimed the unconstitutionality of progress. . . . Let them learn the golden rule of constitutional interpretation. The constitution was made for the American people, not the American people for the constitution. . . .

Let the Republic govern as conditions demand. . . . The Declaration of Independence applies only to people capable of self-government. Otherwise how dared we administer the affairs of the Indians? How dare we continue to govern them today?

. . . And how [else] is the world to be prepared for self-government? . . .

Retreat from the Philippines on any pretext would be the master cowardice of history. It would be the betrayal of a trust as sacred as humanity. It would be a crime against Christian civilization and would mark the beginning of the decadence of our race. And so, thank God, the Republic never retreats. . . .

American manhood today contains the master administrators of the world, and they go forth for the healing of the nations. They go forth in the cause of civilization. They go forth for the betterment of man. They go forth, and the word on their lips is Christ and his peace, not conquest and its pillage. They go forth to prepare the peoples, through decades and maybe centuries of patient effort, for the great gift of American institutions. They go forth not for imperialism, but for the Greater Republic.

Charles S. Olcott, *The Life of William McKinley* (Boston: Houghton, Mifflin Co., 1916)[17]

How the president came to this decision [to demand the cession of the Philippines] was told in a well-authenticated interview at the White House, November 21, 1899. . . . [When] the visitors . . . turned to leave, the president said earnestly:

"Hold a moment longer! . . . Before you go I would like to say just a word about this Philippine business. I have been criticized a good deal about the Philippines but don't deserve it. The truth is I didn't want the Philippines, and when they came to us as a gift from the gods I did not know what to do with them. . . . I sought counsel from all sides—Democrats as well as Republicans—but got little help. . . . I walked the floor of the White House night after night until midnight, and I am not ashamed to tell you gentlemen that I went down on my knees and prayed Almighty God for light and guidance more than one night. And one night late it came to me this way—I don't know how it was but it came: 1. That we could not give them back to Spain—that would be cowardly and dishonorable. 2. That we could not turn them over to France or Germany . . . that would be bad business and discreditable. 3. That we could not leave them to themselves—they were unfit for self-government, and they would soon have anarchy and misrule over there worse than Spain's was. And 4. that there was nothing left for us to do but to take them all, and to educate the Filipinos, and uplift and civilize and Christianize them, and by God's grace do the very best we could by them as our fellowmen for whom Christ also died. And then I went to bed and went to sleep, and slept soundly, and the next morning I sent for the chief engineer of the War Department (our map-maker), and I told him to put the Philippines on the map of the United States." . . .

Editorial from *The Pittsburgh Catholic,* reprinted in *Public Opinion: A Weekly Journal,* Thursday, April 28, 1898[18]

The action of the American government is based on the sublime principle of humanity. This is the bed-rock Christianity, the solid fabric of civilization is builded upon this foundation. By this issue we stand or fall. . . . We challenge the good will of united Christendom and invoke the blessing of the God of battles on what now seems the inevitable struggle. Of the outcome there can be no doubt. It means on this continent the emancipation of Cuba from a blight that has kept that unhappy island in a state of internecine warfare, with but short intervals, for the half century gone, and from which the mother country has been unable to redeem it. The Armenia at our gates must be blotted out and a new republic in the might and majesty of constitutional freedom arise, regenerated and disenthralled from the fetters of an effete foreign domination, to aid the greater republic in carrying out the designs of Providence on this continent for the betterment of the race and the upholding and conserving the rights of the individual MAN.

Henry Van Dyke, *The American Birthright and the Philippine Pottage.* A sermon preached on Thanksgiving day, 1898 (New York: Charles Scribner's Sons [1898][19])

This is the most important Thanksgiving day that has been celebrated by the present generation of Americans. Three and thirty years have rolled away since we gave thanks for the ending of the Civil War. . . . [Now] a signal victory . . . has been granted to our country's arms in a war undertaken for the destruction of the ancient Spanish tyranny in the Western Hemisphere and the liberation of the oppressed people of Cuba.

How reluctantly the American people took up the cross of war after thirty-three years of peace. . . . The call of humanity was the only summons that could have roused them. The cause of liberty was the only cause for which they would have fought. No party, no administration could have received the loyal support of the whole people unless it had written on its banner the splendid motto: "Not for gain, not for territory, but for freedom and human brotherhood!" That avowal alone made the war possible and successful. For that cause alone Christians could pray with a sincere heart . . . and lovers of liberty take up the unselfish sword. The cause is won. The last vestige of Spanish power in the Western Hemisphere is broken. Cuba is free. . . .

But this Thanksgiving day is not significant alone for its causes for gratitude. It is . . . an immensely serious day because it finds us, suddenly and without preparation, face to face with the most momentous and far-reaching problem of our national history.

The question that came upon us at the close of the Revolution was serious: Should the liberated colonies separate or should they unite? But the leaders of the people had long been preparing to meet it. . . . The question that came upon us in the Civil War was urgent and weighty: Could the republic continue to exist "half slave and half free"? But again the minds of the wise and fearless were ready with the well-considered answer. . . . The question that comes upon us today is less urgent, but it is vaster, more fraught with incalculable consequences.

Are the United States to continue as a peaceful republic or are they to become a conquering empire? . . . Have we set the Cubans free or have we lost our own faith in freedom? Are we still loyal to the principles of our forefathers . . . or are we now ready to sell the American birthright for a mess of pottage in the Philippines?

Nine months ago no one dreamed of such a question. Not one American in five hundred could have told you what or where the Philippines were. . . . Six months ago, while Admiral Dewey's triumphant fleet was resting in Cavite Bay, there were not fifty people in the country who regarded his victory as the first step in a career of imperial conquest in the Far East. . . . Without warning, without deliberation, and apparently without clear intention, it has been made the burning issue of the day. . . . And, as if to add to the irony of the situation, political leaders assure us not only that the question has been raised unintentionally but also that it has been already settled involuntarily. . . .

But fortunately, it is not true. There is an old-fashioned document called the American Constitution which was expressly constructed to discourage the unconscious humor of such sudden changes. Before the die is cast, the people must be taken fairly into the game. . . . The question whether the American birthright is to be bartered for the Philippine pottage is still open. . . .

We surely owe the Filipinos the very best we can give them . . . , but it is far from certain that the best thing we can do for them is to make them our vassals. If that were true, our whole duty would not be done . . . until we had annexed the misgoverned Spaniards of Spain also. . . . Does the . . . treatment of the Indians in . . . the United States give us a comfortable sense of pride? . . . Is our success in treating the Chinese problem and the Negro problem so notorious that we must attempt to repeat it on a magnified scale eight thousand miles away? . . . With our unsolved problems staring us in the face, our cities misgoverned and our territories neglected, the cry of today—not the cry of despair but the cry of hope and courage—must be "Americans for America!" . . .

The chief argument against the forcible extension of American sovereignty over the Philippines is that it certainly involves the surrender of our American birthright of glorious ideals.

. . . I do not speak now of our word of honor . . . when we disclaimed any disposition or intention to exercise any sovereignty, jurisdiction, or control over the said islands except for the pacification thereof. . . . Pass it by.

But how can we pass by the solemn and majestic claim of our Declaration of Independence that "government derives its just powers from the consent of the governed"? How can we abandon the principle for which our fathers fought and died? . . .

Anonymous patriots have written to warn me that it is a dangerous task to call for this discussion. . . . The cry today is: "Wherever the American flag has been raised it must never be hauled down." . . . There is one thing that can happen to the American flag worse than to be hauled down. That is to have its meaning and message changed. Hitherto it has meant freedom and equality and self-government, and battle only for the sake of peace. Pray God its message may never be altered. . . .

God save the birthright of the one country on earth whose ideal is not to subjugate the world but to enlighten it.

4

THE ISSUE OF PLURALISM

ON THE DAY of public thanksgiving, December 11, 1783, John Rodgers spoke of the adoption of a constitution as "another instance of the great things our God has done for us," the compact being "that which gives us a national existence and character." By this "great event," he continued, "the thirteen United States became One People."[1] Even though the Articles of Confederation quickly had to be replaced, Americans had good reason to rejoice that a political union had been effected. Nevertheless it was no political compact that made them "one people." The "national existence and character," as has been pointed out, was the product of a long history. Tocqueville made this fact clear when he wrote:

> A government retains its sway over a great number of citizens far less by the voluntary and rational consent of the multitude than by that instinctive, and to a certain extent involuntary, agreement which results from similarity of feelings and resemblances of opinion. I will never admit that men constitute a social body simply because they obey the same head and the same laws. Society can exist only when a great number of men consider a great number of things under the same aspect, when they hold the same opinions upon many subjects, and when the same occurrences suggest the same thoughts and impressions to their minds.[2]

Of much more significance than the written agreement which brought the United States into existence was the process which Crèvecoeur described as "men of all nations" being "melted" into "a new race of men," with common feelings, sentiments, opinions, convictions, and loyalties.[3] This was what made Americans "one people." And it has been a shift from a relatively homogeneous society to what has been called a pluralistic society that provoked a re-examination of American nationality and nationhood in the twentieth century.

THE MELTING POT

The "melting pot" was the word used to describe the process by which immigrants from many lands became assimilated into American life. For the most part, prior to World War I, both older and newer Americans rejoiced in this process which gave them a sense of common nationality. Archbishop Ireland gave an account of the process and expressed the general satisfaction with the merging and emerging identity in an address delivered in France, July 18, 1892. It was Israel Zangwill, however, who gave wide currency to the term with his play, *The Melting Pot,* written in 1908 and performed in New York, Chicago, and Washington the following year.

John Ireland, *The Church and Modern Society* (Chicago: D. H. McBride and Co., 1896)[4]

To this day immigrants are thronging to our shores. On this account the United States affords social science a most interesting field of study. We have in our population representatives of all the nations of the earth—Englishmen, Irishmen, Frenchmen, Germans, Bohemians, Poles, Scandinavians, Italians, Arabs, Syrians, and Chinamen. Well, the number of immigrants is so great that we are beginning to be somewhat fastidious as to the quality. So far, however, the only country whose immigrants we have determined to exclude totally is China. . . . Our workingmen cannot . . . enter into competition with Oriental labor. Moreover, Orientals show no readiness or disposition to assimilate with our American population. . . . As to immigrants from Europe, they with a few exceptions will be welcome in the future as in the past. . . . I have said, with a few exceptions. It is not unknown to us that in some countries of Europe, . . . when a city or a village finds an individual too burdensome, the patriotic authorities say to him: "Go to America." Here we cry halt. . . .

But how, you may ask me, is it possible that the heterogeneous elements brought by immigration to your shores become fused into one people and constitute one undivided nation? How the vast masses of immigrants are assimilated into one people I cannot clearly explain, but it is done. There is something in the air, something in the soil, something in the sweet freedom of our institutions. Almost as soon as immigrants set foot on our shores they love America. They rejoice in the freedom they receive from her. They live of her life. They acquire the spirit of the country. The transformation is particularly noticeable in the children of the immigrants. They form a type of men different from their ancestors. They are Americans.

The first colonists in the New England or northeastern states have, more than any other element of our population, contributed to the formation of the present American type. They have beyond doubt given to our whole population an impress which is ineffaceable, communicated to it a spirit which remains unchanged in the American despite our varied aggregations of types from other countries. But those aggregations have in turn influenced in no small degree our original elements. . . . We shall offer to the world in our growth a new type of humanity. This new type will be more perceptibly differentiated as the years go by. . . . We take from each country its best elements of manhood, and of these elements we build up a new people—the American people. . . .

Israel Zangwill, *The Melting Pot: Drama in Four Acts* (New York: Macmillan Co., 1939 [written in 1908])[5]

DAVID: Oh, I love going to Ellis Island to watch the ships coming in from Europe, and to think that all those weary sea-tossed wanderers are feeling what *I* felt when America first stretched out her great mother-hand to *me!* . . . It was heaven. You must remember that all my life I had heard of

America. . . . All my life America was waiting, beckoning, shining—the place where God would wipe away tears from all faces. . . . To think that the same great torch of liberty which threw its light across the broad seas and lands into my little garret in Russia is shining also for all those other weeping millions of Europe, shining wherever men hunger and are oppressed, . . . shining over the starving villages of Italy and Ireland, over the swarming stony cities of Poland and Galicia. . . . Oh, Miss Revendal, when I look at our Statue of Liberty, I just seem to hear the voice of America crying: "Come unto me, all ye that labor and are heavy laden, and I will give you rest" [Matt. 11:28]. . . .

[*Later David explains further what America means to him.*]

DAVID: America is God's Crucible, the great Melting Pot where all the races of Europe are melting and re-forming! Here you stand, good folk, think I, when I see them at Ellis Island, here you stand in your fifty groups, with your fifty languages, and your fifty blood hatreds and rivalries. But you won't be long like that, brothers, for these are the fires of God you've come to—these are the fires of God. A fig for your feuds and vendettas! Germans and Frenchmen, Irishmen and Englishmen, Jews and Russians—into the crucible with you all! God is making the American. . . .

[*David's uncle asks:*] What true understanding can there be between a Russian Jew and a Russian Christian?

DAVID: What understanding? Aren't we both Americans? . . .

[*In Act III when Vera, a Russian Christian, proposes to marry David, Baron Revendal responds:* Christ save us! You have become a Jewess!

VERA: No more than David has become a Christian. We were already at one—all honest people are. Surely, father, all religions must serve the same God, since there is only one God to serve. . . .

[*At the end of Act IV, David reflects again on the meaning of America.*]

DAVID: There she lies the great Melting Pot—listen! Can't you hear the roaring and the bubbling? There gapes her mouth

—the harbor where a thousand mammoth feeders come from the ends of the world to pour in their human freight. Ah, what a stirring and a seething! Celt and Latin, Slav and Teuton, Greek and Syrian, black and yellow.

VERA: Jew and Gentile.

DAVID: Yes, East and West, North and South, the palm and the pine, the pole and the equator, the crescent and the cross—how the great Alchemist melts and fuses them with his purging flame! Here shall they all unite to build the Republic of Man and the Kingdom of God. Ah, Vera, what is the glory of Rome and Jerusalem, where all nations and races come to worship and look back, compared with the glory of America, where all races and nations come to labor and look forward! Peace, peace, to all ye unborn millions, fated to fill this giant continent—the God of our *children* give you Peace.

A PLURALISTIC SOCIETY

While religious understandings had given the American people a sense of identity, purpose, and mission, thereby uniting them as a people, the process of assimilation did not keep pace with the flow of immigration. Among the elders in every immigrant group there had been some resistance to assimilation, a resistance that received notable reinforcement when the third generation became interested in finding an identity within the heritage represented by their grandparents. This resistance was usually structured within the context of religious communities, largely Roman Catholic and Jewish but also Eastern Orthodox, some Protestant groupings, and a few Oriental faiths. By World War I the "melting pot" concept was increasingly rejected, and within a decade or two it became customary to speak of the United States as a pluralistic society. An early expression of this type of sentiment is represented by Isaac B. Berkson's *Theories of Americanization* (1920), a careful analysis of various types of possible adjustment within American life. The Jew and by inference the Roman Catholic, it was suggested, could live in two worlds at the same time. Leo Pfeffer and Milton Himmelfarb, while not rejecting this stance, in differing ways point to the difficulties in maintaining it.

Isaac B. Berkson, *Theories of Americanization: A Critical Study with Special Reference to the Jewish Group* (New York: Teachers' College, Columbia University, 1920)[6]

[The "Americanization" Theory]. According to this position America is pictured as already populated with a fairly homogeneous type which both in race and culture has Anglo-Saxon affiliations. . . . The main point is that all newcomers from foreign lands must as quickly as possible divest themselves of their old characteristics and, through intermarriage and complete taking over of the language, customs, hopes, aspirations of the American type, obliterate all ethnic distinctions. . . . The foreigners . . . must do all the changing; the situation is not to be changed by them. . . .

"Americanization," in the sense defined here, is the accepted current theory and practice . . . of the most important agencies dealing with this problem. . . . The Educational Alliance, the largest Jewish social settlement in this country, . . . was one of the first to recognize the importance of the problem of the adjustment of the immigrant to the new life in America. . . . It conceived its problem to be the complete de-orientalization of the Russian Jew, the ironing out of all those characteristics which stamped him as a foreigner. . . . The Alliance has remained completely oblivious to the possibilities of cultural and spiritual contribution inherent in the life of the people. . . . Whatever was most vital and spontaneous . . . received no support, and often . . . was suppressed in the single effort to make "good Americans" out of the Russian Jew. . . .

America, it should be remembered, does not exist for the benefit of any one class of persons. . . . The idea that the predominating stock of the inhabitants of the United States is Anglo-Saxon is a myth. The composite American is a multiform hyphenate. . . . To conceive of America as belonging exclusively to one race, because priority of habitation has given it a divine right to possession of the land, is a notion contrary to democracy. . . . Indeed, this minority . . . has stamped its culture ineffaceably upon American life, its language, its political organization and spiritual aspirations. . . . [But] our newcomers had no voice in the formation of these institutions, and to force them upon the immigrant without regard to his consent and without permitting his own personality to modify them in the least is . . . suggestive of tyranny rather than democracy. . . . Even under the conditions of Russian persecution the Jew was permitted to speak his own language and to live in many senses an independent cultural life. . . . The result of such a program of Americanization is a tyranny over the beliefs and minds of men worse than the economic and political slavery from which they fled. . . .

[The "Melting Pot" Theory]. The "Melting Pot" theory agrees with the "Americanization" theory in that both look forward to a disappearance of divergent ethnic strains and cultures within the unity of American life. Both would sever the loyalty to the past lived on foreign soil. But while our first theory tends to look upon Americanism as essentially bound up with Anglo-Saxonism and would give the recent immigrant no part in the development of American culture, the second theory welcomes the contributions that the new racial strains make to American life and looks with favor upon the addition of new cultural elements. Americanism is conceived of as in the making; something representative and growing out of the people that live here rather than a definite completed doctrine. . . . Americanism is a new life to which all can contribute. Out of the present heterogeneity of races a new superior race is to be formed; out of the present medley of cultures a new, richer, more humane civilization is to be created; out of the present ferment a new religion will develop representing the spiritual expression of the new people. . . .

The "Melting Pot" theory is democratic. Not one race is singled out as the standard. All . . . are conceived of as having a contribution to make. . . . From all angles the "Melting Pot" theory is seen to be superior to the "Americanization" theory. . . .

However, self-annihiliation is the price that the "Melting Pot" theory demands. . . . It is by losing their own corporate identity that the foreign groups are conceived of as becoming part of the new nation. The new strains of blood are mingled with the old stock through intermarriage, new folkways to make a new "cake of custom." New ideas are conceived of as enriching the American spiritual heritage. But always the community which has made the contribution itself perishes. . . . Both theories are ultimately alike. They both lead to complete absorption. . . . Both these theories deprive the immigrant groups of the right to perpetuate the group heritage. . . .

[The "Federation of Nationalities" Theory]. Instead of eliminating totally or limiting in some degree the influence of ethnic grouping in favor of a racial and cultural homogeneity, the point of view underlying the "Federation of Nationalities" idea would make the ethnic group paramount and permanent in its influence on American life. . . .

The proper form of government for America in accordance with this underlying concept is a federal republic, its substance "a democracy of nationalities, co-operating voluntarily and autonomously in the enterprise of self-realization through the perfection of men according to their kind" (Horace M. Kallen, "Democracy versus the Melting Pot," *The Nation,* May, 1915, pp. 79–80). No very clear idea of the limitations of such a government is given, but it is emphasized that the unity of America should be of a politico-economic nature. English, too, is to be a common language in the sense of a *lingua franca* necessitated by the politico-economic unity. For the expression of its cultural and spiritual life, however, each group will depend upon the ethnic language, literature, social life, and religion. . . . From this it may be implied that education should be controlled by the ethnic group. . . . Throughout the scheme proposed prevails the analogy of . . . Switzerland where three nationalities with distinct languages and cultures are joined harmoniously under one government. . . .

The simplest and therefore the most telling objection to this type of government organization for the United States is the recognition that it is a notion imported from foreign conditions without realizing that the very considerations which make it valid there are totally different in this country. The analogy . . . is directly inspired by the situation in Switzerland, the British Empire, and old Austria. In all of these . . . there is . . . one set of essential differences. . . . Each ethnic group is fairly well defined and attached to *particular localities.* The land was in all cases possessed by the ethnic group before the government came into existence. . . .

[The "Community" Theory]. The "Community" theory . . . is in reality the formulation of a process already shaping itself among some of our immigrant groups as a result of the confluence of the ethnic will to live with the conditions of American life (see Horace J. Bridges, *On Becoming an American* [Boston: Marshall Jones Co., 1919], Julius Drachsler, *Democracy and Assimilation* [New York: Macmillan Co., 1920], and Israel Friedlaender, *Past and Present: A Collection of Jewish Essays* [Cincinnati: Ark Publishing Co., 1919]). . . . Like the "Federation of Nationalities" theory, . . . this theory insists on the value of the ethnic group as a permanent asset in American life. The "Community" theory differs from the "Americanization" and "Melting Pot" theories in that it refuses to set up as an ideal such a fusion as will lead to the obliteration of all ethnic distinctions. Furthermore, it regards a rich social life as necessary for the development and expression of the type of culture represented by the foreign ethnic group. There is, however, a fundamental difference in what is conceived to be the ultimate sanction for maintaining this identity. . . . In the "Federation of Nationalities" theory the assumed identity of the race is pivotal; the argument is made to rest primarily upon the proposition that "we cannot change our grandfathers." The "Community" theory, on the other hand, would make the history of the ethnic group, its aesthetic, cultural, and religious inheritance, its national self-consciousness, the basic factor. . . .

The definition of nationality in cultural terms gives the clue to the solution of our problem of harmonizing two nationalities dwelling side by side. . . . It points to the preservation of individuality by other means than segregation and reveals a way of retaining loyalty both to the cultural life of the [ethnic group and to the larger political community]. . . . Cultural divergences are not incompatible with allegiance to a common culture. . . .

Accordingly, the "Community" theory of adjustment makes culture the *raison d'être* of the preservation of the life of the group. The School becomes the central agency around which the ethnic group builds its life. In accordance with our theory, the Jews, . . . together with other nationalities, . . . engage in commerce, in political and social life. They take advantage of all opportunities for educational and cultural development offered by the state. They fulfil whatever responsibilities citizenship implies. . . . Over and above this participation in the common life of the country, wherever Jews live in sufficient numbers to make communal life possible, the Jews are conceived of having their own communal life organized with a view to the preservation of that which is essential in the life of the Jewish people—the Torah. . . .

The communal Jewish School . . . becomes the central agency of the community, the institution around which it builds the social life and by means of which it transmits the significant culture of the ethnic group. . . . The function of the complementary schools, as is also the function of the communal organization of which the schools are the agency, is . . . thus to enrich the life of the individual Jew and through him that of the total group. . . . By making the educational agency central and the fundamental means of perpetuating the group, we have chosen the instrument which is directly relevant to that which we wish to preserve, namely, the cultural life of the ethnic group. . . . Culture must have its support in social life and adequate expression in communal institutions. The religious idea with the synagogue, conceived of as a place of worship primarily, as the central communal agency offers too narrow a concept to include the full range of Jewish spiritual life. . . . [The emphasis must be upon] the realistic interests of social life rather than the sentimental outlook which centers about prayer. The culture of the Jewish people, including as it does a language, a literature, and a profoundly spiritual outlook, cannot be confined within the walls of the synagogue. . . .

The "Community" theory, then, would seem to make full provision for the requirements of American life while aiming to contribute to America the finer elements of its ethnic tradition. . . . [It] means concretely that Jewish life in this country must depend mainly upon the existence of a sufficiently large number of Jewish centers. . . .

Leo Pfeffer, "American Individualism and Horace Kallen's Idea," in Horace M. Kallen, *Cultural Pluralism and the American Idea* (Philadelphia: University of Pennsylvania Press, 1956)[7]

I wonder if social philosophers are plagued with the same timidity and lack of assurance in their own propositions that impel lawyers to seek out and magnify even the most tenuous similarity to something that may have been said, the longer ago the better, by other lawyers in the form of judicial decisions. . . . Is it the same felt need for a father-authority or is it simply modesty that requires Professor Kallen to seek to identify cultural diversity with hoary American tradition? For I assume that he employs the term "American idea" as the idea of America rather than the idea for America. If it is the latter, I have no quarrel with Professor Kallen. If it is the former, I suggest that he is unfair to himself and to his monumental and truly original contribution to democratic social thinking. The American motto has never been "Liberty, Equality, and Diversity." On the contrary, it has been *E Pluribus Unum,* with the emphasis on the last word.

Suggestions of the desirability of permanent diversity may perhaps be found here and there among the main currents of early American thought. With a little imagination one can trace the roots of any idea almost anywhere. Professor Kallen, for example, finds much significance in the fact that the original proposal for a Great Seal of the United States envisaged a shield divided into six quarterings symbolizing the six major lands of origin of the American peoples. (I may suggest that perhaps more significance lies in the fact that this proposal was not accepted.) . . .

Actually the generation that brought forth the Declaration of Independence and, fifteen years later the Bill of Rights, was concerned with liberty and equality, not diversity. Whatever concern it had with diversity was an incident of its concern with liberty; and if it thought of diversity at all, it thought of diversity of individuals, not of groups and cultures. It is in this respect that any claim that cultural pluralism is just good old traditional Americanism appears to me to be untenable. For culture necessarily implies cultural groups and associations. It implies, in Professor Kallen's words, "equal liberty, not only for individuals as such but also for their societies and institutions."

Milton Himmelfarb, "Secular Society? A Jewish Perspective," *Daedalus: Journal of the American Academy of Arts and Sciences,* XCVI (1967)[8]

While the secular society in the lands that used to be Christendom is neutral in matters of religion, it is more neutral against Judaism than against Christianity. . . . Nor does this obtain only in lands where the Revolution paused at the bourgeois stage. It obtains also where the Revolution is or calls itself Marxist. Although all religions are equally bad in Russia, one is worse—Judaism. . . .

From this point of view, even a socialist revolution does not go far enough. What is needed is a cultural revolution, or more accurately, a linguistic one. If national languages persist, so will national cultures, and so will the Christianity or the Christian influence—or symbolism or vocabulary—that is so deeply imbedded in Western culture. How can one understand and appreciate Dante, Shakespeare, Donne, Milton, Racine, Pascal, Hegel, Kierkegaard, Dostoevski, Tolstoi, Hawthorne, or Eliot, if one does not understand and appreciate Christianity? . . . It is in the trivialities that we reveal ourselves. . . . In English *crusade* is an O.K. word, . . . but *crusade* is O.K. only from the traditional point of view of West European Christianity, not necessarily from the point of view of modern scholarship and certainly not from the point of view of Slavs, Greeks, Armenians, Moslems, and Jews. For the Jews the crusades meant massacres in Europe and Palestine. . . . Logically, the best way to solve this problem would be to abolish it. Do the languages of the West transmit old Christian memories and habits? Replace them by a new, universal language, a linguistic (and cultural) *tabula rasa*. Zamenhof, the inventor of Esperanto, was a Jew, and his vision included an element of barely modified Jewish messianism. But in no foreseeable future . . . are we likely to find Esperanto substituted for English or French or German or Italian or Russian or Spanish. . . .

From the beginning of Jewish modernity, Jews have had three choices: to be Jews, to be Christians, to be secularists. Many have decided that they cannot conscientiously be Jews because they cannot believe what Judaism requires them to believe: that there is a God, the Creator who revealed himself as Lawgiver to the patriarchs and prophets, that he wishes the children of Israel to preserve themselves in faithful and loving obedience to him, and that all men will yet join them in acknowledging and worshipping him. If a Jew cannot believe this, however freely he interprets it, shall he choose to be a Christian or shall he choose to be a secularist? . . .

The preferred alternative is secularism, the vision of Lessing and Moses Mendelssohn. Only now, two hundred years later, we ought to see in retrospect what Mendelssohn could not see in prospect—that the secularism of the West is not quite neither Christian nor Jewish equally. Especially does it not have equal effects on the children and grandchildren of the ex-Jew and the ex-Christian.

Suppose that the children or grandchildren, in their turn, rebel against *their* fathers and grandfathers; suppose that they become disillusioned with the religion of Reason and turn to one of the traditional religions. Which will that be? Given the culture they have absorbed not only in the mind but also through the pores, the result is not in doubt. . . . [Furthermore,] a Jew who is brought up without religion and who remains without religious feeling may nevertheless marry someone who has such feeling. Statistically the odds are that that person will be a Christian, not a Jew, and that their children will then be Christians. The religious *potential* of our society is Christian. If a secularist Jew, or his child or grandchild, is to be within reach of a Jewish potential—in the second and especially the third generation—he must actively will it, he must make a decision. To be within reach of the Christian potential needs no decision, no act of will. . . .

For two hundred years secularist Jews have tried to evade admitting to themselves that they know what this process is. As experience accumulates with the years, the evasion becomes increasingly difficult. The choice for Jews has not really been whether to be a Jew or a Christian or a secularist; it has been whether to be a Jew or a Christian. Other things being equal, secularism has been, for Jews, a propaedeutic to Christianity.

But Jews know that whatever else they may or may not be, they are not Christians. . . .

Two other questions must be touched on, if not answered: America as specifically American, and the autonomy of the future with respect to the past.

Whatever may be the present state of the old cultural and historical controversy over American uniqueness . . . America is rather special in the Jewish experience. Unlike Europe, America has had no pre-modern past—no Middle Ages, no feudalism, no union of Throne and Altar. Unlike such multinational states as the Hapsburg empire, ethnically diverse America is a unitary nation; but unlike most unitary nations, it has been religiously pluralist from its earliest days, when the pluralism was Protestant. In America the civic equality of the Jews was never an issue and never had to be legislated, at least nationally. A corcllary of the triumph of the American Revolution, so obvious it did not have to be put into words, was that Jews were citizens like all other (white) men. . . . The Jewish folk expression "It's hard to be a Jew" means not only that it is fulfill God's commands as he wishes them to be fulfilled, that minority existence is painful. In America today it is less hard to be a Jew, in the second sense, than ever before, anywhere else.

Specifically, therefore, America is different; but the specific difference is enacted within what is generally common to a West that used to be Christendom. The West has become secular—but not all that secular. . . .

What of the future? Granted that everything said here has been so and is so, it will not necessarily continue to be so. The future may not be completely independent of the past, but neither is it completely dependent. It has its own realm of autonomy and newness—in a word, of futurity. . . . All may yet change, and we may be standing at the edge of a newness that will truly be new. But the probabilities are that the past will not give up its old habit of putting its mark on the future.

CIVIL RELIGION

Jewish exponents were not alone in seeking to create and perpetuate a pluralistic society. Many Roman Catholics became equally assiduous in an attempt to foster a separate and distinct cultural life, establishing a separate school system and organizing separate fraternal, philanthropic, youth, labor, veterans, and other groupings to provide a full and complete cultural and social life of their own. This was a difficult enterprise, made more difficult with the separation being bridged at the political, economic, and often at the residential level. It also left untended the question of that which, beyond the separate loyalties, binds the nation together and makes of individual citizens a people.

Confronted by the need for a bond of unity, many Americans began to turn back to the old concept of "general" or "civil" religion which William Penn had expounded in 1675 and which most leaders of the Revolutionary era had accepted as axiomatic in American life. Based on the Puritan distinction between the realm of "nature" and the realm of "grace," civil religion was that religion which was available (i.e., needing no special revelation) and common to all men. Roger Williams had taken this civil religion for granted as the ground of the civil order in Rhode Island, and at the end of the seventeenth century John Locke had explicated it as a basic constitutional principle.[9] The moral law (the Ten Commandments and the Sermon on the Mount) bulked large in this civil religion, but in its American manifestation an emotional element was introduced. The concept of civil religion as the ground of a common political order was broadened to include the notion of "spiritual religion," religion freed of all ecclesiastical trappings.

Spiritual religion was variously understood. Evangelical Protestants thought of it as the free operation of the Spirit that had been so conspicuous a feature of the colonial revivals. In 1798 "brethren of different denominations," following the procedure established in the colonial period, joined in concerted prayer for a spiritual quickening that would unite the Christians of the nation in the communion of Christ's earthly kingdom. From such ardent longing came the great revivals of the Second Awakening. Then, as the unity of the nation became increasingly threatened, the strong conviction was expressed that a "true American union" could be made secure only by the "vitalized and harmonious action" of individual Christians voluntarily cooperating in revivals, missionary endeavors, and a vast array of benevolent enterprises.[10] Some Americans were less sure than others that revivals would unify the nation, but almost everyone accepted the notion that the nation had a soul, that this soul was one, and that there was a spiritual union among Americans which existed independently of formal religious experience or affiliation.

Civil religion, while variously interpreted in nineteenth-century America, drew heavily in all its formulations upon major Protestant motifs for understanding the identity, mission, and destiny of the nation. In twentieth-century America, with its broadening spectrum of religious belief, this was much less true. For a time the emphasis upon a pluralistic society caused the notion of civil religion ("religion in general") to be either neglected or scorned. And when discussion of the concept was revived, much less prominence was given to specifically Protestant and even biblical themes. The major stress was upon value systems associated with a democratic society.

Sidney E. Mead and J. Paul Williams were among the first to give serious attention in mid-twentieth-century America to the issue of civil religion. Both insisted that distinctions should be made between private religion, denominational or church religion, and public or civil religion. A similar understanding of the American situation was proposed by Will Herberg in *Protestant-Catholic-Jew: An Essay in American Religious Sociology* (1955). Robert N. Bellah, on the other hand, pointed beyond past expressions of civil religion in America to a possible reconstruction of civil religion to take into account the necessities of a global society.

William Penn, *England's Present Interest* (1675)[11]

I am now come to the . . . question propounded, viz. the Sincere Promotion of General and Practical Religion, by which I mean the Ten Commandments or moral law, and Christ's Sermon on the Mount with other heavenly sayings excellently improved and earnestly recommended by several passages in the disciples which forbid evil not only in deed but thought, and enjoin purity and holiness as without which no man, be his pretenses what they are, shall ever see God. In short, general, true, and requisite religion in the apostle James' definition is "to visit the widow and the fatherless, and to keep ourselves," through the universal grace, "unspotted of the world" [Jas. 1:27]. This is, as the most sacred, so the most easy and probable way to fetch in all men professing God and religion. For . . . every persuasion acknowledges this in words, be their lives never so incongruous with their confession. And this being the *unum necessarium,* that one thing only requisite to make men happy here and hereafter, why should men sacrifice their accord in this great point for their unity in minute or circumstantial things that . . . would signify little or nothing either to the good of human society or the particular comfort of any individual in that world which is to come? . . . O how decent, how delightful, would it be to see mankind . . . of one accord at least in the weighty things of God's practical law. 'Tis want of practice and too much prate that hath made way for all the incharity and ill-living that is in the world. No matter what men say, if the devil keeps the house. . . . Men are not to be reputed good by their opinion (nor is that, nor ought it to be, offensive to the government), but practice is what must save or damn temporally or eternally. Christ, in his representation of the Great Day, doth not tell us that it shall be, "Well said," or "Well talked," but "Well done, good and faithful servant" [Matt. 25:21]. Truly it is high time that men should give better testimony of their Christianity, for cruelty hath no share in Christ's religion and coercion upon conscience is utterly inconsistent with very nature of his kingdom. . . .

In short, the promoting of this general religion by a severe reprehension and punishment of vice and encouragement of virtue is the interest of our superiors in several ways: 1. In that it meets with and takes in all the religious persuasions of the kingdom. "Penal laws for religion is a church with a sting in her tail." Take that out and there is no fear in the people's love and duty. . . . 2. Next, a promotion of general religion, it being in itself practical, brings back again ancient virtues. Good living will thrive in this soil. Men will grow honest, trusty, and temperate. We may expect good neighborhood and cordial friendship. . . . 3. The third benefit is that men will be more industrious, more diligent in their lawful callings, which will increase our manufacture, set the idle and poor to work for their livelihood, and enable the several countries with more ease and decency to maintain the aged and impotent among them. . . . 4. It will render the magistrate's province more facile and government a safe as well as an easy thing. . . . Lastly, Heaven will prosper so natural, so noble, and so Christian an essay, which ought not to be the least consideration with a good magistrate; and the rather because the neglect of this practical religion hath been the ruin of kingdoms and commonwealths among heathens, Jews, and Christians. . . .

Sidney E. Mead, "Thomas Jefferson's 'Fair Experiment'—Religious Freedom," *The Lively Experiment: The Shaping of Christianity in America* (New York: Harper & Row, 1963)[12]

We now turn to the important question of the real difference between Establishment and religious freedom. . . . Establishment rested upon two basic assumptions: that the existence and well-being of any society depends upon a body of commonly shared religious beliefs—the nature of man, his place in the cosmos, his destiny, and his conduct toward his fellow men—and that the only guarantee that these necessary beliefs will be sufficiently inculcated is to put the coercive power of the state behind the institution responsible for their definition, articulation, and inculcation. . . .

Religious freedom did not mean giving up the first assumption, that is, the necessity for the commonly shared basic religious ideas. It meant only the rejection of the second assumption, namely, that the institution(s) responsible for their inculcation must have the coercive power of the state behind it (them). . . . Looked at in this fashion, religious freedom can be seen to have had some very profound and far-reaching implications that perhaps were not too clearly grasped at the time. . . .

From the viewpoint of the society and the state . . . there will be a multiplicity of religious groups, or "sects" as the rationalists consistently called them. Each and every sect will inculcate in its own way the basic religious beliefs that are essential. This is what Jefferson thought had been demonstrated in New York and Pennsylvania. There religion is well supported, he said, "of various kinds, indeed, but all good enough; [because] all sufficient to preserve peace and order." . . .

Much more important, however, is the fact that Jefferson's theory implies that the limits even of religious freedom are to be defined by the "public welfare." Apparently the eighteenth-century leaders who fathered the new government with its experiment in religious freedom did not have to wrestle with any outstanding practical consequences of this view. . . . Beginning as the founders did with the assumption that the basic religious beliefs they held were merely the essentials of every religion, they naturally concluded that all religious groups teach and inculcate them under whatever peculiar disguise they may adopt. Hence they could hardly envisage a time when some or even all the religious groups might not teach them at all, or might not teach and inculcate them adequately for the support of the public welfare.

Here, then, is a troublesome lacuna in the theory. But it seems a fair conclusion that (since the public welfare was to set the limits even of religious freedom, and the public welfare is a matter for the state to define) the way was left open for the state, if and when it judged that the religious sects were inadequate or derelict in the matter, to defend itself by setting up the institutions or machinery necessary to guarantee the dissemination and inculcation of the necessary beliefs. . . .

Perhaps the most striking power that the churches surrendered under religious freedom was control over public education which traditionally had been considered an essential aspect of the work of an established church if it was to perform its proper function of disseminating and inculcating the necessary foundational religious beliefs. Ideally . . . [the churches might have continued] to possess such control, since, dividing the population among themselves, each in its own way would inculcate the basic beliefs (the "essentials of every religion") common to all and necessary to the general welfare.

But for many and complex reasons this proved completely impracticable in the United States. . . . And so somewhat by default the state took over what had traditionally been part of the work of the church. If we ask, Why the rise of compulsory free public education? must it not be said that prominent among the reasons was a desire to make possible and to guarantee the dissemination and inculcation among the embryo citizens of the beliefs essential to the existence and well-being of the democratic society? . . .

The state in its public education system is and always has been teaching religion. It does so because the well-being of the nation . . . demands this foundation of shared beliefs. . . .

In this sense the public school system of the United States *is* its established church. . . . In this context onc can understand why it is that the religion of many Americans is democracy—why their real faith is the "democratic faith"—the religion of the public schools. Such understanding enables one to see religious freedom and separation of church and state in a new light.

One of the most provocative contributions to the discussion of these matters is contained in the final chapter of a book published in 1952 with the title *What Americans Believe and How They Worship*. The author, Professor J. Paul Williams, proposes that in order to meet the present crisis "governmental agencies must teach the democratic ideal *as religion*." This is essentially an appeal for a State Church in the United States, and his arguments for it largely parallel those traditionally used to defend Establishments. They are worth examining for they suggest that Americans may now have to . . . face some of the implications of religious freedom that were almost forgotten. . . .

"A culture," he argues, "is above everything else a faith, a set of shared convictions, a spiritual entity," and its continued health and well-being depends upon the maintenance of this faith in the hearts and minds of the people. Hence "systematic and universal indoctrination is essential in the values on which a society is based, if that society is to have any permanence or stability." This will be recognized as the first assumption underlying an established church.

In the present crisis, he goes on to say, with democracy threatened from all sides "Americans do not even have a clear common conception of what the democratic ideal is," and hence "America runs a grave danger from lack of attention to the spiritual core which is the heart of her national existence. If we are to avoid this danger, democracy must become an object of religious dedication. Americans must come to look on the democratic ideal (not necessarily the American practice of it) as the Will of God or, if they please, the law of Nature." This means the articulation, dissemination, and inculcation of beliefs. And in order to achieve this "it will be necessary to mobilize many agencies," among which "the churches and synagogues are obviously first on the list."

But although these religious institutions are already doing quite a bit to bolster democracy, Dr. Williams sees little reason to suppose that they can or will do the job that is necessary on a broad enough scale or fast enough, for "the churches receive but voluntary attention [and that from "but half the population"]; the government may require attention [of "all the population"]." This will be recognized as appeal to the second assumption underlying an established church—the institution responsible for inculcating the basic beliefs must have behind it the coercive power of the state. Naturally Dr. Williams turns to the public school system. No other agency, he argues, is in as strategic a position to teach democracy and to bring "the majority of our people to a religious devotion to the democratic way of life." But whatever agencies may be enlisted, "we must find ways to awaken in the hearts of multitudes of Americans a devotion to democratic ideals like the devotion given by ardent believers in every age to the traditional religions," even though this means "giving the power of wholesale religious indoctrination into the hands of politicians. . . ."

As for those who object on one ground or another, Dr. Williams' answer is clear and concise. He steps forthrightly into the way left open by the founding fathers. "But at those points where religion is a public matter, those areas which contain the ethical propositions essential to corporate welfare, society will only at its peril allow individuals and sects to indulge their dogmatic whims." For Dr. Williams, religious freedom means primarily the "freedom to follow conscience in private worship."

It is hard to understand why the publication of these views . . . apparently attracts little attention. . . . Perhaps concern for religious freedom is being drowned in a sea of religious indifference. . . . [Or perhaps] knowledge of history is so eroded that Dr. Williams' position seems utterly foreign and implausible and [therefore] is not taken seriously. . . .

I think it ought to be taken seriously because it has real historical roots in our tradition. What Dr. Williams seems to be saying is that we have . . . found that Jefferson [and his supporters] were over optimistic in supposing the many sects, armed only with persuasive power, would be effective in inculcating the religious and moral principles necessary for order in government and obedience to the laws. They have failed. Therefore the government in self-defense must step in and do the job. . . . The well-being of the commonwealth must determine the limits even of religious freedom. Democracy, in a state of siege, must ask that "governmental agencies . . . teach the democratic ideal as religion."

This argument ought to be answered if possible, not ignored.

Robert N. Bellah, "Civil Religion in America," *Daedalus,* XCVI (1967)[13]

While some have argued that Christianity is the national faith, and others that church and synagogue celebrate only the generalized religion of "the American Way of Life," few have realized that there actually exists alongside of and rather clearly differentiated from the churches an elaborate and well-institutionalized civil religion in America. . . . This religion—or perhaps better, this religious dimension—has its own seriousness and integrity and requires the same care in understanding that any other religion does.

Kennedy's inaugural address . . . serves as an example and a clue with which to introduce this complex subject. . . . [There] are three places in this brief address in which Kennedy mentioned the name of God. If we could understand why he mentioned God, the way in which he did it, and what he meant to say in those three references, we would understand much about American civil religion. . . .

Let us consider first the placing of the three references. They occur in the two opening paragraphs and in the closing paragraph, thus providing a sort of frame for the more concrete remarks that form the middle part of the speech. Looking beyond this particular speech, we would find that similar references to God are almost invariably to be found in the pronouncements of American presidents on solemn occasions. . . .

It might be argued that the passages . . . reveal the essentially irrelevant role of religion in the very secular society that is America. The placing of the references . . . indicates that religion has "only a ceremonial significance." . . . But we know enough about the function of ceremonial and ritual in various societies to make us suspicious of dismissing something as unimportant because it is "only a ritual." What people say on solemn occasions need not be taken at face value, but it is often indicative of deep-seated values and commitments that are not made explicit in the course of everyday life. . . .

It might [also] be countered that the very way in which Kennedy made his references reveals the essentially vestigial place of religion today. He did not refer to any religion in particular. He did not refer to Jesus Christ, or to Moses, or to the Christian church; certainly he did not refer to the Catholic Church. In fact, his only reference was to the concept of God, a word which almost all Americans can accept but which means so many different things to so many different people that it is almost an empty sign. . . .

These questions are worth pursuing because they raise the issue of how civil religion relates to the political society. . . . President Kennedy was a Christian, more specifically a Catholic Christian. Thus, his general references to God do not mean that he lacked a specific religious commitment. But why, then, did he not include some remark to the effect that Christ is the Lord of the world or some indication of respect for the Catholic Church? He did not because these are matters of his own private religious belief and of his relation to his own particular church; they are not matters relevant in any direct way to the conduct of his public office. . . .

Considering the separation of church and state, how is a president justified in using the word *God* at all? The answer is that the separation of church and state has not denied the political realm a religious dimension. Although matters of personal religious belief, worship, and association are considered to be strictly private affairs, there are, at the same time, certain common elements of religious orientation that the great majority of Americans share. These have played a crucial role in the development of American institutions and still provide a religious dimension for the whole fabric of American life, including the political sphere. This public religious dimension is expressed in a set of beliefs, symbols, and rituals that I am calling the American civil religion. The inauguration of a president is an important ceremonial event in this religion. It reaffirms, among other things, the religious legitimation of the highest political authority.

Let us look more closely at what Kennedy actually said. First he said, "I have sworn before you and Almighty God the same solemn oath our forebears prescribed nearly a century and three quarters ago." . . . Beyond the Constitution . . . the president's obligation extends not only to the people but to God. In American political theory, sovereignty rests, of course, with the people, but implicitly and often explicitly, the ultimate sovereignty has been attributed to God. . . . What difference does it make that sovereignty belongs to God? Though the will of the people as expressed in majority vote is carefully institutionalized as the operative source of political authority, it is deprived of an ultimate significance. The will of the people is not itself the criterion of right and wrong. There is a higher criterion in terms of which this will can be judged; it is possible that the people may be wrong. The president's obligation extends to this higher criterion.

When Kennedy says that "the rights of man come not from the generosity of the state but from the hand of God," he is stressing this point again. It does not matter whether the state is the expression of the will of an autocratic monarch or of the "people"; the rights of man are more basic than any political structure. . . .

But the religious dimension in political life as recognized by Kennedy not only provides a grounding for the rights of man which makes any form of political absolutism illegitimate, it also provides a transcendent goal for the political process. This is implied in his final words that "here on earth God's work must truly be our own." . . . The whole address can be understood as only the most recent statement of a theme that lies very deep in the American tradition, namely the obligation, both collective and individual, to carry out God's will on earth. . . . That this very activist and non-contemplative conception of the fundamental religious obligation, which has been historically associated with the Protestant position, should be enunciated so clearly in the first major statement of the first Catholic president seems to underline how deeply established it is in the American outlook. . . .

The words and acts of the founding fathers . . . shaped the form and tone of the civil religion as it has been maintained ever since. Though much is selectively derived from Christianity, this religion is clearly not itself Christianity. . . . The God of the civil religion is . . . on the austere side, much more related to order, law, and right than to salvation and love. Even though he is somewhat deist in cast, he is by no means simply a watchmaker God. He is actively interested and involved in history, with a special concern for America. Here the analogy has much less to do with natural law than with ancient Israel; the equation of America with Israel in the idea of the "American Israel" is not infrequent. . . . Europe is Egypt; America, the promised land. God has led his people to establish a new sort of social order that shall be a light unto all the nations. . . .

What we have, then, from the earliest years of the republic is a collection of beliefs, symbols, and rituals with respect to sacred things and institutionalized in a collectivity. This religion—there seems no other word for it—while not antithetical to and indeed sharing much in common with Christianity, was neither sectarian nor in any specific sense Christian. . . . Nor was the civil religion simply "religion in general." While generality was undoubtedly seen as a virtue by some . . . , the civil religion was specific enough when it came to the topic of America. Precisely because of this specifity, the civil religion was saved from empty formalism and served as a genuine vehicle of national religious self-understanding.

But the civil religion was not . . . , with the exception of a few radicals like Tom Paine, ever felt to be a substitute for Christianity. There was an implicit but quite clear division of function between the civil religion and Christianity. Under the doctrine of religious liberty, an exceptionally wide sphere of personal piety and voluntary social action was left to the churches. But the churches were neither to control the state nor to be controlled by it. The national magistrate, whatever his private religious views, operates under the rubrics of the civil religion as long as he is in his official capacity. . . .

The civil religion has not always been invoked in favor of worthy causes. On the domestic scene, an American-Legion type of ideology that fuses God, country, and flag has been used to attack nonconformist and liberal ideas and groups of all kinds. Still, it has been difficult to use the words of Jefferson and Lincoln to support special interests and undermine personal freedom. . . .

With respect to America's role in the world, the dangers of distortion are greater and the built-in safeguards of the tradition weaker. . . . Never has the danger been greater than today. The issue is not so much one of imperial expansion, of which we are accused, as of the tendency to assimilate all governments or parties in the world which support our immediate policies or call upon our help by invoking the notion of free institutions and democratic values. Those nations that are for the moment "on our side" become "the free world." . . . The civil religion has exercised long-term pressure for the humane solution of our greatest domestic problem, the treatment of the Negro American. It remains to be seen how relevant it can become for our role in the world at large. . . .

The civil religion . . . is also caught in another kind of crisis, theoretical and theological, of which it is at the moment largely unaware. "God" has clearly been a central symbol in the civil religion from the beginning and remains so today. . . . In the late-eighteenth century this posed no problem; even Tom Paine . . . was not an atheist. . . . But today . . . the meaning of the word *God* is by no means so clear or so obvious. . . . If the whole God symbolism requires reformulation, there will be obvious consequences for the civil religion, consequences perhaps of liberal alienation and of fundamentalist ossification that have not so far been prominent in this realm. The civil religion has been a point of articulation between the profoundest commitments of the Western religious and philosophical tradition and the common beliefs of ordinary Americans. It is not too soon to consider how the deepening theological crisis may affect the future of this articulation. . . .

In conclusion it may be worthwhile to relate the civil religion to the most serious situation that we as Americans now face. . . . This is the problem of responsible action in a revolutionary world, a world seeking to attain many of the things, material and spiritual, that we have already attained. Americans have, from the beginning, been aware of the responsibility and the significance our republican experiment has for the whole world. . . .

Every president since [Franklin D.] Roosevelt has been groping toward a new pattern of action in the world, one that would be consonant with our power and our responsibilities. . . . There seems little doubt that . . . the attainment of some kind of viable and coherent world order would precipitate a major new set of symbolic forms. So far the flickering flame of the United Nations burns too low to be the focus of a cult, but the emergence of a genuine trans-national sovereignty would certainly change this. It would necessitate the incorporation of vital international symbolism into our civil religion, or, perhaps a better way of putting it, it would result in American civil religion becoming simply one part of a new civil religion of the world. It is useless to speculate on the form such a civil religion might take though it obviously would draw on religious traditions beyond the sphere of Biblical religion alone. Fortunately, since the American civil religion is not the worship of the American nation but an understanding of the American experience in the light of ultimate and universal reality, the reorganization entailed by such a new situation need not disrupt the American civil religion's continuity. A world civil religion could be accepted as a fulfillment and not a denial of American civil religion. Indeed, such an outcome has been the eschatological hope of American civil religion from the beginning. To deny such an outcome would be to deny the meaning of America itself.

Behind the civil religion at every point lie Biblical archetypes: Exodus, Chosen People, Promised Land, New Jerusalem, Sacrificial Death and Rebirth. But it is also genuinely American and genuinely new. It has its own prophets and its own martyrs, its own sacred events and sacred places, its own solemn rituals and symbols. It is concerned that America be a society as perfectly in accord with the will of God as men can make it, and a light to all the nations.

It has often been used and is being used today as a cloak for petty interests and ugly passions. It is in need—as is any living faith—of continual reformation, of being measured by universal standards. But it is not evident that it is incapable of growth and new insight. . . .

Appendix
THE ENGLISH HERITAGE

THE REIGN of Queen Elizabeth (1558–1603) marked the maturing of England's national self-consciousness. Elizabeth was the English Deborah who ushered in England's days of glory. This was the age of Drake and Raleigh and Shakespeare, the age when English literature flowered and the Spanish Armada was defeated, the age when recalcitrant elements finally came to share esteem for "good Queen Bess" and pride of being English. But the glory was only one facet of the new national self-consciousness. A more important element was the strong conviction that England had a God-given vocation to fulfill.

Elizabeth's reign was a time when returning exiles devoted their energies to making clear England's identity and mission as a chosen people. Evidence of God's favor was rehearsed, and Englishmen were reminded again and again that it had been England's vocation for a thousand years to be the bearer and custodian of true apostolic religion.

After Elizabeth's death, the perils as well as the privileges of England's role as a nation in covenant with God were spelled out with precision and persuasiveness by the preachers and publicists of the Puritan Revolution which began with the meeting of the Long Parliament in 1640. During these years ancient liberties became closely intertwined with true religion as part of the legacy England was called upon to preserve for the world. Following the Restoration of 1660, spokesmen of religious dissent and opposition politics continued to remind England of her heritage and vocation. The Glorious Revolution of

1688 was a vindication of their efforts. The vindication, as is true of most political settlements, was ambiguous at some points of detail, and opposing parties continued to be locked in debate as each sought to make clear the specific implications of England's religious and political self-understanding.

THE ELECT NATION

At the conclusion of a European tour in 1605, Edwin Sandys published *A Relation of the State of Religion . . . in the Several States of these Western Parts of the World* in which he noted:

> The first and chief means whereby the reformers of religion prevail in all places was their singular assiduity and dexterity in preaching, especially in the great cities and palaces of princes. . . .
>
> A second thing whereby the Protestant part hath so greatly enlarged itself hath been. their well educating of youth especially in the principles of Christian religion and piety. . . .
>
> A third course that much advantageth the Protestant's proceedings was their offers of disputations with their adversaries in all places. . . ., a thing which greatly assured the multitude of their soundness whom they saw so confident in abiding the hazard of trial. . . .
>
> The last means I will here speak of [that] were used in setting forward this reformation of religion was the diligent compiling of the histories of those times and actions, and especially the martyrology of such as rendered by their deaths a testimony of that truth which was persecuted in them.

These "memories and stories" of "celestially inspired courage" displayed amid the "furious flames" of martyrdom, Sandys continued, were "set out in sundry places with pictures" to "imprint" upon the reader's mind a "more lively" sense of commiseration for the persecuted and an equally lively detestation of the persecutors.[1]

The "martyrology" to which Sandys referred was John Foxe's "Book of Martyrs" or *Acts and Monuments of Matters Most Special and Memorable Happening in the Church with an Universal History of the Same.* While not the first response to

Elizabeth's accession, it was the most influential. It did more to shape the mind of Englishmen than any book except the Bible. Written initially by Foxe while an exile on the Continent during the reign of "Bloody Mary," the "Book of Martyrs" was first published in English in 1563. Its publication was sponsored by the Elizabethan authorities, and every device was used to entice and aid the reader. It was introduced with an essay on "the utility of the story." There were titles, subtitles, running heads, marginal notes, a full index with directions how to use it, a chronological digest, a calendar of martyrs, a table to help the "unlearned" translate Roman into Arabic numerals, and a profusion of vivid and dramatic woodcuts. At the end of the first volume, the story thus far was recapitulated in a brief pictorial history with a minimum of text entitled "The Image of the True Catholic Church of Christ." Small wonder that Foxe's history was destined to be republished again and again in revised, expanded, and abbreviated editions.

The 1559 Latin edition of the "Book of Martyrs" had begun with the story of John Wyclif, the significance of the story being memorably summarized a century later by Thomas Fuller: "The corpse of John Wyclif had quietly slept in his grave about one and forty years" when the Council of Constance "ordered that his bones . . . be taken out of the ground and thrown far off from any Christian burial." In obedience thereto, his bones were taken from the grave, burned to ashes, and cast "into the Swift, a neighboring brook running hard by. Thus this brook hath conveyed his ashes into the Avon, Avon into Severn, Severn into the narrow seas, they into the main ocean. And thus the ashes of Wyclif are the emblem of his doctrine which now is dispersed all the world over."[2]

In the 1563 English edition, the tribulations which accompanied and flowed from the dawning light marked by Wyclif's preaching were placed within the context of the age-old conflict between God and Satan. An account was given of the several ages or dispensations of the church, of the early Christian persecutions, of the first establishment of the faith in Britain, of the valiant deeds in England of Alfred the Great and Edward the Confessor, of the betrayal of the church and the loosing of Satan in the time of Gregory VII and his successors, of the reign of Antichrist and the subversion of English liberties which followed the Norman victory in 1066, of continuing struggles against the agents and allies of Rome, and finally of God's gracious deliverance of England from the toils of Satan through his handmaiden Elizabeth. By 1570 Foxe's book had been so expanded that it took more than one thousand folio pages to get to the time of Mary Tudor, whose reign provided the bulk of the martyrdoms which Foxe described so vividly.

Unfortunately the themes explicated by Foxe are so interwoven with his massive documentation that they cannot be represented by brief selections. The prefatory materials of the 1589 abridgment by Timothy Bright, however, gave some indication of what readers understood the "Book of Martyrs" to be saying. Foxe's own account of the introduction of Christianity to Britain and his summary statement of God's subsequent visitations are also included.

The most uninhibited response to Elizabeth's accession was John Aylmer's *An Harborowe* [Harbor] *for Faithful and True Subjects,* published at Strassburg in 1559. Aylmer, later to be Bishop of London, also was in exile under Mary and for a time helped Foxe translate his "Book of Martyrs" into Latin. The impetus for his treatise was the publication of John Knox's *The First Blast of the Trumpet against the Monstrous Regiment of Women.* A stirring denial of the right of women to rule, Knox's *Blast of the Trumpet* at the time of its composition seemed an appropriate counter to the persecutions carried out under the aegis of Mary Tudor, Mary Stuart, Mary of Guise, and Catherine de Medici, but it proved to be one of the most ill-timed propagandist tracts in history. To the dismay of other exiles, Knox's polemic came from the press just as Mary Tudor died and was succeeded by her half-sister Elizabeth. Believing Elizabeth would prove to be an instrument to bring papal tyranny in England to an end and that she would both reform the church and restore the faith, the exiles quickly dissociated themselves from Knox's *Blast.* Aylmer's disavowal was the most vigorous, and it concluded with a rousing summons to obedience which played upon every patriotic sentiment and emotion. Characterized by an extreme emphasis upon God's special relationship to England, Aylmer's hurriedly written tract was perhaps as ill-considered as Knox's was ill-timed. Still, in a very vivid way, it gives insight into the more boistrous expressions of England's sense of self-identity.

In contrast to Aylmer's uninhibited appeal to national pride and more akin to Foxe's emphasis upon the responsibilities and perils of England's privileged position as God's elect champion and upon Elizabeth's unparalleled opportunity to forward the cause of the godly was the Dedication of the Geneva Bible to "the most virtuous and noble Queen Elizabeth." The Geneva Bible, published in 1560, also used every device to entice and aid the reader. It too had woodcuts, introductions, subheads, running titles, and marginal notes. Ease of reading was further facilitated by its quarto size and by the replacement of black-letter printing with the more legible Roman or Italian type. Moreover, chapters were divided into verses for purposes of ready reference. Even after the publication of the Authorized or King James Version of the Bible in 1611, the Geneva Bible remained for many years the most popular translation of the Scriptures in England. The translation was the work of English exiles at Geneva. Echoing in its notes and headings many of the themes of biblical interpretation that informed Foxe's "Book of Martyrs," the Geneva Bible did much to give form and content to England's understanding of her national vocation.

An Abridgement of the Book of Acts and Monuments of the Church Written by that Reverend Father, Master John Foxe, and now abridged by Timothy Bright (London, 1589)

TO THE CHRISTIAN READER:

Considering the great use and profit of that worthy book of *Acts and Monuments* . . . and by reason of the largeness of the volume and great price how the most were bereaved of the benefit of so necessary an history, I often wished some man would take the pains to draw the same into an abridgement that both those that are busied in affairs or not able to reach to the price of so great a book might also have use of the history. . . . But seeing hitherto nothing done that way . . . , I ventured upon the labor myself. . . . I do exhort thee, gentle reader, the rather for my abridgement's sake to buy and use [the large book]. For, as the copiousness of that notable work hath hid the rich treasures of the same through charge of price and men's affairs, so this my labor may give thee an . . . appetite to know further, whereof thou mayest here take, as it were, a taste. I assure thee in my opinion there is not a book under the Scriptures more necessary for a Christian to be conversant in.

There is no burgess of a city that hath care of his corporation [city] but would be glad to know how in times past the world went with his corporation, that thereby he may understand the better how to behave himself therein as occasion shall serve. . . . Even so it becometh much more Christians that are citizens of the church of Christ and have a community in that body to know not only the laws of this city, which is the Word of God, but also what hath befallen [it], either good or bad. . . . This commonwealth of the church . . . giveth great variety of examples of God's providence, of his mercy, of his fatherly chastisements and correction, and of that holy faith which hath ministered invincible strength of constancy and patience . . . in the midst of all storms of trial. . . . When I say in this abridgement thou mayest read these things, I mean much more in the large volume where all matters lie open at the full and whereto, I pray thee, let this my labor be, as it were, an introduction. . . .

The History is divided into five parts.

1. The first is of the suffering of the church, 300 years after Christ.

2. The growing and flourishing time of the same, other 300 years.

3. The declining time, other 300 [years] until the loosing of Satan about the thousandth year after Christ.

4. The time of Antichrist, which continueth in full swing 400 years.

5. The time of reformation, these latter 288 years.

A special note of England.

England, the first kingdom that universally embraced the gospel.

Constantine, the first Christian emperor (who utterly destroyed the idolatry of the Gentiles and planted the gospel throughout the world), an Englishman.

John Wyclif, that first manifestly discovered the Pope and maintained open disputation against him, an Englishman.

The most noble prince, King Henry VIII, the first king that renounced the Pope.

The worthy prince, King Edward VI, the first king that utterly abolished all popish superstition.

Her royal majesty [Elizabeth], our most gracious sovereign, the very maul [hammer] of the Pope and a mother of Christian princes, whom the Almighty long preserve over us.

England, the first that embraced the gospel, the only establisher of it throughout the world, and the first reformed.

John Foxe, *Acts and Monuments of Matters Most Special and Memorable Happening in the Church with an Universal History of the Same* . . . , the eighth time newly imprinted. 3 vols. (London, 1641)[3]

Now, because the tying up of Satan giveth to the church some rest and to me some leisure to address myself to the handling of other stories, I mind therefore, Christ willing, in this present book . . . to prosecute such domestical histories as more nearly concern this our country of England and Scotland . . . , beginning first with King Lucius, with whom the faith first began here in this realm as some writers doth hold.

And forasmuch as here . . . doth rise a great controversy in these our popish days concerning the first origin and planting of the faith in this our realm, it shall not be greatly out of our purpose somewhat to stay and say of this question: Whether the

Church of England first received the faith from Rome or not? The which . . . being so granted, it little availeth the purpose of them which would so have it. For be it that England first received the Christian faith and religion from Rome, both in the time of Eleutherius their bishop 180 years after Christ and also in the time of Augustine whom Gregory sent hither 600 years after Christ, yet their purpose followeth not thereby that we must therefore fetch our religion from thence still as from the chief wellhead and fountain of all godliness. And yet as they are not able to prove the second, so neither have I any cause to grant the first, that our Christian faith was first derived from Rome, which I may prove by six or seven good conjectural reasons.

Whereof the first I take of the testimony of Gildas, our countryman, who in his history affirmeth plainly that Britain received the gospel in the time of Tiberius, the emperor under whom Christ suffered, . . . and saith moreover that Joseph of Arimathea . . . was sent of Philip the Apostle from France to Britain about the year of our Lord 63 . . . and laid the first foundation of Christian people among the Britain people. . . .

The second reason is out of Tertullian who, living . . . somewhat before the time of this Eleutherius . . . , manifestly importeth the same, where . . . testifying how the gospel was dispersed abroad by the sound of the apostles . . . at length cometh to . . . the borders of Spain with divers nations of France, there . . . reciteth also the parts of Britain which the Romans could never attain to and reporteth the same now to be subject to Christ. . . .

The third probation I deduct out of Origen . . . , whereby it appeareth that the faith of Christ was sparsed [dispersed] here in England before the days of Eleutherius.

For my fourth probation I take the testimony of Bede where he affirmeth that in his time and almost a thousand years after Christ, here in Britain Easter was kept after the manner of the East Church in the full of the moon what day in the week soever it fell on, and not on the Sunday as we do now. Whereby it is to be collected that the first preachers in this land have come out of the east part of the world where it was so used rather than from Rome. . . .

For my seventh argument moreover I may make my probation by the plain words of Eleutherius in whose epistle written to King Lucius we may understand that Lucius had received the faith of Christ in this land before the king sent to Eleutherius for the Roman laws. . . .

By all which conjectures it may stand probably to be thought that the Britons were taught first by the Grecians of the East Church rather than by the Romans. . . . In a few words to conclude this matter, if [it should] so be that the Christian faith and religion was first derived from Rome to this our nation by Eleutherius, then let them but grant to us the same faith and religion which then was taught at Rome and from thence derived hither by the said Eleutherius, and we will desire no more. . . .

If leisure of time or haste of matter would suffer me a little to digress unto more lower times and to come more near home, the like examples I could also infer of this our country of England concerning the terrible plagues of God against the churlish and unthankful refusing or abusing the benefit of his truth.

First, we read how God stirred up Gildas to preach to the old Britons and to exhort them unto repentance and amendment of life, and afore to warn them of plagues to come if they repented not. What availed it? Gildas was laughed to scorn and taken for a false prophet and a malicious preacher. The Britons with lusty courages, whorish faces, and unrepentant hearts, went forth to sin and to offend the Lord their God. What followed? God sent in their enemies on every side and destroyed them and gave their land to other nations.

Not many years past God, seeing idolatry, superstition, hypocrisy, and wicked living used in this realm, raised up John Wyclif to preach repentance. . . . His exhortations were not regarded. He with his sermons were despised. His books and he himself after his death were burnt. What followed? They slew their right king and set up three wrong kings in a row, under whom all the noble blood was slain and half the commons . . . with their own sword in fighting among themselves . . . and the land brought half to a wilderness. O extreme plagues of God's vengeance.

Since that time, even of late years, God once again having pity of this realm of England raised up his prophets, namely, William Tyndale, Thomas Bilney, John Frith, Doctor Barnes, Jerome Garrett, Anthony Person, with divers others, which both with their writings and sermons earnestly labored to call us to repentance that by this means the fierce wrath of God might be turned away from us. But how were they intreated? . . . They themselves were condemned and burnt as heretics. . . . Whether anything since that time hath chanced to this realm worthy of the name of a plague [e.g., Mary Tudor], let the godly wise judge. If God hath deferred his punishment . . . , let us not therefore be proud and high-minded but most humbly thank him for his tender mercies and beware of like ungodly enterprises hereafter. . . .

Of this I am sure, that God yet once again is come on visitation to this Church of England, yea, and that more lovingly and beneficially than ever he did before. For in this visitation he hath redressed many abuses and cleansed his church of much ungodliness and superstition and made it a glorious church if it be compared to the old form and state. And now how grateful receivers we be? With what heart, study, and reverence we embrace that which he hath given? That I refer either to them that see our fruits or to the sequel which peradventure will declare it. . . .

John Aylmer, *An Harbor for Faithful and True Subjects* (Strassburg, 1559)[4]

For the safeguard of your country, if you be called to the wars, grutch [complain] not nor groan at it. Go with good wills and lusty courages to meet them in the field rather than to tarry till they come home to you and hang you at your own gates. Play not the milksops in making curtsy who shall go first, but show yourselves true Englishmen in readiness, courage, and boldness. And be ashamed to be the last. Fear neither French nor Scot. For first you have God and all his army of angels on your side [a marginal note observes "God is English"]. You have right and truth, and seek not to do them wrong but to defend your own right. Think not that God will suffer you to be foiled at their hands, for your fall is his dishonor. If you lose the victory, he must lose the glory. For you fight not only in the quarrel of your country but also and chiefly in defense of his true religion and of his dear son Christ. . . .

What people be they with whom we shall match. Are they giants? Are they conquerors or monarchs of the world? No, good Englishman, they be effeminate Frenchmen, stout in brag but nothing in deed. They be such as you have always made to take to their heels . . . , saving that William of Normandy crept in among us through the civil war of two brethren, Harold and Tostig. And yet, what did he? He left his posterity to reign which were rather by time turned to be English than the noble English to become French, as our tongue and manners at this day declareth, which differeth very little from our ancestors the Saxons. . . . Thus have we nothing to dismay us but all things to encourage us. God to fight for us, the strength of our land, the courage of our men, the goodness of our soil. . . . Now, therefore, it is our duties to be in every wise obedient. . . .

Do you not hear how lamentably your natural mother, your country of England, calleth upon you for obedience? . . .

"I have been and am glad of you. I delight and rejoice in you above all over nations. In declaration whereof I have always spued out and cast from me Danes, French, Norwegians, and Scots. I could brook none of them for the tender love that I bare unto you, of whom I have my name. I never denied to minister to you by my singular commodities which God hath lent me for you, as corn and cattle, land and pasture, wool and cloth, lead and tin, flesh and fish, gold and silver, and all my other treasures. I have poured them out among you and enriched you above all your neighbors. . : . Besides this, God hath brought forth in me the greatest and excellentest treasure that he hath for your comfort and all the world's. He would that out of my womb should come that servant of his, your brother John Wyclif, who begat [John] Hus, who begat [Martin] Luther, who begat truth. What greater honor could you or I have than it pleased Christ, as it were in a second birth, to be born again of me among you? [A marginal note comments: "Christ's second birth in England"]. And will you now suffer me, or rather by your disobedience purchase me, to be a mother without my children? . . . Stick to your mother as she sticketh to you. Let me keep in quiet and feed, as I have done, your wives, your children, and your kinsfolks. Obey your mistress and mine which God hath made lady [queen] over us, both by nature and law. You cannot be my children, if you be not her subjects. . . ."

Thus good, truehearted Englishmen, speaketh your country unto you, not in word but in deed. Wherefore give no dull ear to hear, nor hearken to any vain blasts or voices which may draw you from the love of your country and the defense of your sovereign. . . .

The Bible and Holy Scriptures Contained in the Old and New Testament . . . with Most Profitable Annotations (Geneva, 1560)

To the Most Virtuous and Noble Queen Elizabeth . . . , your humble subjects of the English church at Geneva wish grace and peace from God the Father through Jesus Christ our Lord.

. . . The marvelous diligence and zeal of Jehoshaphat, Josiah, and Hezekiah are by the singular providence of God left as an example to all godly rulers to reform their countries and to establish the Word of God with all speed lest the wrath of God fall upon them for the neglecting thereof. For these excellent kings did not only embrace the Word promptly and joyfully, but also procured earnestly and commanded the same to be taught, preached, and maintained through all their countries and dominions, binding them and all their subjects both great and small with solemn protestations and covenants before God to obey the Word and to walk after the ways of the Lord. . . . As well priests as judges were appointed and placed through all the cities of Judah to instruct the people in the true knowledge and fear of God and to minister justice according to the Word, knowing that except God by his Word did reign in the hearts and souls all man's diligence and endeavors were of none effect. For without this Word we cannot discern between justice and injury, protection and oppression, wisdom and foolishness, knowledge and ignorance, good and evil. . . .

Most gracious queen, . . . the eyes of all that fear God in all places behold your countries [counties, i.e., realm] as an example to all that believe, and the prayers of all the godly at all times are directed to God for the preservation of your majesty. For considering God's wonderful mercies toward you at all seasons, who hath pulled you out of the mouth of the lions and how that from your youth you have been brought up in the Holy Scriptures, the hope of all men is so increased that they cannot but look that God should bring to pass some wonderful work by your grace to the universal comfort of his church. . . . This Lord of lords and King of kings, who hath ever defended his [own], strengthen, comfort, and preserve your majesty that you may be able to build up the ruins of God's house to his glory, the discharge of your conscience, and to the comfort of all them that love the coming of Christ Jesus our Lord.

From Geneva. April 10, 1560.

[A woodcut, showing the Israelites at the Red Sea, with the Egyptian army behind them and the pillar of cloud before them, appears on the title pages of both the Old Testament and the New Testament. Above the woodcut is the text: "Fear ye not. Stand still and behold the salvation of the Lord which he will show to you this day" (Exod. 14:13). Below the cut is the text: "The Lord shall fight for you; therefore hold your peace" (Exod. 14:14). Framing the cut at either side is the text: "Great are the troubles of the righteous, but the Lord delivereth them out of all" (Ps. 34:19). The same woodcut appears in the text opposite Exodus 14:10 and is accompanied by the explanation: "When the dangers are most great, then God's help is most ready to succor. For the Israelites had on either side of them huge rocks and mountains, before them the sea, behind them the most cruel enemies, so that there was no way left to escape by man's judgment."]

THE COVENANTED NATION

Foxe's "Book of Martyrs" made it plain that the favor bestowed on England could be and would be withdrawn if a churlish and disobedient people refused to repent and mend their ways. As the Geneva Bible was careful to emphasize, God had committed himself to ancient Israel by way of a covenant. So it was with England. England had become God's chosen instrument. God's mercies were freely bestowed, but they were not unconditional. His visible blessings presupposed a faithful and obedient people. Otherwise England would be an ineffective instrument and prove itself unworthy of God's continued favor. Still God had not chosen lightly and would not quickly nor easily forsake the people by whom he intended to effect his purposes. Again and again in miraculous ways he had preserved England. And again and again by chastisements and judgments he had recalled England to its vocation. But Englishmen were never to become so presumptuous as to count on God's continued indulgence. Fully aware that God could raise up new "children of Abraham" (Matt. 3:9), Elizabethan preachers and their successors in the seventeenth century repeatedly summoned England to repentance and amendment of life.

Fast days, days of humiliation and prayer, were a means of publicly summoning people to repentance. A practice derived from the Scots and explicitly related to the biblical "Day of Atonement," fast days were community affairs undertaken "at the appointment of them which, under Christ, have the government of the places where the fast is holden."[5] They lasted from evening to evening, with the community assembling both morning and afternoon for preaching and prayer. They were proclaimed for a specific purpose, usually to avert some impending calamity. During the 1570's public fasts, with the active encouragement of Archbishop Edmund Grindal, were held at various points in the kingdom, with the preachers exhorting the people to repentance and reform lest they receive just punishment for their sins. And on January 10, 1580 [1581], at the beginning of the parliamentary session, the House of Commons voted that a national fast day be held. The members were ordered to assemble in the Temple church "to have preaching and to join together in prayer, with humiliation and fasting, for the assistance of God's Spirit in all their consultation" and "for the preservation of the queen's majesty and her realms." The queen, however, was not pleased with "so great a rashness in that house as to put in execution such an innovation without her privity and pleasure first made known to them," whereupon the House acknowledged its offense and craved forgiveness.[6] Nevertheless, the practice persisted on a local and even on a diocesan basis.[7] And in the crisis of 1640 one of the first acts of the Long Parliament was to appoint a day of fasting, humiliation, and prayer. The day appointed, by some quirk of fate, was the anniversary of Elizabeth's accession.

A monthly fast day became a fixed feature of the Long Parliament's proceedings throughout its lengthy existence, and in 1643 the king began appointing his own fast days to counteract those of parliament. Since the parliamentary fast days were being used to foment rebellion, the king declared that they were not to be countenanced. Yet, "being desirous to express our own humiliation and the humiliation of our people for our own sins and the sins of the nation," we "are resolved to continue a monthly fast but not on the day formerly appointed." The king, therefore, commanded that "from henceforth no fast be held on the last Wednesday of the month," but that "in all churches and chapels, etc. there be a solemn fast religiously observed on the second Friday in every month."[8]

The king's action is testimony to the power of the concept of a covenanted nation as it was dramatized by the parliamentary fast days. Nowhere is that concept more plainly set forth than in the sermons which were preached to the House of Commons at these monthly observances. Indeed, the occasional days of thanksgiving which were appointed to mark some remarkable deliverance served the same purpose, for in the hands of the preachers the reason for thanksgiving was an indication of God's favor and thus became a further reason for repentance and reform.

Stephen Marshall, Cornelius Burges, and Edmund Calamy were the most noted of the parliamentary preachers. Selections from Burges and Calamy have been used because their fast-day sermons are representative and more easily excerpted. Marshall, the most famous of the three, was frequently given the afternoon assignment. This meant that his sermons, of necessity, carried forward the thought of the morning and took the form more of rousements than sustained argument and coherent discourse.

In contrast to the extended exposition of the fast-day sermons, the practical implications for national morale of the notion of a covenanted people were spelled out tersely and briefly in *The Soldier's Pocket Bible* of 1643, which rehearsed the "qualifications" of "a fit soldier to fight the Lord's battles." The "qualifications" are drawn from Scripture, but they were selected and grouped in such a manner as to reveal the pattern of God's ways with his people. Significantly, all but seven of the 125 verses assembled in *The Soldier's Pocket Bible* are from the Old Testament. It is noteworthy that it was reprinted by the American Tract Society during the American Civil War, the Spanish-American War, and World War I.

Cornelius Burges, *A Sermon Preached to the Honorable House of Commons . . . at their Public Fast, November 17, 1640* (London, 1641)[9]

That great apostle Saint Paul, when he had to do with wise men, held it a point of wisdom to pass by some things which he would not have waived among meaner capacities. His practice shall be my precedent. . . . How weak and unworthy soever I myself be, yet I am now to speak to wise men who need not so much to be catechized touching the nature as to be incited and quickened to the principal use of a religious fast, which consisteth not solely in such drawing near to God by extraordinary prayer and humiliation as may produce a total divorce from our lusts, but also (and that more principally) in particular, formal, solemn, entire engaging and binding of ourselves by an indissoluble covenant to that God whose face and favor we seek and implore. . . . To provoke both myself and you at this time to the due performance of this . . . duty, I have thought fit, in a very plain and familiar way . . . , to work and chafe into all our hearts the strength and spirit of that good word of God which you shall find written for our instruction in the prophecy of Jeremiah: "They shall ask the way to Zion with their faces thitherward, saying: 'Come and let us join ourselves unto the Lord in an everlasting covenant that shall not be forgotten' " (Jeremiah 50:5). Which words are part of a prophecy . . . uttered and penned by Jeremiah about the fourth year both of the Babylonish captivity and of the tributary reign of Zedekiah.

The occasion [is] this. The prophet, having labored about thirty years to humble Judah by continual ringing in her ears the doleful tidings of a sore captivity approaching, could not be believed. But, when once the quick and sad sense of their bondage under the Chaldean had forced them to an acknowledgement of the truth of his prophecies, he found it as hard a task to work their hearts to any expectation of deliverance. . . .

The main beam which stuck in their eyes to hinder their sight of deliverance was the greatness and invincible potency of the Chaldean monarchy (then in her pride) and more especially the strength of Babylon, the queen and mistress of that puissant empire. How could they hope to be delivered when she that commanded the world detained them? . . .

To cure them, therefore, of this desperate desponsion of mind, the Lord stirred up this prophet to foretell the total and final subversion and ruin of Babylon and of that whole monarchy, and further to declare from God that the desolation thereof should be the dissolution of the captivity of Judah in it. . . .

What should be the means of such an unexpected destruction? An army from the north of the Medes and Persians. . . .

This northern army [like the Scottish army poised at Berwick-upon-Tweed] should be the confusion of Babylon. The confusion of Babylon should prove the restoring of the church (verse 3). And the restoring of the church should produce a covenant. . . .

The issue and consequent of the ruin of Babylon was the return of the captive Jews from thence to Jerusalem and a renewing covenant with him that had showed such mercy on them. For, "in those days and in that time, saith the Lord, the children of Israel shall come, they and the children of Judah together, going and weeping, they shall go and seek the Lord their God. They shall ask the way to Zion with their faces thitherward, saying: 'Come and let us join ourselves to the Lord in an everlasting covenant that shall not be forgotten' " (verses 4–5). They should go not so much to repossess their ancient patrimony and inheritance, thereby to grow rich in the world, as to seek and find the Lord their God, and that with a resolution to enter into covenant with him, even such a covenant as should never be forgotten but daily remembered and carefully performed.

You see the context. . . . The chief and only point of instruction which I shall . . . press upon you . . . is plainly this, that *when God vouchsafes any deliverance to his church, especially from Babylon, then is it most seasonable and most necessary to close with God by a more solemn, strict, and inviolable covenant to be his and only his for ever*. . . .

What was it for which Judah and Israel became captives but the breach of the covenant? "They kept not the covenant of God," saith the Psalmist (Psalms 78:10). And how so? Because they did not remember it. . . . He then that would not break covenant must not forget it, but mind and perform it. Otherwise it is like vowing unto God and not paying, which is worse than not to vow at all. . . .

I proceed to the . . . reasons why upon receipt of any deliverance, but more especially from Babylon, people should enter into such a covenant with God. . . .

1. Because God at no time so much as when he bestows

upon his people some notable deliverance gives such clear hints and demonstrations of his willingness to strike an everlasting covenant with them. . . . It is the nature of God where he bestows one benefit to add more. . . . Where he once opens his hand to take a people into his protection, he opens his heart to take them into his bosom. Where he puts forth his power to rescue a people, he puts out his heart to make them his own if they have the eyes to discern the opportunity. . . .

Now then, shall God at such a time be so willing and desirous to enter covenant with men and shall they think it too much for them to be in covenant with him? Shall he be fast bound to them and they left free to sit loose from him? Indeed, this is that which our corrupt nature would willingly have. People would fain be their own men, which yet in truth is to be the greatest slaves. Necessary therefore it is for men upon receipt of any deliverance to renew covenant with God who is pleased to honor them so far as to be in covenant with them. For these two are relatives, and even go together: "I will be their God, and they shall be my people" [II Cor. 6:16]. . . .

2. As God is pleased to enter into covenant with his people, so is he first in the covenant. God requires no man to bind himself by covenant to him till the Lord first strike a covenant with his soul. As "we love him because he loved us first" [I John 4:19], so we enter into covenant with him because he first entered into covenant with us. "I will be their God." He is the first bound. . . . And then, and not till then, it follows, "they shall be my people." . . . Now God no way so much declares his willingness to be in covenant and to be first in it as by deliverances. . . . It is an hard case when men will not follow where God leads.

3. In deliverances God more especially manifesteth his fidelity in keeping covenant with his people even when they have broken covenant with him and forfeited all into his hands. When God delivers a people out of any strait, doth not that usually suppose some folly of theirs going before and provoking him to cast them into that affliction? When upon their cry, he is pleased to deliver them. . . .

Again, fourthly and lastly, all our hopes of a full deliverance . . . will be delayed . . . and the next deliverance will stick in the birth and want strength to bring forth, if we come not up to a covenant for deliverances already received. If God have delivered us once, he will do it no more (or if he do somewhat to hold us up by the chin that we sink not, yet will he hold us down from the throne that we reign not) till we come up actually and fully in this point of covenanting with him. . . . He that hath obtained most and greatest deliverances will ere long stand in need of more. Now one thing is necessary to draw down more . . . , and that is to enter into a solemn covenant with the Lord upon consideration of what he hath done already. . . .

Some think it bootless thus to close in with God after an evil is over. When God's hand is heavy upon them, sense of smart compels them . . . to do somewhat to confess their sins, to humble themselves, and to seek God. . . . But so soon as he takes his hand off from them, they cast all care away. . . .

Others, if . . . they arrive at some hopes and opportunities . . . of freeing the land of the great instruments of all their evils, they conceit strongly that, if this be done, all is done. If but some of the Nimrods [Gen. 10:8] who have invaded their laws and liberties be pulled down . . . , the many (who do nothing towards any reformation of themselves) rejoice and promise to themselves great matters. Now, think they, there will be an end to all our miseries and we shall see golden days. . . . Oh, brethren, deceive not yourselves. If this be all you look at, if upon opening this door of hope, this be all you aim at to secure yourselves against oppressors and never think of closing with God . . . , you may perhaps [go] far in pursuit of your own designs . . . , but let me tell you from God that this will never do the deed till the covenant . . . be resolved on and solemnly entered into by all those that expect any blessing from [this parliament]. . . . Not this nor all the parliaments in the world shall ever be able to make us happy . . . till the Lord hath even glued and married us all unto himself by mutual covenant. . . .

Consider that whatever work God calls you to, ye will never buckle thoroughly to it till you have entered into covenant with him. An apprentice boy who goes to a master upon trial only, his mind is now on, then off again. Sometimes he could like the trade; by and by his mind hangs after his mother at home or after some other course of life, and he never sets close to his business till he be bound. . . . And thus also it will be with you. You have much work under your hands and are like to have more. And I hope you desire to do all in truth of heart for God and not for ends of your own. But let me tell you, this will never be done thoroughly till once you be married to him by solemn covenant. . . .

Remember and consider that this day, even this very day, the 17th of November, 82 years sithence [ago], began a new resurrection of this kingdom from the dead, our second happy reformation of religion by the auspicious entrance of our late royal Deborah (worthy of eternal remembrance and honor) into her blessed and glorious reign. . . . Consider, I beseech you, that it was not without a special providence that this your meeting was cast upon this very day (for I presume little did you think of the 17th of November when you first fixed on this day for your Fast) that, even from thence, one hammer might be borrowed to drive home this nail of exhortation, that the very memory of so blessed a work begun on this very day might thoroughly inflame you with desire to enter into a covenant and so to go forward to perfect that happy reformation which yet in many parts lies unpolished and unperfect. . . . If you would indeed honor her precious memory, yea, honor God and yourselves, and not only continue the possession of what she (as a most glorious conduit pipe) hath transmitted to us but perfect the work, set upon this duty of "joining ourselves to the Lord in an everlasting covenant that shall not be forgotten." . . .

Thus, if you do, God shall be set up, religion advanced, your grievances removed. You shall hear no more such complainings in our streets. All blessings shall follow, not yourselves alone, but the whole kingdom. . . . Then shall the whole nation and the children which are yet unborn praise and bless the Lord for this parliament and your endeavors in it.

Edmund Calamy, *England's Looking-Glass, presented in a sermon before the Honorable House of Commons, December 22, 1641* (London, 1642)[10]

This text [Jer. 18:7-10] may fitly be called a looking-glass for England and Ireland, or for any other kingdom whatsoever, wherein God Almighty declares what he can do with nations and kingdoms, and what he will do.

1. What he can do. He can "build and plant" a nation. And he can "pluck up, pull down, and destroy" a nation. And when a kingdom is in the depth of misery, he can in an "instant," if he but speak the word, raise it up to the top of happiness. And when it is in the height and zenith of happiness, he can in another instant speak a word and throw it down again into an abyss of misery.

2. What he will do. God will not always use his prerogative but will first "speak" before he strikes. He will first "pronounce" judgment before he executeth judgment. And "if that nation against which he hath pronounced the evil" of punishment "turn from their evil" of sin, "then will God repent of the evil he intended to do unto them." And not only so, but he will "build and plant" that nation and of a barren wilderness make it a fruitful paradise. But if "that nation do evil in God's sight and will not obey his voice, then will God repent of the good wherewith he would have benefited them," and pull down what he hath built and pluck up what he hath planted and of a fruitful paradise make it a barren wilderness.

By all this it appears that, as this day is a national day and this honorable assembly a national assembly, so this text is a national text every way suitable for the occasion about which we are met. . . . From the words thus explained, I gather these four doctrinal conclusions.

1. That God hath an absolute power over all kingdoms and nations, to pluck them up, pull them down, and destroy them as he pleaseth.

2. That though God hath this absolute prerogative over kingdoms and nations, yet he seldom useth this power but first he gives warning.

3. If that kingdom against which God hath threatened destruction repent and turn from their evil, God will not only not destroy that kingdom but build it and plant it. Or thus: National repentance will divert national judgments and procure national blessings.

4. That when God begins to build and plant a nation, if that nation do evil in God's sight, God will repent of the good he intended to do unto it. . . .

To turn from sin is a key to unlock all the chests of God's mercies. . . . A repenting faith . . . ties God's hands and charms his wrath. There is no thunderbolt so great, no wrath so furious in God, but repentance will abolish it. . . .

I have here a large field of matter for a year rather than a day, but as a little boat may land a man into a large continent so a few words may suggest matter sufficient to a judicious ear for a whole life's meditation. . . . I will only . . . beseech you to turn the doctrine into practice and to express the sincerity of your repentance by two duties which are as the two poles upon which our turning from sin doth move—by humiliation and reformation. Humiliation for sins past. Reformation for the time to come. "Humiliation without reformation is a foundation without a building; reformation without humiliation proves often a building without a foundation." Both of them together comprehend the essentials of this great duty which is the very quintessence of practical divinity. . . .

Now mark the doctrine. When God begins to build and plant, if that nation do evil, God will un-build what he hath built, pluck up what he hath planted. . . . For you must know that God repents as well of his mercies as of his judgments. When God hath made Saul king and he proved stubborn and disobedient, God repented that ever he made him king. When God saw that the wickedness of the old world was great upon the earth, he was grieved at the very heart and repented that ever he made man. . . . When the people of Israel were come out of

Egypt and very near Canaan, because they brought an evil report upon the land of Canaan and murmured, the Lord repents of what he had done and carries them back again forty years journey through the vast howling wilderness.

Reason: 1. Because God's covenant with a nation is conditional. . . . 2. Because that sin is so pernicious to a kingdom that where sin rules, there God and his mercy will not abide. . . .

It is God only that can build and plant a nation. He is the only architect that can build our waste places. . . . He is the only gardener to pluck up our weeds and to plant useful and fruitful trees in the orchard of this nation. And if he please, he can do it, and that in an instant with a word of speaking. . . . If we turn from our evil ways, God will perfect his building and finish his plantation. He will make us a glorious paradise, an habitation fit for himself to dwell in. He will set up his ordinances after a purer manner, and watch over us for good from the beginning of the year to the end of it. . . .

Edmund Calamy, *God's Free Mercy to England, presented as a precious and powerful motive to humiliation in a sermon before the House of Commons, February 23, 1641* [1642] (London, 1642)[11]

We are here met this day to keep a day of humiliation. . . . It cannot be denied but that God hath done much for England and that England hath done much against God. Now my purpose is to lay the sins of England against God in one scale and the mercies of God to England in the other scale, and to call upon you this day to be humbled and ashamed and broken in heart before the Lord that ever you should sin against such a God. . . .

God doth sometimes show mercy to a nation when it least deserves it and least expects it. . . .

My desire is that this doctrine may be a looking-glass for this nation in which we may behold the several miracles of mercy that God hath bestowed upon us, a nation not worthy to be beloved and yet beloved above all nations of the world. God hath made us like Saul, taller by the head in mercies than all other nations. . . .

There was indeed a time when this island was . . . worshipping stocks [stumps] and stones, even the devil instead of God. . . . But it pleased God presently after the death of Christ to send the Christian religion among us. Christ made haste to convert England. Some say that James the brother of John, some Simon Zelotes, some that Peter and Paul, but all agree that Joseph of Arimathea preached the gospel here, and here he died. And that which makes much for the mercy of God to this happy island, the first Christian king that ever was in the world was King Lucius, a Briton. And the first Christian emperor was born in England, even Constantine the Great. And when we came afterwards to be woefully drowned with popish heresies and idolatry, the first king that ever shook off the subjection to Antichrist after he was discovered by Luther was Henry VIII. . . . We have enjoyed the gospel of peace and the peace of the gospel for almost a hundred years. . . .

In this century God hath multiplied deliverances upon deliverances. We have had our '88 [defeat of the Armada] and our Gunpowder deliverances, but . . . the mercies of these two last years do far exceed all the mercies that ever this nation did receive since the first reformation. . . . Give me leave to name some few of them. First, the happy pacification between Scotland and England. God hath freed us from civil wars which of all wars are most uncivil. . . . Secondly, the mighty turn that God hath made in this kingdom for the better. . . . We were like firebrands in the fire, like birds in the snare, but God Almighty hath made a blessed turn of things for the better. The enemies are thrown into the dens and dungeons they prepared for the godly. . . . Fourthly, the great hope we have of a reformation of the church and state. . . . Fifthly, the many grievous yokes that God hath freed us from . . . , from civil yokes and from spiritual, from monopolies, from the late canons . . . , from the Star Chamber, and from the terrible High Commission . . . , from those two terrible oaths, the oath *ex officio* and the oath of the late canons [*et cetera* oath]. . . .

These mercies . . . are so great and so wonderful as that . . . I can hardly forbear from turning this day of humiliation into a day of thanksgiving. . . .

Give me leave now, Right Honorable, to make two uses of . . . these mercies. . . . Let God have the glory of all his mercies. . . . This I speak . . . because I preach to them whom God hath made one of the instruments of all our mercies. You are the golden pipes through which these mercies come to us, and you must be as golden pipes in suffering the praise to pass through you, not reserving any to yourselves. . . . And we must give God the glory of his mercies, so we must give glory to God with all his mercies. We must improve England's mercies to the glory of the God of England. . . . As God hath done singular and extraordinary things for us, let us do some singular and extraordinary service for God. He hath made England a miracle of mercy; let England be a miracle of obedience. . . .

Observe that national mercies come from free grace, not from free will; not from man's goodness, but from God's goodness. . . . If any shall ask, how it comes to pass that England hath been like Noah's ark safe and secure, when all other nations have been drowned with a sea of blood, . . . no other answer can be returned but God's free grace and mercy. "I will have mercy upon whom I will have mercy" [Rom. 9:15]. "May I not do what I will with mine own" [Matt. 20:15]? . . . Be it known unto you, O house of England, it is not for your sakes, for you are a stiffnecked people, but for my holy name's sake.

But doth not God indent and covenant with a nation upon its repentance to show mercy? How then is God's mercy free?

Repentance itself is of God's free grace. . . . [And] repentance is not the cause for which God spares a nation but only a qualification of that nation which God will spare. . . . If England's mercies come from free grace, let not England presume upon God's mercies as if entailed upon them and their posterity. For it is as free for God to take away his mercies as it was free to give them. . . . If England's mercies come from free grace, let England serve God freely. God loves a free people, a free-will offering. . . .

The contemplation of God's free mercy to nations and persons ought to be a mighty incentive and a most effectual argument to make them ashamed and ashamed; ashamed for sin for the time past and ashamed to sin for the time to come. . . . And this is the argument, Right Honorable, which I spread before you this day to help forward the work of humiliation. . . . There is great reasons why the mercies of God should make us ashamed for sin and ashamed to sin. . . . Because every new mercy we receive from God is a new kindness, and the more kindnesses we sin against, . . . the more shame to be so unkind to that God that is so kind to us. . . . Because every new mercy is a new obligation to obedience, and the more obligations we sin against, the more shame it is to commit sin. . . . Because every new mercy we receive from God is a new talent (for mercies are talents betrusted with us by God as stewards for which we must give a severe and strict account . . .), and the more talents we sin against, the greater is our sin and the more shame to commit it. . . . This makes the least sin of us in England greater than the greatest sin of Germany or of Ireland because God hath dealt more mercifully with us than with them. . . . There is no sin that doth more provoke God to anger or sooner cause him to destroy a nation, and to destroy it utterly, than this sin: to sin after mercy, under mercy, and with mercies. . . .

If the beginnings of hope that now appear, these inklings of better days, will not work upon us to humble us for and from sin, God will take away all our hopes and all his mercies from us and give them to a nation that will make better use of them. . . .

Edmund Calamy, *England's Antidote against the Plague of Civil War, presented in a sermon before the House of Commons, October 22, 1644* (London, 1645)[12]

Among all the texts that are in the Bible, there is no one text more suitable to these times than this that I have read unto you:

"But now God commands all men to repent" [Acts 17:30]. God hath been preaching repentance to England by the ministry of his Word almost these hundred years, but England hath turned a deaf ear to God's preaching repentance, not only by his Word but by the sword, for the sword hath a voice as well as the Word (Micah 6:9). And the sword speaks louder than the Word. God is riding throughout all England upon his "red and bloody horse" [Zech. 1:8?], thundering out repentance to every city, country, town, and family. And that which was the last speech of Master Bradford when he was burning at the stake is now become the voice not only of the Word of God but of the Sword of God: "Repent, O England, repent, repent." . . .

If any shall object and say that the doctrine of repentance is a doctrine that we all know already, I answer: If you know this doctrine so well, the more shame you practice it so little. . . . I could heartily wish that all the godly ministers of England would combine together never to leave preaching the sword-removing and land-preserving doctrine of repentance till they had persuaded all the people of England to repent and till God should be pleased upon our repentance, for Christ's sake, to turn away the judgments that are now upon us. . . .

God doth now use such an argument to persuade us to repentance the like of which he never yet did use since England was England. God's argument is this: Repent, O ye lords and commons, or else I'll give you over to beggary. Repent or else I'll give you over to popery, I'll give you over to slavery. Repent or I'll plunder your houses, I'll give up your wives and daughters to be deflowered. Repent or else I'll burn your cities. Repent or else I'll remove the gospel from you." . . . These are killing days. These are dying days. . . . Now the patience of God is at an end. Now the heavy wrath of God lies upon England. "Now the axe is laid at the very root of the tree" [Luke 13:9]. God hath been holding up his axe for many years against England, but now God is hewing down the tree of England at the very roots. It is high time now we should begin to repent. . . . Repentance is the only way to remove the man-devouring and land-devouring judgment that is now upon us. I say it is the only way, for so saith Christ: "Except ye repent, ye shall all perish" (Luke 13:5). . . . Mistake me not. I do not say, God will remove the bloody sword for our repentance. But this I say, God will not remove it without our repentance, and upon our repentance he will remove it. . . .

True repentance is a medicine made of Christ's blood that must have five ingredients in it. And if any one of these ingredients be wanting, the medicine will not avail us unto salvation. It is a golden chain that must have five links, and if one link be wanting, the chain is of little use. The five links of this golden chain are: First, godly sorrow for sin. Secondly, a hearty confession of sin. Thirdly, a sincere endeavor to forsake all sin. Fourthly, satisfaction for sin. Fifthly, a turning to God by new obedience. . . .

Now what remains but, first, that all you that pretend to a right repentance be persuaded to examine yourselves whether you have this medicine with the five ingredients, this golden chain with the five links. . . . Secondly, labor to put on this golden chain this day. . . . The Lord give you hearts to do it. Repentance is Christ's gift. . . . Sue him for it, and he will bestow it upon you. And be sure to remember this truth of God, if any one link of this chain be wanting, thou canst not be saved. For I am not now preaching of points in difference between us and the papists or between Protestant and Protestant, but of those things which all will confess to be true. If any one of these ingredients be out of the medicine, this medicine of repentance will do thee no good. . . .

The Soldier's Pocket Bible, containing the most if not all those places contained in Holy Scripture which do show the qualifications of his inner man . . . , which Scriptures are reduced to several heads and fitly applied (London, 1643)[13]

A soldier must be valiant for God's cause. . . .

A soldier must put his confidence in God's wisdom and strength. . . .

A soldier must consider and believe God's gracious promises. . . .

A soldier must consider that sometimes God's people have the worst in battle as well as God's enemies. . . .

Soldiers and all of us must consider that though God's people have the worst of it yet it cometh of the Lord. . . .

For the iniquities of God's people, [they] are delivered into the hands of their enemies. . . .

Therefore both soldiers and all God's people upon such occasions must search out their own sins. . . .

Especially let soldiers and all of us upon such occasions search whether we have not put too little confidence in the arm of the Lord and too much in the arm of the flesh. . . .

And let soldiers and all of us consider that to prevent this sin and for the committing of this sin, the Lord hath ever been accustomed to give the victory to a few. . . .

And let soldiers and all of us know that the very nick of time that God hath promised us help is when we see no help in man. . . .

Wherefore, if our forces be weakened and the enemy strengthened, then let soldiers and all of us know we have a promise of God's help which we had not when we were stronger, and therefore let us pray more confidently. . . .

And let soldiers and all of us know that if we obtain any victory over our enemies, it is our duty to give all the glory to God. . . .

TRUE RELIGION AND SAXON LIBERTIES

The conflict in England between king and parliament was precipitated by a dual concern for true religion and constitutional liberties. The godly readily recognized that their rights and liberties as Englishmen served as a major defense against what they regarded as the incursions of Rome. The intermingling of the two concerns was exhibited both in parliamentary debates and in Puritan sermons. Furthermore, although a more thoroughly reformed religious uniformity was presupposed by almost everyone at the outset of the Long Parliament, it was soon discovered that differences of opinion with regard to ecclesiastical order made the desired uniformity difficult to achieve. A growing number of Englishmen, unwilling to impose a forced worship upon any of the godly who had hazarded life and fortune in the parliamentary cause, began to link religious toleration to the other rights of Englishmen. As the American Revolution was later to be fought in the name of "liberty, both civil and religious," so Cromwell's troops became united in defense of "the good old cause" of religious toleration.

John Goodwin, Jeremiah Burroughes, and Hugh Peters were among the preachers who exhibited a marked preoccupation with the liberties of Englishmen. All three were conspicuous figures with close connections to New England. Hugh Peters had been in Massachusetts, where he had been pastor at Salem and a founder of Harvard. He had helped to draft the laws of the colony, and had been sent back to England in 1641 as the colony's agent. In England he became a noted army chaplain and frequently was sent to carry tidings of battle to parliament.

Bernard Bailyn has shown that the eighteenth-century heirs of the Puritan Revolution, sparked by Thomas Hollis, had more to do with shaping the political convictions of the American colonists than John Locke. Grounding their thought "in pessimism concerning human nature and in the discouraging record of human weakness," they became effective transmitters of the earlier Puritan admiration of the English constitution as a balance of powers designed to protect the natural rights of men by placing an effective check upon the power to oppress.[14] Bailyn's stress upon the role of eighteenth-century propagandists, however, should not obscure the continuing influence of a little book by William Penn in determining the mind-set of the American colonists. Penn was an earlier product of the Puritan Revolution, and his handbook, *English Liberties; or The Free-born Subject's Inheritance* (1682) went through many editions. Long attributed to Henry Care, it now seems reasonably certain that *English Liberties* was Penn's own handiwork.[15] After the three initial imprints of 1682, new editions were printed in 1691, 1692, 1700, and 1719. These London printings were followed by two American editions in 1721 (Boston) and 1774 (Providence, Rhode Island). In addition, a rewritten version, *British Liberties; or, The Free-born Subject's Inheritance,* was published in London in 1766.

English Liberties was a handbook designed to help Dissenters manage their own defense when hailed before the courts. They were reminded of their ancient Saxon liberties, and the *Magna Charta* and other basic documents, with appropriate commentaries, were reproduced for their use. The conduct of jury trials was discussed, and technicalities which could be utilized to deflect attempts to suppress dissenting activity were given due attention. Basically, however, *English Liberties* was a compendium of the fundamental rights and privileges of all Englishmen. It was this latter aspect that led William Penn to publish the first portion of *English Liberties* in Philadelphia in 1687. He gave this excerpt from the larger book the title *The Excellent Privilege of Liberty and Property, Being the Birthright of the Free-born Subjects of England*. His purpose, Penn explained in a preface, was to let those "who may not have leisure from their plantations to read large volumes" know "what is their native right and inheritance," hoping thereby to "raise up noble resolutions in all the freeholders in these new colonies not to give away anything of liberty and property that at present they do (or of right as loyal English subjects ought to) enjoy." He urged the new settlers to heed "the good example of our ancestors and understand that it is easy to part with or give away great privileges but hard to be regained if once lost."[16]

Prior to the revolution of 1689 in Massachusetts, when Governor Edmund Andros was ejected, all the basic arguments concerning the rights of Englishmen were rehearsed. This was before the publication of either Locke's *Two Treatises on Government* or Sidney's *Discourses concerning Government*. At this critical juncture, Penn's *English Liberties* would have been immediately relevant. There was, of course, the truncated Philadelphia edition of 1687, but more important is the fact that all three publishers of the first London edition of 1682 (George Larkin, John How, and Benjamin Harris) had connections with the New England book-trade. Indeed, Benjamin Harris was in Boston at the time, having set up shop there in 1686, becoming printer to the Mathers and the governor, and gaining fame as the author and publisher of *The New England Primer*.

In 1700, after having returned to London, Harris brought out a revised edition of *English Liberties*. The material dealing with religious dissent had been outdated by the accession of William and Mary, so this was deleted and the 1700 edition was transformed into a general legal handbook by adding material dealing with various mundane matters such as directions for justices of the peace, constables, and coroners. Since "law books," as William Penn had pointed out, were scarce in the colonies, it may be assumed that this small compendium or handbook was widely used. Daniel Dunlany, Sr., at least, made use of it when he drafted his *Right of the Inhabitants of Maryland to the Benefit of the English Laws* (Annapolis, 1728).[17]

John Goodwin, *Anti-Cavalierism; or, Truth Pleading as well the Necessity as the Lawfulness of this Present War* (London, 1642)[18]

Since we are fallen upon the mention of those men who are ready . . . to fall upon us and our lives and liberties, both spiritual and civil, upon our estates, our gospel and religion, and all that is or ought to be dear or precious unto us . . ., give me leave in that which remains to stir you up from the greatest to the least, both young and old, rich and poor, men and women, to quit yourselves like men. . . . O let it be as an abomination unto us . . . not to be active . . . to make our lives and our liberties and our religion good against that accursed generation that now magnifieth themselves. . . .

To rise up in your own defense, in the defense of your lives, your estates, your liberties, your wives, your children, your friends, your laws, your religion against those who, without any lawful authority or warrant either of God or men, are risen up with all their might and all their power to make havoc and spoil and ruin of us all is no ways offensive either in the sight of God or reasonable men. . . .

As the cause recommended to you is every ways justifiable, so is it a matter of the highest and deepest concernment unto you. . . . All your interest, relations, and concernments in this world are bound up in it; yea, it narrowly concerns you in relation to the world which is to come. . . .

1. For your estates. These are already designed by your enemies for a reward and recompense of their labor and travail in procuring your ruin. . . .

2. For your liberties. This is another precious possession . . . , and this likewise will certainly be oppressed and seized upon and turned into a miserable slavery and bondage. . . .

3. For your wives and children. . . . Neither are they like to find any better quarter . . . than your liberties and estates. . . .

4. That honorable senate of both houses of parliament . . . , to whose unwearied labors and diligence and faithfulness and zeal and expense, under God, you and your whole nation owe your lives and liberties, both spiritual and temporal, . . . these are like to perish and be cut off by the right hand of iniquity if that generation of men . . . ever get the upper hand. We know it is this assembly that have stood by you and stuck close to your liberties and the truth and purity of that religion you profess, that are the bulwark and defense against the furious impressions of those wicked men. . . .

5. And lastly, for matter of this world's concernment, what do you think of your lives themselves if those men of blood shall carry the day? . . .

But behold greater things than these. Your spiritual concernments also are like to suffer . . . if Gog and Magog prevail, if ever you come to be at the allowance of Cavaliers, papists, and atheists . . . for the things of heaven. . . . Those golden pipes by which heaven and earth are, as it were, joined together and have lively communion each with other (I mean your pure ordinances of worship . . .) will be cut off, and others of lead laid in their stead. . . . If you shall desire at any time to be rained upon by a shower of life and peace from heaven, you must repair again to the woods and mountains or to the covert of some close and secret place where you must eat the bread of your souls in peril of your lives as your forefathers did in Queen Mary's days. . . .

All our own concernments and the concernments of all our dear brethren in the faith throughout the land are bound up in the business. . . . So are the like concernments of others of our brethren also . . . in other lands and kingdoms bound up likewise herein. . . . There is a common report of a strange sympathy between Hippocrates' twins that they always cried together and laughed together. And doubtless there is some such sympathy between all the reformed churches (as we call them) in these parts of the world, amongst which likewise I comprehend those plantations of our brethren of this land in America and other western parts. . . . I do not speak here of that inward or spiritual sympathy . . . between all the true and living members of the mystical body of Christ though never so remote asunder, but of that mutual dependency which the outward affairs and conditions of everyone hath upon the condition of the other, so that the prosperity and well established peace of any one hath an influence into and contributes more or less towards the like establishment of the other. . . .

Now, then, this is that which I say and hold forth to your Christian and godly considerations . . ., that the action wherein the church and people of God in the land are now engaged . . . will . . . be of very remarkable concernment to all the saints of God. . . . If through your zeal and forwardness and faithfulness to advance it, and the blessing of God upon it, your present service shall prosper, your light will be like the "lightning which," as our Savior saith, "shineth from the East even unto the West" [Matt. 24:27]. The heat and warmth and living influence thereof shall pierce through many kingdoms great and large, as France, Germany, Bohemia, Hungary, Poland, Denmark, Sweden, with many others, and find out all the children of God and all that are friends to the kingdom of heaven, and will be a cheering and refreshing to them. . . .

Now, then, inasmuch as God hath set you this day as the sun in the firmament of heaven from when he hath an opportunity and advantage to send forth his beams and to furnish and fill the world with his light and influence . . ., I beseech you, do not betray this first-born opportunity of heaven. Look upon it as a great and solemn invitation from God himself unto you to do greater things for the world . . . than ever you did unto this day or . . . than any particular Christian state ever did or is like to do while the earth stands. God hath prepared and fitted a table for you large enough . . . that you may feast and give royal entertainment to the whole household of faith almost through the whole world at once. . . .

Jeremiah Burroughes, *The Glorious Name of God, the Lord of Hosts* (London, 1643)[19]

If God be "the Lord of Hosts," . . . there is no war to be undertaken but for God and according to God's will. . . . But if any shall say, we are afraid we go not by the commission of "the Lord of Hosts" because we go against the king, [and ask] doth God give commission for subjects to fight against the king? For answer . . . :

First, it is not against the king, it is defensive only, to defend our lawful liberties, our estates, which we inherit as truly as the king inherits anything he has. The law of nature and Scripture teacheth us to defend ourselves from violence and wrong. God hath not put man and whole kingdoms into a worse condition than brute creatures, and yet they by an instinct of nature defend themselves against man that would hurt them. . . .

Secondly, it is not against the king but for the king. It is for the preservation of true regal power in the king and his posterity. It is to rescue him out of the hands of evil men who are his greatest enemies. The Scripture bids that "the wicked should be taken from the throne of the king" [Prov. 25:5]. . . .

Thirdly, that which is done is not done against the power of the king. His power is that which the laws of the land invests him withal. The Scripture bids us "be subject to the higher powers" (Rom. 13:1). It doth not bid us to be subject to the *wills* of those who are in highest place. If we be either actively or passively subject to the laws of that country wherein we live, we fulfill the very letter of that Scripture that commands us to be "subject to the highest powers." Wherefore that which is now done is not against the king though it be against the personal command of [the] king. When we speak of a king, we mean such a man invested with a regal power by the laws and constitutions of that country he is king of. Now if nothing be done against this power that the laws and constitutions of our country invests him with, then nothing can be said to be done against the king. . . .

But may we go against the command of the king?

It is not against his authoritative command. Many, if not most, men mistake in this. They think the authoritative commands of the king chiefly consist in his personal verbal commands, but the truth is, his authority is in his commands by his officers' seals and courts of justice. We may appeal from his personal verbal command to his command in his courts of justice, and whatsoever is his command in one court of justice may be appealed from to a superior court, and so to the highest, and there we must rest.

But the king says that this which is done is done against the law.

If when the most inferior court of justice determines anything to be law, it is not the king's personal dissent and saying that it is not law that disannuls it but the judgment of some superior court. Then if the highest court in the land, which is the parliament, shall judge a thing to be law, surely the personal dissent of the king and saying it is not law cannot disannul it.

But although the parliament tells us that what they do is law, yet they do not show where that law is. Where shall we find it extant?

We are to know that our commonwealth is governed not only by statute law but by the common law. Now this common law is nothing else but *recta ratio,* right reason, so adjudged by judges appointed thereunto by law. And this is various as cases do occur, so that although some precedents, some general maxims of this law be extant, yet if new cases arise then there must be determination according to the nature of such a new case, which determination by such as are appointed judges is now law although it were nowhere written before. And certainly we have now such things fallen out as no former time can show precedents of, as that a king should go from his parliament . . . , that a king should take up arms. . . . These things were never heard of since England was a kingdom. Therefore we can expect no precedents of what determinations there can be in these cases, and some determination we must have or else we shall run to confusion.

This is the way of determining cases that fall out in the

common law. First, the determination must not be against any statute law. . . . Secondly, it must be according to some general maxims of that law. Now this is one great maxim of it, *Salus populi suprema lex,* the safety of the people is the supreme law. . . . Thirdly, when any inferior judge makes this determination against any party that thinks himself wronged, he makes his appeal to the King's Bench. If at the King's Bench that be judged law against a man which he thinks is not right, then he hath a writ of appeal . . . to the next parliament. So that it is apparent by the frame of government in our kingdom that the parliament is supreme judge of what is *recta ratio,* right reason, in cases of difficulty and controversies. . . .

There is no country in the world where countrymen such as we call the yeomandry, yea, and their farmers and workmen under them, do live in that fashion and freedom as they do in England. In all other places they are slaves in comparison. . . . In England every freehold hath an influence into the making and consenting every law he is under, and enjoys his own [property] with as true a title as the nobleman enjoys whatsoever is his. . . . Such is the constitution of the government of this kingdom that the commons of the land, choosing so many to represent them, have that power that they may so moderate the government by nobility and monarchy that neither of them may grow into a tyranny. . . .

These things being so obvious to every man's thoughts that one can hardly be a man to understand anything but he must needs think of those things, how then is it possible that the kingdom should not generally rise up with indignation against these men who are thus risen up to make such spoil and waste in the kingdom? Although they do not yet stir in many places, hoping there may be some help of these things some other way, but if they see there can be no other help, . . . indignation must rise throughout the kingdom. Men will never suffer themselves to be baffled out of their religion, their liberties, their estates, on this fashion. . . .

Wherefore the conclusion from all is [this]: There is nothing required of you in this service by both houses of parliament but what you may with a good conscience undertake by commission from this great general, "the Lord of Hosts." . . .

What is this bondage that the spirit of a Christian will not, should not bear?

There is a natural slavery that, as a man, he should not, he will not be subject to, that is in these three things: 1. To give up his own propriety in what he hath so as whatsoever God and nature hath given him should not be his own but wholly at the will of another. 2. Subjection to that government that he no way either by himself or others hath ever yielded consent unto, neither is bound to by the law of God in his Word nor by the law of nature. 3. To be in such a condition as that whatsoever service he does, he shall receive nothing for it by way of justice but merely out of favor. This is slavery which an ingenuous spirit cannot bear.

And as a Christian, he will not subject his conscience to any, but reserves that to do his homage unto God by it.

Hugh Peters, *God's Doings and Man's Duty, opened in a sermon preached before both Houses of Parliament . . . at the last thanksgiving day, April 2, 1645* (London, 1646)[20]

To improve what I have spoken in the doctrinal part, truly the Lord hath rightly timed his favors. . . . He it is that hath . . . raised help for you out of the very dust. External motive he hath had none from us who are not the loveliest people in the world. He hath from himself over-awed men, poured contempt upon princes, . . . met the proud in their full career and withered their arm. . . . Parliament is not destroyed, the city stands, the gospel is preached. . . . We hear not the rattling of their arms nor the neighing of their horses in our streets. . . . In a word, you have the army you wished for and the successes you desired.

O the blessed change we see that can travel now from Edinburgh to the Land's End in Cornwall, who not long since were blocked up at our doors. To see the highways occupied again, to hear the carter whistling his toiling team, to see the weekly carrier attend his constant mart. . . . Methinks I see

Germany lifting up her lumpish shoulder, and the thin-cheeked Palatinate looking out a prisoner of hope; Ireland breathing again that not only lay bed-rid but the pulse beating deathward; the over-awed French peasant studying his long lost liberty; the Netherlanders looking back upon their neighboring England who cemented their walls with their blood and bought their freedom with many, many thousands of good old Elizabeth shillings. . . . Dumb rhetoric is best. I could even stand silent and give you time to wonder. And this God is your God, and I trust will be your guide for ever. . . . "The Lord hath preserved the faithful, and plenteously rewarded the proud doer" [Ps. 31:23]. . . .

And so I pass in the last place to the first words of my text, which will be the reverse or the other side of our present business. . . . Lord, what wouldst thou have from thy servants? . . . David lets you know God's mind: "O love the Lord, ye his saints." . . .

But you may ask . . . how would I desire this affection to be manifested? I answer, there is a love in imitation. And, indeed, those we love most we make our copies to write after. Then be pleased to mind the text again: "He preserveth the faithful and plenteously rewardeth the proud doer." There is your pattern. Imitation calls upon you to preserve the faithful and to reward the proud doer. And these two look like the main interests of this state. . . .

If you hear politicians abroad, what they say [is] . . . that we should have continued the patrons of the Protestant cause (as the king of Spain of the Catholic) and so have preserved the faithful, which Germany and Rochelle would have thanked us for. And secondly, we should have rewarded the proud, i.e. kept our war at a distance, . . . and by this time (it may be) we might have dried up Euphrates, I mean possessed the whole West Indies, which with little time and help from these parts may be accomplished. . . . Doubtless much love of imitation will be showed to God in recovering these two interests abroad.

And, if I might not be thought a designer, I wish it at home. Why should not the faithful be preserved? For the love of God do it. I speak not for myself . . . , nor do I bring any petition from your army. They never have nor ever will be burdensome to you by petitions, but since you have trusted them with your own lives and estates, they are contented willingly to trust you again with their liberties. . . . Can you bind those hands which, lately armed, procured the liberty and safety of the kingdom? . . .

I fear not all the contentions among us, but pride I fear, the mother, midwife, nurse of all contentions. I hear much of differences, opinions, sects, heresies. And truly, I think they would be less if we did not think them so many. One error, and but one, our Savior gives caution about. . . . He says, "Beware of the leaven of the pharisees" [Mark 8:15], and if we knew what that leaven were it would help us in these fears. . . . Leaven hath three properties: 1. It sours. 2. It toughens or hardens. 3. It swells the lump. Therefore, that opinion which sours men's spirits against their brethren . . . , that swells them and prides them, that hardens them and makes tough and not easily entreated; beware of that opinion as of the leaven of the pharisees. . . . You shall ever find pride the fomenter of differences. I beseech you, therefore, reward the proud doer and spare not. But those opinions that find a soul in a lowly frame, and after received keep the soul so and carry it to Christ, they need not trouble state nor church. . . . Be not offended if I leave this caution with you . . . , ever beware of a spirit of domination. . . .

It concerns us this day that our love appear in our praises. . . . We have had so many victories and mercies that we have even wanted time for our solemn acknowledgments. . . . I wish your children, and so ages to come, may be taught his praises. Since you so abound in matter, I pray [you] convey it to after ages that they may love the God of their fathers. Tell your little ones this night the story of 45 [1645], the towns taken, the fields fought. Tell them of near 30,000 prisoners taken this last year, 500 pieces of ordnance. Tell them of the little loss on our side. Be sure to let them know it was for the liberties of English subjects you fought. Charge them to preserve the liberties that cost you so dear, but especially the liberties purchased by the blood of Christ. And above all, let them know that the God of heaven is the God of England and hath done all. . . . I wish we knew God better that we might love him more. O love the Lord in his praises, and praise him for his love. . . .

I dare not add more, time is so exceedingly exceeded. . . .

[William Penn], *English Liberties; or, The Freeborn Subject's Inheritance, containing, Magna Charta, the Petition of Right, the Habeas Corpus Act, and divers other most useful statutes, with large comments upon each of them* (London: Printed by G. Larkin for John How, [1682])[21]

The Proem

The constitution of our English government (the best in the world) is no arbitrary tyranny like the Turkish grand seignoir's or the French king's whose wills (or rather lusts) dispose of the lives and fortunes of their unhappy subjects, nor an oligarchy where the great ones (like fish in the ocean) prey upon and live by devouring the lesser at their pleasure, nor yet a democracy or popular state (much less an anarchy) where all confusedly are hail fellows well met; but a most excellently mixt or qualified monarchy where the king is vested with large prerogatives sufficient to support majesty and restrained only from doing himself and his people harm (which would be contrary to the very end of all government and is properly a weakness than power), the nobility adorned with privileges to be a screen to majesty and a refreshing shade to their inferiors, and the commonality too so guarded in their persons and properties by the sense of law as renders them free men, not slaves.

In France and other nations, the mere will of the prince is law, His word takes off any man's head, imposes taxes, seizes any man's estate, when, how, and often as he lists. And if one be accused or but so much as suspected of any crime, he may either presently execute him, or banish or imprison him, at pleasure. Or if he will be so gracious as to proceed by form of laws, if any two villains will but swear against the poor party, his life is gone. Nay, if there be no witnesses, yet he may be put to the rack, the tortures whereof make many an innocent person confess himself guilty, and then with seeming justice he is executed. Or if he prove so stout as in torments to deny the fact, yet he comes off with disjointed bones and such weakness as renders his life a burden to him ever after.

But in England the law is both the measure and the bond of every subject's duty and allegiance, each man having a fixed fundamental right born with him as to freedom of his person and property in his estate, which he cannot be deprived of but either by his consent or some crime for which the law has imposed such a penalty or forfeiture. For all our kings take a solemn oath at their coronation "to observe and cause the laws to be kept." . . . Likewise all our judges take an oath wherein, amongst other points, they swear "to do equal law and right to all the king's subjects, rich or poor, and not to delay any person of common right for the letters of the king or of any other person, or for any other cause, but if any such letters come to them, they shall proceed to do the law, the same letters notwithstanding." Therefore, said Fortescue, who was first chief justice and afterwards lord chancellor to King Henry VI, in his book *De laudibus legum Angliae,* chap. 9, . . . : "The king of England cannot alter nor change the laws of his realm at his pleasure. For why? He governeth his people by power not only royal but also politic. If his power over them were only regal, then he might change the laws of his realm and charge his subjects with tallage and other burdens without their consent. . . . But from this much differeth the power of a king whose government is politic, for he can neither change laws without the consent of his subjects nor yet charge them with impositions against their wills. Wherefore his people do frankly and freely enjoy and occupy their own goods, being ruled by such laws as they themselves desire." Thus Fortescue, with whom accords Bracton, a reverend judge and law-author in the reign of Henry III. . . . And on the same score, Judge [John] Vaughn, speaking of our fundamental laws which are coeval with the government, sticks not to say: "The laws of England were never the dictates of any conqueror's sword or the placita [decree] or good will and pleasure of any king of this nation, or, to speak impartially and freely, the results of any parliament that ever sat in this land." . . .

Tis true, the law itself affirms, "the king can do no wrong," which proceeds not only from a presumption that so excellent a person will do none, but also because he acts nothing but by ministers which (from the lowest to the highest) are answerable for their doings. So that, if a king in passion should command A. to kill B. without process of law, A. may yet be prosecuted by indictment or upon an appeal (where no royal pardon is allowable) and must for the same be executed, such command notwithstanding.

The original happy frame of government is truly and properly called an "Englishman's liberty," a privilege not to be exempt from the law, but to be freed in person and estate from arbitrary violence and oppression. "A greater inheritance," said Judge [Edward] Coke, "is derived to every one of us from our laws than from our parents." For without the former, what would the latter signify? And this birthright of Englishmen shines most conspicuously in two things: 1. Parliaments. 2. Juries.

By the first, the subject has a share by his chosen representatives in the legislative (or law-making) power, for no new laws bind the people of England but such as are by common consent agreed on in that great council.

By the second, he has a share in the executive part of the law; no causes being tried nor any man adjudged to lose life, member, or estate but upon the verdict of his peers (or equals), his neighbors and of his own condition.

These two grand pillars of English liberty are the fundamental vital privileges whereby we have been and are preserved more free and happy than any other people in the world. And we trust we shall ever continue so. For whoever shall design to impair, pervert, or undermine either of these do strike at the very constitution of our government, and ought to be prosecuted and punished with the utmost zeal and rigor. To cut down the banks and let in the sea, or to poison all the springs and rivers in the kingdom, could not be a greater mischief. For this would only affect the present age, but the other will ruin and enslave all our posterity. . . .

Notes on *Magna Charta*

This excellent law holds the first place in our statute books, for though there were, no doubt, many Acts of Parliament long before this, yet they are not extant. Tis called *Magna Charta,* or the Great Charter, not in respect of its bulk, but in regard of the great importance and weight of the matters therein contained. It is also styled *Charta Libertatum Regni,* the Charter of the Liberties of the Kingdom; and upon good reason, saith Coke in his Proem, is so called from the effect . . . , because it makes and preserves the people free.

Though it run in the style of the king as a charter, yet, as my Lord Coke well observes on the . . . [last] chapter, it appears to have passed in parliament, for there was then a fifteenth [a subsidy] granted to the king by the bishops, earls, barons, free tenants, and people, which could not be except in parliament. . . .

Likewise, though it be said here that the king hath given and granted these liberties, yet these must not be understood as mere emanations of royal favor or new bounties granted which the people could not justly challenge or had not a right unto before, for the Lord Coke at divers places asserts, and all lawyers know, that this charter is for the most part only declaratory of the principal grounds of the fundamental laws and liberties of England. No new freedom is hereby granted, but a restitution of such as lawfully they had before, and to free them of what had been usurped and encroached upon by any power whatsoever. And therefore you may see this charter often mentions *sua jura* (their rights) and *libertates suas* (their liberties), which shows they had them before and that the same now were confirmed.

As to the occasion of this charter, it must be noted that our ancestors, the Saxons, had with a most equal poise and temperament very wisely contrived their government and made excellent provisions for their liberties and to preserve the people from oppression. And when William the Norman made himself master of the land, though he be commonly called the conqueror, yet in truth he was not so, and I have known several judges that would reprehend any gentleman at the bar that casually gave him that title. For though he killed Harold the Usurper and routed his army, yet he pretended right to the kingdom and was admitted by compact, and did take an oath to observe the laws and customs.

But the truth is, he did not perform that oath as he ought to have done, and his successors . . . likewise made frequent encroachments upon the liberties of their people. But especially King John made use of so many illegal devices to drain them of money that, wearied with intolerable oppressions, they resolved to oblige the king to grant them their liberties and to promise the same should be observed, which King John did in Runnymede . . . by two charters, one called . . . the Charter of Liberties . . . , the other, the Charter of the Forest. . . .

But by ill counsel he quickly began to violate them as much as ever, whereupon disturbances and great miseries arose both to himself and to the realm. The son and successor of this King John was Henry III who, in the nineteenth [ninth] year of his reign, renewed and confirmed the said charters. . . .

The twenty-ninth chapter [of this Great Charter], NO FREEMAN SHALL BE TAKEN, etc. [imprisoned, dispossessed, outlawed, exiled, destroyed, except "by the due course and process of law"] deserves to be written in letters of gold. And I have often wondered the words thereof are not inscribed in capitals on all our courts of judicature, town halls, and most public edifices. They are the elixir of our English freedoms, the storehouse of all our liberties. . . .

[William Penn], *The Excellent Privilege of Liberty and Property, Being the Birthright of the Freeborn Subjects of England* [Philadelphia, 1687]

To the Reader

It may reasonably be supposed that we shall find in this part of the world many men, both old and young, that are strangers in great measure to the true understanding of that inestimable inheritance that every freeborn subject of England is heir unto by birthright. I mean that unparalleled privilege of liberty and property beyond all the nations in the world beside. And it is to [be] wished that all men did rightly understand their own happiness therein, in pursuance of which I do here present thee with that ancient garland, the fundamental laws of England, bedecked with many precious privileges of liberty and property, by which every man that is a subject of the crown of England may understand what is his right and how to preserve it from unjust and unreasonable men; whereby appears the eminent care, wisdom, and industry of our progenitors in providing for themselves and posterity so good a fortress that is able to repel the lust, pride, and power of the noble as well as ignorance of the ignoble; it being that excellent and discrete balance that gives every man his even proportion, which cannot be taken from him, nor be dispossessed of his life, liberty, or estate, but by the trial and judgment of twelve of his equals or law of the land, upon the penalty of the bitter curses of the whole people. So great was the zeal of our predecessors for the preservation of these fundamental liberties (contained in these charters) from encroachment that they employed all their policy and religious obligations to secure them entire and inviolate. . . .

The chief end of the publication hereof is for the information and understanding (what is their native right and inheritance) of such who may not have leisure from their plantations to read large volumes. And beside, I know this country is not furnished with law books, and this being the root from whence all our wholesome English laws spring, and indeed the line by which they must be squared, I have ventured to make it public, hoping it may be of use and service to many free men, planters and inhabitants, in this country to whom it is sent and recommended, wishing it may raise up noble resolutions in all the freeholders in these new colonies not to give away anything of liberty and property that at present they do (or of right as loyal English subjects ought to) enjoy, but take up the good example of our ancestors and understand that it is easy to part with or give away great privileges but hard to be regained if once lost. And therefore all depends on our prudent care and actings to preserve and lay sure foundations for ourselves and the posterity of our loins.

NOTES

PREFACE

1. Hezekiah Niles, *Principles and Acts of the Revolution in America, or, An Attempt to Collect and Preserve Some of the Speeches, Orations, and Proceedings . . . Belonging to the Revolutionary Period* (Baltimore: William Ogden Niles, 1822), p. iv.

2. Hans Kohn, *The Idea of Nationalism* (New York: Macmillan Co., 1945), pp. 179, 574, 635.

INTRODUCTION

1. *The Works of Benjamin Franklin,* ed. Jared Sparks, Vol. IV (Boston: Hilliard, Gray and Co., 1837), pp. 41–42.

2. Claude H. Van Tyne, *The Causes of the War of Independence* (London: Constable and Co., 1922), p. 303.

3. Hans Kohn, *The Idea of Nationalism* (New York: Macmillan Co., 1945), p. 286.

4. Henry Parker, *Jus Populi: or, A Discourse wherein Clear Satisfaction Is Given concerning the Right of Subjects as the Right of Princes* (London, 1644), p. 15.

5. Yehoshva Arieli, *Individualism and Nationalism in American Ideology* (Cambridge: Harvard University Press, 1964), p. 19.

6. *Ibid.,* 20. John Jay could have explained to Tocqueville why Americans held common opinions. Writing the Federalist Paper No. II, Jay commented: "Providence has been pleased to give this one connected country to one united people, a people descended from the same ancestors, speaking the same language, professing the same religion, attached to the same principles of government, very similar in their manners and customs." H. B. Danson (ed.),

The Federalist (New York: Charles Scribner's Sons, 1867), pp. 7–8.

7. Carl Bridenbaugh, *Vexed and Troubled Englishmen, 1590–1642* (New York: Oxford University Press, 1968), p. 401.

8. *Works of Benjamin Franklin,* Vol. IV, p. 42.

9. E. F. Humphrey, *Nationalism and Religion in America* (Boston: Chipman Law Publishing Co., 1924), p. 40.

10. J. Hector St. John [Michel-Guillaume Jean de Crèvecoeur], *Letters from an American Farmer* (London, 1782), p. 51.

11. Jonathan Edwards, "Thoughts on the Revival of Religion in New England" (1740), *The Works of President Edwards* (8th ed.; New York: Leavitt, Trow and Co., 1859), Vol. III, p. 419; "A Humble Attempt to Promote Explicit Agreement and Visible Union of God's People in Extraordinary Prayer for the Revival of Religion and the Advancement of Christ's Kingdom," *ibid.,* p. 462. George Bancroft, *Literary and Historical Miscellanies* (New York: Harper and Brothers, 1857), p. 470.

12. Bernard Faÿ, *The Revolutionary Spirit in France and America* (London: Allen and Unwin, 1928), p. 22.

13. C. H. Van Tyne, *The War of Independence: American Phase* (London: Constable and Co., 1929), p. 72.

14. *Burke's Speech on Conciliation with America,* ed. F. G. Selby (London: Macmillan and Co., 1912), pp. 17–21. Kohn, *The Idea of Nationalism,* pp. 265–267.

15. *The Letters and Speeches of Oliver Cromwell,* ed. Sophia C. Lomas (London: Methuen Co., 1904), Vol. II, p. 509; Vol. III, pp. 30–31. For a discussion of the principle of segregation, the distinction between the realm of nature and the realm of grace, in Puritan thought, see A. S. P. Woodhouse (ed.), *Puritanism and Liberty* (London: J. M. Dent and Sons, 1938), Introduction, pp. 38–43, and George L. Hunt (ed.), *Calvinism and the Public Order* (Philadelphia: Westminster Press, 1965), pp. 115–116, 118–124.

16. Kohn, *Idea of Nationalism,* pp. 166–168.

17. *Ibid.,* pp. 167, 168.

18. Richard Bland, *An Inquiry into the Rights of the British Colonies* (Williamsburg, 1766), p. 7. James Otis, *The Rights of the British Colonies Asserted* (Boston, 1764), p. 31.

19. Bernard Bailyn (ed.), *Pamphlets of the American Revolution, 1750–1776* (Cambridge: Harvard University Press, 1965), Vol. I, pp. 55–84.

20. *Ibid.,* p. 84.

21. *Ibid.*, p. 57.

22. *The Works of John Adams,* ed. C. F. Adams (Boston: Little, Brown and Co., 1850–1856), Vol. X, p. 286.

23. Perry Miller, "From the Covenant to Revival," in James W. Smith and A. Leland Jamison (eds.), *Religion in American Life* (Princeton: Princeton University Press, 1961), Vol. I, pp. 350–353.

1. THE AMERICAN IDENTITY

1. *The Works of John Adams,* ed. C. F. Adams (Boston: Little, Brown and Co., 1850–1856), Vol. X, pp. 282–284.

2. Albert J. Beveridge, *The Meaning of the Times and Other Speeches* (Indianapolis: Bobbs-Merrill Co., 1908), pp. 20, 24. Matthew Simpson, *Western Christian Advocate,* July 11, 1849, as quoted by J. E. Kirby, "Matthew Simpson and the Mission of America," *Church History,* XXXVI (1967), 303. John Ireland, *The Church and Modern Society* (Chicago: D. H. McBride and Co., 1896), p. 356. Philip Schaff, *America,* ed. Perry Miller (Cambridge: Harvard University Press, 1961), pp. 54, 88–89, 107, 116–117.

3. Alexander Whitaker confessed that "many of the men sent hither have been murderers, thieves, adulterers, idle persons, and what not besides." *Good News from Virginia* (London, 1613), p. 11. John Hammond wrote: "The country is reported to be . . . a nest of rogues, whores, dissolute and rooking [dishonest] persons. At the first settling and many years after, it deserved most of the aspersions (nor were they then aspersions but truths). It was not settled at the public charge, but . . . by adventurers whose avarice and inhumanity brought these inconveniences which to this day brands Virginia. Then were jails emptied, youth seduced, infamous women drilled in." *Leah and Rachel; or, Two Fruitful Sisters, Virginia and Maryland* (London, 1656), p. 7. William Crashaw, the eager clerical promoter of Virginia, was confident that it did not matter greatly what the character of "the generality of them that go in person" was, since "we find that the most disordered men that can be raked up . . . if they be removed . . . from the licentiousness and too much liberty of the states where they have lived, into . . . a harder course of life . . . and to a strict form of government and severe discipline, do often become new men." *A Sermon Preached before . . . the Lord La Warr, Lord Governor and Captain of Virginia* (London, 1610). Even if Crashaw's con-

fidence was not overly sanguine, contemporary accounts of the early settlers did not lend themselves to the fashioning of a noble epic.

4. For a perceptive discussion of colonial history writing, see Richard S. Dunn, "Seventeenth-Century Historians in America," in James M. Smith (ed.), *Seventeenth-Century America: Essays in Colonial History* (Chapel Hill: University of North Carolina Press, 1959), pp. 196–221.

5. Thomas Budd, *Good Order Established in Pennsylvania and New Jersey* (Cleveland: Burrows Brothers, 1902), p. 76.

6. Stephen Marshall, *A Peace-Offering to God* (London, 1641), p. 51

7. Urian Oakes, *New England Pleaded With and Pressed to Consider those Things which Concern Her Peace* (Cambridge, Mass., 1673), p. 23. Thomas Shepard, *Eye-Salve; or, A Watchword from our Lord . . . to His Church* (Cambridge, Mass., 1673), pp. 15–16.

8. Since New England historians made such generous use of Bradford's manuscript, to check one of them against another is often to check Bradford against Bradford.

9. *Bradford's History of Plymouth Plantation, 1606–1646,* ed. W. T. Davis (New York: Charles Scribner's Sons, 1908), pp. 23–25, 30, 32, 44, 46, 48–49, 78–80, 95–97, 106–107, 244–245, 272.

10. Pp. 4–8, 20, 22.

11. William Stoughton, *New England's True Interest* (Cambridge, Mass., 1670), pp. 10, 17, 25. Thomas Shepard, *Eye-Salve,* p. 33. John Higginson's "Attestation," in Cotton Mather, *Magnalia Christi Americana* (London, 1702).

12. Perry Miller, *The New England Mind: From Colony to Province* (Cambridge: Harvard University Press, 1953), p. 32.

13. Of the committee members identified, 11 were from New England and 19 from other colonies.

14. Preface.

15. *Collections of the Massachusetts Historical Society,* 3rd ser., Vol. VII (Boston: Charles C. Little and James Brown, 1838), pp. 44–47.

16. Pp. 3–5, 7, 14–18, 20.

17. *Journals of Congress,* Vol. I, *Containing the Proceedings from September 5, 1774 to January 1, 1776* (Philadelphia: R. Aitken, 1777), pp. 117–118.

18. *Ibid.,* Vol. II, *Containing the Proceedings in the Year 1776* (Philadelphia: R. Aitken, n.d.), pp. 93–94.

19. *Ibid.*, Vol. III, *Containing the Proceedings from January 1, 1777 to January 1, 1778* (Philadelphia: John Dunlap, n.d.), pp. 467–468.

20. *Ibid.*, Vol. IV, *Containing the Proceedings from January 1, 1778 to January 1, 1779* (Philadelphia: David Claypoole, n.d.), p. 138.

21. *Ibid.*, Vol. V, *Containing the Proceedings from January 1, 1779 to January 1, 1780* (Philadelphia: David C. Claypoole, 1787), pp. 106–107.

22. *Resolutions, Acts, and Orders of Congress,* Vol. VI, *For the Year 1780* (Printed by John Dunlap), p. 217.

23. Pp. 50–51, 53–54.

24. Pp. 57–58.

25. J. D. Richardson (ed.), *A Compilation of the Messages and Papers of the Presidents* (Washington: Bureau of National Literature and Art, 1910), Vol. I, p. 370. Gilbert Chinard, *Thomas Jefferson: the Apostle of Americanism* (Boston: Little, Brown and Co., 1929), p. 86.

26. *New England's Memorial,* p. 152.

27. F. G. Selby (ed.), *Burke's Speech on Conciliation with America* (London: Macmillan Co., 1912), p. 21.

28. *Journals of Congress,* Vol. I (1774–1776), pp. 3, 14, 55, 143.

29. Pp. 9–10, 17–18.

30. Pp. 15–16, 22–25, 27–28.

31. Pp. 8–9, 17–19, 21, 24, 26, 45–55, 62–63.

32. Pp. 38–44. Quite apart from the revolt against Andros, the Glorious Revolution of 1688 was no distant event to the colonists. Gilbert Burnet's sermon before the House of Commons and the declaration at Nottingham were both reprinted in Boston.

33. The reference would appear to be to Cotton Mather's *Eleutheria; or, An Idea of the Reformation in England . . . with Predictions of a More Glorious Reformation and Revolution at Hand* (London, 1698), which asserts: "That part of the English nation which values its true English liberty . . . will not much longer permit the truest friends of English liberty to be suppressed, abused, and incapacitated merely to please the humors of a faction who have always done all they can to betray that English liberty" (p. 16). Although printed ten years later, *Eleutheria* makes sense only within the context of the situation in 1688.

34. Pp. 1–2, 6–8, 12, 43, 45–46.

35. Pp. 16–27, 29–32.

2. MISSION AND DESTINY

1. Samuel K. Lothrop, *Oration Delivered before the City Authorities of Boston, July 4, 1866* (Boston: Alfred Mudge and Son, 1866), pp. 7–8.

2. John Rodgers, *The Divine Goodness Displayed in the American Revolution* (New York, 1784), p. 30. M. C. Tyler, *The Literary History of the American Revolution, 1763–1783* (New York: G. P. Putnam's Sons, 1900), Vol. II, p. 315.

3. For "asylum" image, see John Winthrop, "Arguments for the Plantation of New England," *Winthrop Papers,* Vol. II, 1623–1630 (Boston: Massachusetts Historical Society, 1931), p. 114; William Penn, *The Excellent Privilege of Liberty and Property* (Philadelphia: Philobiblon Club, 1897), p. xii; Daniel Neal, *History of New England* (London, 1747), Vol. I, Dedication, Vol. II, p. 254; C. H. Van Tyne, *The American Revolution* (New York: Harper and Brothers, 1905), p. 333; Thomas Paine, *Common Sense,* in *The Political and Miscellaneous Works of Thomas Paine* (London: R. Carlile, 1819), Vol. I, pp. 21, 23; J. Hector St. John [Crèvecoeur], *Letters from an American Farmer* (London, 1782), p. 49: Marquis de Condorcet, "The Influence of the American Revolution on Europe (1786)," *William and Mary Quarterly,* 3rd. ser., XXV (1968), 93.

4. See Winthrop's "Model of Christian Charity," *supra* 23; and J. D. Richardson, *A Compilation of the Messages and Papers of the Presidents* (Washington: Bureau of National Literature, 1910), Vol. II, p. 1223, Vol. XVIII, p. 8352. The terms "experiment" and "example" are to be found everywhere. For William Penn's early usage of the terms, see Robert Proud, *The History of Pennsylvania* (Philadelphia, 1797–1798), Vol. I, p. 169.

5. Richardson, *Compilation of the Messages . . . of the Presidents,* Vol. II, p. 1527. Paul L. Ford (ed.), *The Writings of John Dickinson,* Vol. I (Philadelphia: Historical Society of Pennsylvania, 1875), p. xx.

6. See Frontispiece of Increase Mather, *Icabod* (Boston, 1702), and C. F. Adams (ed.), *The Works of John Adams* (1850–56), Vol. IX, pp. 599–600.

7. *Memoirs of the Historical Society of Pennsylvania* (Philadelphia, 1834), Vol. III, pp. 291–292. *Works of John Adams,* Vol. IV,

p. 293. A. K. Weinberg, *Manifest Destiny: A Study of Expansionism in American History* (Baltimore: Johns Hopkins Press, 1935), p. 55.

8. John White, *The Planter's Plea* (London, 1630), pp. 1–3. John Cotton, *God's Promise to His Plantation* (London, 1630), pp. 4–6.

9. Weinberg, *Manifest Destiny*, pp. 64, 168. James Parton, *Life of Andrew Jackson* (New York: Mason Brothers, 1860), Vol. III, p. 658.

10. Tyler, *Literary History of the American Revolution*, Vol. II, p. 305. John Howard Pugh, *The Success and Promise of the American Union* (Philadelphia: King and Baird, 1865), pp. 20–22.

11. Richardson, *Compilation of the Messages . . . of the Presidents*, Vol. II, pp. 1223–24; Vol. VI, pp. 688–689. *Writings and Speeches of Daniel Webster* (Boston, 1903), Vol. XVI, p. 423. Allan Nevins (ed.), *The Letters of Grover Cleveland* (Boston: Houghton, Mifflin Co., 1933), pp. 491–492.

12. Editions were printed in both Springfield, Massachusetts, and Norfolk, Virginia, in 1806.

13. Pp. 5–11, 13–16, 21.

14. Pp. 15–16, 20–21.

15. Pp. 5–7, 9–10, 14–17, 20–23, 34–37, 48, 52, 55–56, 68–69.

16. 2nd ed., pp. 4–5, 26–29, 31.

17. Hans Kohn, *The Idea of Nationalism* (New York: Macmillan Co., 1945), pp. 313–314.

18. *Works of John Adams*, Vol. I, p. 230. G. S. Phillips, *The American Republic and Human Liberty Foreshadowed in Scripture* (Cincinnati: Poe and Hitchcock, 1864), p. 12. Nathaniel West, *Establishment in National Righteousness and Present Causes for Thanksgiving* (New York: John F. Trow, 1861), pp. 20–22, 36.

19. George Bancroft, *Memorial Address on the Life and Character of Abraham Lincoln* (Washington, D.C.: L. Towers, [1866]), p. 14.

20. W. A. Clebsch, "Christian Interpretations of the Civil War," *Church History*, XXX (1961), 221.

21. Pugh, *Success and Promise of the American Union*, pp. 171–173.

22. Pp. 5–7, 9–17, 19–27.

23. J. D. Richardson (ed.), *A Compilation of the Messages and*

Papers of the Presidents (Washington: Bureau of National Literature and Art, 1910), Vol. V, pp. 3211–12.

24. *Ibid.*, p. 3343.

25. *Ibid.*, pp. 3477–78.

26. *Pennsylvania Packet,* November 27, 1781, reprinted in E. F. Humphrey, *Nationalism and Religion in America* (Boston: Chipman Law Publishing Co., 1924), pp. 128–129.

27. Pp. 57–58, 118–119, 138–140, 147, 149–150, 154–158. The selections are from three addresses: "The Mission of Catholics in America," "Human Progress," and "Patriotism."

28. Facsimile in *Jewish Encyclopedia* (New York: Funk and Wagnalls Co., 907), Vol. XII, p. 348.

29. Daniel J. Boorstin (ed.), *An American Primer* (Chicago: University of Chicago Press, 1966), Vol. I, p. 459.

3. THE RENOVATION OF THE WORLD

1. John Aylmer, *An Harborowe for Faithful and True Subjects* (Strassburg, 1559), no pagination. Jeremiah Burroughes, *A Sermon Preached before . . . the House of Peers* (London, 1646), pp. 44–45.

2. James T. Peck, *The History of the Great Republic* (New York: Broughton and Wyman, 1868), p. 562.

3. Josiah Strong, *Our Country,* ed. Jurgen Herbst (Cambridge: Harvard University Press, 1963), p. xi. M. E. Curti, *The Growth of American Thought* (New York: Harper & Row, 1943), p. 261.

4. Printed as an Appendix to Heman Humphrey, *The Promised Land* (Boston: S. T. Armstrong, 1819).

5. Lyman Beecher, *A Plea for the West* (Cincinnati: Truman and Smith, 1835), pp. 9–10, 42, 45–46.

6. Pp. 3–6, 11–14, 16–18, 28–29.

7. The text is from Lyman Beecher, *Sermons Delivered on Various Occasions* (Boston: T. R. Marvin, 1828), pp. 293–305.

8. Pp. 467–473, 475–479.

9. A. K. Weinberg, *Manifest Destiny: A Study of Expansionism in American History* (Baltimore: Johns Hopkins Press, 1935), pp. 275–277.

10. Frederick Merk, *Manifest Destiny and Mission in American History* (New York: Alfred A. Knopf, 1963), p. viii.

11. See title page and preface of 1891 edition. In England an

abridged edition was published under the title *The United States and the Future of the Anglo-Saxon Race* (1889).

12. Josiah Strong, *Expansion under New World Conditions* (New York: Baker and Taylor Co., 1900), p. 213.

13. Merk, *Manifest Destiny*, pp. 242–244, 247.

14. Pp. 159–161, 163, 165–166, 170–180. The copyright is 1885, but Strong said it was published in 1886.

15. These sentences have been transposed from Strong, *ibid.*, 176–177.

16. Privately printed, pp. 3–16.

17. Vol. II, pp. 109–111.

18. Vol. XXIV (Jan.–June, 1898), p. 519.

19. Pp. 1–7, 11–12, 14–16.

4. THE ISSUE OF PLURALISM

1. John Rodgers, *The Divine Goodness Displayed in the American Revolution* (New York, 1784), p. 28.

2. Alexis de Tocqueville, *Democracy in America* (New York: Alfred A. Knopf, 1945), Vol. I, p. 392.

3. J. Hector St. John [Crèvecoeur], *Letters from an American Farmer* (London, 1782), p. 52.

4. Pp. 354–357.

5. Pp. 30–33, 41–42, 124, 184–185.

6. Pp. 55–57, 61–62, 73, 75–76, 78–80, 91, 97–98, 101–106, 221.

7. Pp. 159–160.

8. Pp. 224–230.

9. See George L. Hunt (ed.), *Calvinism and the Public Order* (Philadelphia: Westminster Press, 1965), pp. 115–116, 118–124.

10. See C. R. Keller, *The Second Great Awakening in Connecticut* (New Haven: Yale University Press, 1942), pp. 1–2; and Robert Baird, *Religion in America* (New York: Harper and Brothers, 1844), pp. 129–183.

11. Pp. 55–58.

12. Pp. 62–71. For a more detailed and systematic analysis, see S. E. Mead, "The Post-Protestant Concept and America's Two Religions," *Religion in Life*, XXXIII (1964), 191–204, and "The Nation with the Soul of a Church," *Church History*, XXXVI (1967), 262–283.

13. Pp. 1–5, 7–8, 14–16, 18–19.

APPENDIX: THE ENGLISH HERITAGE

1. Edwin Sandys, *A Relation of the State of Religion* (London, 1605), no pagination.

2. Thomas Fuller, *The Church History of Britain,* 6 vols. (Oxford: University Press, 1845), Vol. II, pp. 423–424.

3. Vol. I, pp. 137–138, 41–42.

4. No pagination.

5. *The Holy Exercise of a True Fast Described Out of God's Word* (London: John Harison and Thomas Man, 1580), p. 49. The first edition was entitled, *A Very Godly and Learned Treatise of the Exercise of Fasting Described Out of the Word of God* (London: John Day, 1580). Subsequently it was reprinted as part of *Two Treatises* (London: Harison and Man, 1610). Although attributed to Thomas Cartwright, it is possible that Thomas Cooper, Bishop of Lincoln, was the author. Cooper's active sponsorship of fasts at Stamford, the publication by John Day, and the relationship of the treatise to parliamentary action give plausibility to the latter conjecture. Also influential in promoting fast days was Nicholas Bownde, *The Holy Exercise of Fasting* (Cambridge: John Legat, 1604). For a discussion of fasting, see Daniel Neal, *The History of the Puritans* (London: William Baynes and Son, 1822), Vol. I, p. 297; Vol. III, pp. 37–39, and Patrick Collinson, *The Elizabethan Puritan Movement* (Berkeley: University of California Press, 1967), pp. 216–217.

6. Neal, *History of the Puritans,* Vol. I, p. 297.

7. Bownde, *Holy Exercise of Fasting,* Dedicatory Epistle.

8. Neal, *History of the Puritans,* Vol. III, p. 38.

9. Pp. 1–4, 20–27, 29, 40, 42–43, 45–46, 55–56.

10. Pp. 1–3, 25–26, 54–55, 58–59.

11. Pp. 1–6, 8, 11–13, 17–18, 21–24, 26, 30, 45.

12. Pp. 1–2, 9, 11, 13, 37, 43–44.

13. Pp. 2–3, 5, 7–10, 13–15.

14. Bailyn, *Pamphlets of the American Revolution,* Vol. I, 24, 29, 31, 35–38.

15. For a discussion of Penn's authorship, see W. S. Hudson, "William Penn's *English Liberties:* Tract for Several Times," *William and Mary Quarterly,* XXVI (1969), 578–85.

16. Preface. This interest of Penn was maintained, as is evident

by his publication of Bulstrode Whitelocke's *Memorial of the English Affairs from the Supposed Expedition of Brute to this Island to the End of the Reign of King James I. Published from his original manuscript . . . by William Penn, Esq., Governor of Pennsylvania* (London, 1709), with the stated purpose of making it "easy for every Englishman to know his country, its settlement, constitution, customs, laws; the performance of kings and princes thereof, as also of our parliaments and national assemblies, that we may have a true idea of their legal power and our legal liberty."

17. Penn, *The Excellent Privilege of Liberty and Property,* Preface. Bailyn, *Pamphlets of the American Revolution,* Vol. I, p. 742, note 9.

18. Pp. 2–3, 24–26, 28–29, 31, 33–34.

19. Pp. 26–35, 42, 51–53, 59, 68, 73–74.

20. Pp. 15–16, 18, 24–32, 34, 36–38, 42 ff.

21. Pp. 1–5, 19–22.